Reinterpreting Property

Reinterpreting Property

Margaret Jane Radin

The University of Chicago Press
Chicago and London

MARGARET JANE RADIN is a professor of law at Stanford University.

The University of Chicago Press, Chicago 60637
The University of Chicago Press, Ltd., London
© 1993 by The University of Chicago
All rights reserved. Published 1993
Printed in the United States of America
02 01 00 99 98 97 96 95 94 93   1 2 3 4 5
ISBN: 0-226-70227-8 (cloth)

Library of Congress Cataloging-in-Publication Data

Radin, Margaret Jane.
    Reinterpreting property / Margaret Jane Radin.
        p.   cm.
    A collection of essays by the author, some which were originally published in various
periodicals.
    Includes index.
    1. Property.   2. Law—Philosophy.   I. Title.
K720.R33   1993
340'.1—dc20   93-4908
                                                                              CIP

For Amadea and Wayland

Contents

Acknowledgments

These essays were written between 1981 and 1992. For the most part they are reproduced as first published, except that some footnotes have been abridged or deleted. Footnotes have not been updated, except in a few cases, mostly to provide appropriate cross references within this volume. Rarely I have added a footnote in brackets where I now feel my text should be added to or contradicted, but mostly I have resisted the temptation.

"Property and Personhood" (chapter 1) was first published in 34 *Stanford Law Review* 957–1015 (1982). Except for minor stylistic matters, the text is unchanged. Some footnotes have been abridged or deleted. Reprinted with permission of the *Stanford Law Review*.

"Residential Rent Control" (chapter 2) was first published in 25 *Philosophy and Public Affairs* 350–380 (1986), and is reprinted, with minor stylistic changes, with permission of Princeton University Press.

"Problems for the Theory of Absolute Property Rights" (chapter 3) is adapted from two essays, "The Consequences of Conceptualism," first published in 41 *University of Miami Law Review* 239–244 (1986), and "Time, Possession, and Alienation," first published in 64 *Washington University Law Quarterly* 739–579 (1986). The latter piece was commissioned by the Liberty Fund, Inc., for a conference on "Time, Property Rights, and the Common Law," held in November 1985, and the former was written in response to a conference held in January 1986, also sponsored by the Liberty Fund, Inc., on "Takings of Property and the Constitution." Only minor revisions have been made to the texts. A brief introduction and conclusion have been added. Some footnotes have been abridged or deleted. Reprinted with permission of the *University of Miami Law Review* and the *Washington University Law Quarterly*.

"The Liberal Conception of Property: Crosscurrents in the Jurisprudence of Takings" (chapter 4) was published in 88 *Columbia Law Review* 1667–1698 (1988). Except for minor stylistic matters, the text is unchanged. Some footnotes have been abridged or deleted. The *Columbia Law Review* version is an adaptation and expansion of "The Constitution and the Liberal Conception of Property," chapter 8 in *Judging the Constitution: Critical Essays on Judicial Lawmaking,* edited by Michael W. McCann and Gerald L. Houseman, published by Scott, Foresman & Co. division of Little Brown & Co. (1989). Reprinted with permission of the *Columbia Law Review* and Scott, Foresman & Co.

"Diagnosing the Takings Problem" (chapter 5) was first published as chapter 10 in *NOMOS XXXIII, Compensatory Justice,* edited by John W. Chapman, published by the New York University Press (1991). Minor corrections have been made to the text. Reprinted with the permission of the New York University Press.

"Government Interests and Takings: Cultural Commitments of Property and the Role of Political Theory" (chapter 6) is an adapted version of an essay commissioned for a conference sponsored by Albany Law School on "Compelling Government Interests: The Mystery of Constitutional Analysis," held in September 1991. The essay was first committed to *Public Values in Constitutional Law,* edited by Stephen E. Gottlieb and to be published by the University of Michigan Press (September 1993). Inclusion here is with permission of the University of Michigan Press.

"The Rhetoric of Alienation" (chapter 7) was written in 1986 for a colloquium on property and rhetoric. It is published here for the first time, with minor revisions.

All but one of these essays were written while I was on the faculty of the University of Southern California Law Center. I appreciate USC's summer research support grants, as well as Stanford's since 1990. At Stanford my research was supported by a bequest from the Claire and Michael Brown Estate. I can no longer name all the people at USC whose ideas and arguments helped to form mine, but I remain grateful to that institution and to my colleagues there for the extraordinary scholarly community that made this work possible. For thoughtful responses to these essays during their gestation, I am grateful as well to a lot of other academics who think about property. I do not mean that *expressio unius est exclusio alterius* when I mention Frank Michelman in particular. Over the years his readings have been both sympathetic and critical in the way a writer hardly dares hope for. Special thanks to

Thomas C. Grey, whose unerring ear for decent prose greatly improved the introduction; to John Tryneski, Senior Editor, the University of Chicago Press, whose idea this project was; and (they know why) to Layne L. Britton, Barbara Herman, Kathleen M. Sullivan, and Jeanne M. Wilson. I dedicate this collection to my children because of what they have taught me.

Introduction: Property and Pragmatism

Some writers say, I have been told, that when an essay is more than two years old, there can be no presumption that it has anything to do with one's views. The essays in this book range from eleven years old to one. The younger ones are much more recognizable to me as being mine. For a while I hoped someday to knit all of these essays together into a book to be entitled "Property and Personhood." It turned out that there is too much water under the bridge, intellectually speaking, for that to be possible. If I were starting the project now, there is too much I would do differently. Yet the essays are loosely connected by certain recurring themes.

One main theme in these essays is the personality theory of property. The personality theory is an aspect of traditional liberal thought about property. It elaborates the notion that ownership is bound up with self-constitution or personhood. It connects ownership with central ideological commitments of liberal thought, particularly with notions of freedom and individualism. In reconsidering the personality theory I have juxtaposed it with two other main aspects of liberal property theory, the labor theory stemming from Locke and the economic theory stemming from Bentham. I have also often recurred to questions about how these ideological strands are played out in American property law in general, and especially in American constitutional property law. In these inquiries jurisprudential questions are never far from view. To what extent and in what way are these ideological commitments of liberal culture integral with the law?

Another main theme is a species of pragmatism. Although I did not at the time of the earlier essays consciously name myself a pragmatist, it has always seemed important to me to focus on the nonideal nature of property practices and institutions, on the situated, and second-best, working out of liberal ideological commitments in practice. It has always seemed important to me to connect theory with specific legal practices, such as landlord-tenant law or takings of property without just compensation. As I wrote and learned about these matters, I was led to a more explicit commitment to philosophical pragmatism. This commitment in turn led to more explicit reflections about the interrelationship between law and the cultural commitments of property. It also led to reflections about the language of property: the role of property rhetoric in the social construction of selves.

I

"Property and Personhood" (chapter 1) resulted from my experience in my first few years of teaching property law. Again and again, study of cases revealed that we—students, the teacher, and the judge who wrote the opinion—perceived the strength of property claims differently depending upon who advanced them and under what circumstances. When individuals credibly claimed real attachment to their property in some personal sense, their legal claims to that property were by and large treated as weightier than claims where economic return to investment was the only plausible connection between the claimant and the property. No distinction between different types of property claims ever became explicit in the cases. But exceptional cases where the distinction was ignored—the famous *Peevyhouse*[1] is a good example—were greeted by many students with gut-level outrage, not merely disagreement. Feelings about the distinction ran deep, yet there were no modern theoretical works that focused on it. Hence the essay starts out by saying that the relationship between property and personhood "has commonly been both ignored and taken for granted in legal thought."

In "Property and Personhood" I wanted first of all to point out the tacit legal and cultural understanding that there are two kinds of property—I should have said two kinds of property relationships—and I wanted to show how broad that understanding is, how it cuts across many fields of law. I used the label "personal" to denote the kind of property that individuals are attached to as persons, and I used the label "fungible" to denote the kind of property that individuals are not attached to except as to a source of money. (Perhaps I should have called property that is bound up with personhood "constitutive" rather than "personal," since "personal property" already means something else.)

Although the tacit legal and cultural understanding I wanted to point out does seem to create a dichotomy (two kinds of property), in another sense it is a great oversimplification to reduce to two the types of relationships between individuals and things. In "Property and Personhood" I noted that we could think of a continuum ranging "from a thing indispensable to someone's being to a thing wholly interchangeable with money." I went on to say that where a dichotomy telescoping the continuum to its two endpoints is useful, it is because "within a given social context certain types of person-thing relationships are understood to fall close to one end or the other of the continuum."[2] I then gave the example of resident home ownership as personal property.

This is implicitly a pragmatic approach. I said that it would be "useful" to describe at least part of the social world in terms of the two categories of property relationships, even though these descriptions do not exhaust either the universe of different property relations that exist (or can exist) or the nuances of any particular existing property relation. This approach gives rise to a number of questions that I did not then answer. The general question is, "useful" for what? (What problem is best solved by understanding the social world this way?) The general question leads to a number of more particular ones. What makes it appropriate to omit from this analysis the property relations that are not perspicuously described by these categories? What makes it appropriate to omit from this analysis the nonproperty relations that are also understood as constitutive of personhood? How should we think about property owned by nonpersonal entities like corporations? Once the tacit conventional understanding of the dichotomy between two kinds of property is made explicit, is a critique of it needed? (What makes it appropriate to accept this conventional understanding, at least in some contexts?) In this introduction I will consider these questions. I will also consider certain types of responses to my essays from both the right and the left, and speculate about where further investigation of property and personhood might fruitfully focus.

II

The "useful for what?" question leads to another: whether there is a sharp distinction between fact and value. It leads there because in "Property and Personhood" I said that the personhood perspective is useful in both a descriptive and a prescriptive way: it can explain certain aspects of existing property institutions and practices, and it can help either to justify or critique those institutions and practices. I now recognize it as a characteristic pragmatist move to elide explanation and justification in this way. But the move often seems merely a confusion to nonpragmatists.

Both descriptive and evaluative understandings are constructed from the totality of the circumstances in which we find ourselves. Our circumstances include, blurred together, both the problems we need tools to solve and our visions and desires for a better future. Observations about the world we face "out there" help to construct our values, and our values help to construct our observations about the world. As Hilary Putnam has recently said, "This insistence on the total entanglement of the particular with the universal, the so-called factual with the so-called normative, is at the heart of pragmatism."[3] Pragmatism "walks a knife edge": it is fallibilist (anti-essentialist) but not skeptical.[4] In one of the later essays in this book, "Government Interests and Takings: Cultural Commitments of Property and the Role of Political Theory" (chapter 6), I showed how our description of the existence of particular property rules and regimes is mixed up with our evaluation of the justice or injustice of those rules and regimes.

In "Property and Personhood" I was not yet prepared to say much about this pragmatist move, however. When we observe that someone's personhood is bound up with an item of property, does that mean that this is good? Clearly not always, but then how can we distinguish good from bad property relations? In my essay, I said that even if someone is bound up with a "thing," we nevertheless should not treat that "thing" as personal "when there is an objective moral consensus that to be bound up with that category of 'thing' is inconsistent with personhood or healthy self-constitution."[5] I said that I wished to eschew "natural law or simple moral realism," yet make "objective judgments about property for personhood," and concluded that "consensus must be a sufficient source of objective moral criteria."[6]

I would put it differently now, after some years of wrestling with pragmatist ideas. First of all, I would no longer use the word "objectivity" so unselfconsciously. (Indeed, "objectivity" does not appear in this unproblematized way in any essay after the first.) It is not that the word is without meaning for a pragmatist. There are indeed things that we experience as existing apart from us and outside our control. But the word has too much baggage in the history of modern Western thought. The baggage is essentialism, the kind of traditional philosophical realism that the pragmatist denies.

Second, I would no longer use the word "consensus" to describe the kind of strong entrenchment of concepts like personhood in our culture and discourse. ("Consensus" does not appear in the essays written after

"Property and Personhood.") I was groping for a vocabulary in which to express the pragmatic understanding of objectivity: shared understandings that are, for now, too entrenched to be revisable by individuals, and are experienced by individuals as coming from outside themselves. "Objective moral consensus" was a particularly unfortunate phrase in which to try to express this entrenchment because the foundationalist baggage attached to "objectivity" implied for most readers a kind of transcendent reality divorced from the activities of human beings.

Thus, "objectivity" seemed to contradict what is implied by "consensus," which has its own baggage having to do with groups of individuals entering into a social contract. To most readers, "consensus" seemed to imply a naive kind of conventionalism. It seemed to suggest that normative understandings are determined by taking a survey of people's views, or asking people to vote. It seemed to imply a crass skepticism about values—that they amount to no more than the winning sum of people's "subjective" preferences. In retrospect it appears to me that the phrase "objective moral consensus" represents an early attempt to erode the fact/value dichotomy by simply picking one word from column A (essentialism, "objectivity") and one word from column B (skepticism, "consensus"). The choice of this phrase was unfortunate because I could not metamorphose the philosophical baggage of the last few centuries just by linking its opposites and declaring their opposition dissolved.

Third, I would no longer make "health" ("healthy self-constitution") the criterion by which we distinguish good from bad property attachments, although I am not as distant from this usage as from "objective consensus." The concept of "health" is ordinarily understood as both regulative (normative) and descriptive, so its use will not be confusing even to readers who have not yet questioned the philosophical received wisdom about the fact/value dichotomy. Yet I now think it will advance the argument much better to speak directly about human flourishing, rather than health.

By the time of "Residential Rent Control" (chapter 2), having made progress toward a pragmatist view (but still not naming it as such), I had seen the problems with the notion of objectivity and was no longer speaking in terms of consensus. There I said that "an ultimate context-dependency of the distinction between good and bad object-relations, and thus of the choice of the moral categories of personal property, can be admitted without thereby rendering the matter subjective or conventional."[7] Rather than speaking of "healthy" property relations, I spoke of *justifiable* property relations. And I connected justifiable property relations with the notion of human flourishing, though merely with a gesture rather than a full-fledged consideration of either human flourishing or the nature of the connection.

To what extent do "we" possess a persuasive conception of human flourishing? Or is the concept of human flourishing too deeply contested to admit of one conception that is properly "ours"? In light of this conception (or, these conceptions), what property relations—if any—are appropriate? These are questions I would want to address if I began my project today, and that I hope will be addressed in the future, either by me or by others.

III

The connection between human flourishing and property relations is a central subject of liberal property theory. In my essays I did not address the issue of whether private property *must* exist—whether justice, or human flourishing, requires the existence of private property. As a pragmatist, I started in the middle, within a property system. Starting from where we are, I argued that we could be truer to the ideals of individuality and freedom by which we justify property if we admitted the existence of, and regulated ourselves normatively by, the distinction between personal and fungible property. For example, I argued that we could be truer to the entrenched ideal of equal treatment of persons if we admitted that an apartment could be a tenant's home in the same sense as an owned house could be an owner's home, and then treated the interests of residential tenants like the interests of homeowners in certain respects.

The arguments stay situated in our practices and institutions, in our historical and cultural circumstances. At the same time, in making these arguments I referred to a theoretical heritage (Locke, Kant, Hegel) that largely understood itself in a more transcendent way. Understandably, some readers understood me to be saying that private property is necessarily part of some timeless and transcendent ideal theory of justice. I conceived of my project as more immanent, closer to the ground, but still I found the theoretical heritage relevant.

The history of liberal property theory is part of the circumstances in which we find ourselves; it contributes to the entrenched understanding that ownership is connected to individuality and freedom. The British branch of that theoretical history, from Smith and Hume through Bentham and Mill, still connects with a common understanding that freedom involves free markets. This branch of liberal theory supports the law and economics movement. In the economic view, private property is justified because it is necessary to create, through internalization of benefits, incentives to productive activity. As the nations of Eastern Europe try to develop market societies in the 1990s, this is the branch of liberal theory that occupies the foreground of discussion. Yet in these essays I was not concerned primarily with the economic theory of property, but rather with property and personhood. The German branch of our theoretical history about property, from Kant through Marx, is, I still think, very interesting to juxtapose with our common understanding that property—property relations—can be constitutive of personhood.

My view that persons can become bound up with external objects can be related to Hegel, who argued in his *Philosophy of Right* that placing the will into an object takes the person from abstract to actual. It can also be related to Kant, who argued in his *Rechtslehre* that property was necessary to give full scope to the free will of persons: they must have control over objects in order fully to constitute themselves as persons. Indeed the view can be related as well to Marx, who thought that we become fully human through working up the world outside us. We fulfill ourselves and our "species being," he thought, through possessing the natural world, though not as private property.[8] Marx had rejected the capitalist aspect of the prior tradition, the claim that private property must exist, but not its romantic aspect, the claim that people constitute themselves as individuals vis-à-vis a natural world.

Among the scholarly population there are many who have devoted their life work to an understanding of Kant, or Hegel, or Marx. Since I am not among them, I do no more than point out certain resonances between these texts and the cultural/legal understanding I am trying to illuminate. In "Property and Personhood" I should perhaps have said more about Kant;[9] I should perhaps have said less about Hegel. I am not in a position to offer a full-fledged interpretation of Hegel on his own terms, in his own historical context, and in light of all of his work. Because I focused on what he said about property in his section on "Abstract Right," it was open for readers to think I misunderstood

Hegel as holding that the property relationship is something unmediated between the person and the object, rather than always a matter of social mediation.

Neither Kant nor Hegel (who is very Kantian in his passages on "Abstract Right") thought property—or contract, or any of the other juridical relationships of abstract right—to be anything but socially mediated. Indeed, Kant's point about property was that property must become a juridical (i.e., socially mediated) relationship precisely because it is crucial to the full scope of the will of persons, and thus related to the moral law. I did not mean to argue that "property" was a matter between an individual and an object alone in the universe. Instead I wanted to plug into a socially constructed understanding involving connection between persons and things that matter to them. I did not mean to take Hegel as a theoretical foundation for my view, but only as a suggestive text. Thus I said: "The idea of embodied will, cut loose from Hegel's grand scheme of absolute mind, reminds us that people and things have ongoing relationships which have their own ebb and flow, and that these relationships can be very close to a person's center and sanity."[10]

In "Residential Rent Control" (chapter 2) I noted that my view "blurs or bridges the subject/object dichotomy in a way I believe Hegel did not."[11] In "The Rhetoric of Alienation" (chapter 7) I suggested that Hegel was ambivalent about the subject/object dichotomy because his commitment to the market society (requiring free alienation of private property) reinscribed the dichotomy even as other aspects of his theory undercut it. Whether Hegel did or did not reinscribe the subject/object dichotomy is a matter of serious controversy among Hegelians. On the one hand, his reference to the "initial gulf" between subject and object in the section on "Abstract Right" implies that this gulf is *aufgehoben* (transcended) in later, more actualized stages of theory and history. On the other hand, it is hard to see how he can argue in "Abstract Right" that whatever is external to personhood is required to be alienable, while whatever is internal to personhood is required to be inalienable, without presupposing at least an "initial" sharp divide between what is external and what is internal to the person. Then if the relationships described in "Abstract Right" are supposed to remain intact, even after they are *aufgehoben* in later stages, it may seem that the internal/external distinction must also remain.

I did not intend my remarks to adjudicate this Hegelian controversy.

In my writings I found Hegel's text on property suggestive for exposing my view, and several times returned to it, but in the end the project of intellectual history—getting the best interpretation of Hegel—is not the primary one that engages me. My project is a cultural description/ critique of American institutions of property and the legal discourse in which they are couched. My view is that our culture of property in its relationship to persons is best understood as blurring the traditional subject/object dichotomy, regardless of Kant's or Hegel's views about the matter. It is best understood as socially constructed, because of the need for a shared language and culture before property understandings can be conceivable, regardless of Kant's or Hegel's views about the matter.

Kant in fact (at least according to the dominant understandings of him) is the principal author of the subject/object dichotomy. According to this understanding, Kant divided the universe into two completely disjunct realms. One, the realm of persons, is made up of autonomous entities that are ends in themselves, that possess free will, that are capable of giving to themselves the moral law according to the categorical imperative, and that must be treated with respect according to the dignity of their status as persons. The other, the realm of objects, is made up of heteronomous entities that are not ends in themselves, that do not possess free will, that are not subject to the moral law, and that are manipulable at the will of persons. For Kant, property—that is, the possibility of *title* over and above mere possession—is necessary precisely in order to extend the realm in which persons may exercise their free will by manipulating objects to their own ends.

Just as the blurring of the traditional distinction between empirical and normative (fact and value) is a pragmatist project, so too is the blurring of the traditional distinction between subject and object. My attempt to develop a view of property and persons that blurs the subject/ object distinction is therefore another pragmatist aspect of my project.[12] In fact, my view can be understood as blurring both the subject/object distinction and the subjective/objective distinction. These have slightly different connotations. The subject/object distinction calls to mind the disjunction between persons and things, and the subjective/objective distinction calls to mind the disjunction between what is "inside" the will of a person (arbitrary, merely a matter of preference or desire) and what is "outside" in the world of objects (fixed, mind-independent reality).

The pragmatist breakdown of these categories consists in showing that each is an exaggerated caricature; or, in the manner of deconstruction, that if they are constructed in this exaggerated way, each must permeate the other. What exists "inside" a person doesn't spring from nothing; it is constructed out of interactions with other people and things (culture and the natural world). What exists "outside" a person isn't a timeless mind-independent absolute; it is constructed out of the perspectives of culture as we meet problems and create tools—ontological as well as technological—to solve them. The border between "inside" and "outside" is not usefully conceptualized as a permanent fissure in the universe.

The word "property" crosses over the traditional divide by means of the pun that I discuss in "The Rhetoric of Alienation" (chapter 7). When "property" means an attribute of a person, it is "inside" (on the subject side). When it means a thing that a person has the right to control, it is "outside" (on the object side). As long as we can maintain a perfect disjunction between what counts as a thing "outside" the person, to be manipulated, and what counts as an attribute "inside" the person, part of the entity doing the manipulating, we can also maintain the traditional divide. But I think there are cases where we do not maintain such a perfect disjunction. Things that we see as mostly "outside" can also, at the same time, be seen as partly "inside"—can become to some extent assimilated to the attributes of the person. Another way to put this is that the person's context, as we understand it, can to some degree become inseparable from the person. This is how I think the traditional subject/object distinction becomes blurred.

The blurring of the subject/object distinction coalesces with the blurring of the subjective/objective distinction once we come to see that even what we feel to be wholly "inside" ourselves is socially mediated, and even what we feel to be wholly "outside" ourselves is influenced by the perspectives we draw from our history and the circumstances that now confront us. The subjective/objective distinction returns us to the problem I discussed earlier: When we observe that someone's personhood is bound up with an item of property, does that mean that this is automatically good? Clearly not, but then a procedure for distinguishing good from bad entanglements between persons and things seems to be required. Readers of my early essays who thought that entanglements between persons and things were wholly "subjective" wondered if there could be an "objective" procedure which could distinguish among them.

My answer to this is roughly that the entanglements, *when we can see them, and see them as appropriate,* are not "subjective" in the sense such readers had in mind. While there cannot be a procedure that is "objective" in the sense they had in mind, our ability to see and understand entanglements between persons and things is not wholly separate from any procedure by which we judge them as appropriate or inappropriate. In "Government Interests and Takings" (chapter 6), I used examples in the spirit of Wittgenstein to show that we attribute mental states to other persons (and entities), and make judgments about their appropriateness or inappropriateness, based upon our shared cultural understandings of what persons (and other entities) are supposed to be like. If someone's attributed mental states, or her actions as we comprehend them, seem inappropriate to us under the circumstances, we will judge that she has a screw loose. These shared understandings can often be entrenched enough to be experienced as quite "objective" once we drop the essentialist baggage from that word. It is such shared understandings that enable us to observe and judge personal property relationships. (We are still left with the problem of critique: Can we ever get a foothold from which to argue that our shared understandings, however entrenched, are wrong? I will return to this question below.)

IV

Let me turn to the topic of whether the categories of "personal" and "fungible" property are perspicuous. Are they useful for understanding and evaluating our legal/moral culture of property? Some of the questions that arise in this regard are as follows. (1) The categories seem to be drawn with natural persons in mind, yet most property in our society is held by nonpersons; what should we say about property of churches or business corporations or universities or Indian tribes? (2) Many non-property relationships (e.g., relationships with other persons, religious commitments) can be constitutive of personhood; does it make sense to construct categories that divide these constitutive relationships into property relationships, on the one hand, and every other kind, on the other? (3) Perhaps property relationships are experienced as personal in some contexts and fungible in others; are the categories too rigid? (4) Even if the categories are perspicuous across a significant range of cases, courts may not be institutionally appropriate to try to put them into practice; do we really want to encourage judges to make distinctions between personal and fungible property?

Property of persons and nonpersons. In spite of the fact that most holdings in today's society are intangible and the largest proportion of holdings are owned by institutions or entities other than persons, the standard ideology of property stubbornly pictures property as a tangible object—indeed, usually land—owned by a natural person. Let me refer to this as the conservative (or classical liberal) ideology. In this conservative ideology, land ownership is thought to undergird individuality and liberty for persons. In the ideology, land ownership mythologically becomes ownership, and the ideology then mythologically extends to whatever we normally denominate property. One of the things I hoped to accomplish by disaggregating the category of "property" into personal and fungible was to make it clear that only a small fraction of everything we accept as property could possibly be justified by the conservative standard ideology of individual liberty and self-constitution. In other words, I wanted to show that the purported justification of all property holding could at best only be a justification of a small part of it. (It would be possible to argue, and many conservatives do argue, that even fungible property is necessary for self-constitution and liberty—but this is like arguing that people need money in order to be persons. The argument is more comfortable for welfare-rights liberals than for the traditional ideologists of private property.)

In the contemporary era the conservative ideology of property is allied to a market ideology. The market ideology pictures business entities as purely rational economic actors—that is, as profit-maximizing black boxes. Corporations are normally not conceptualized as having collective identities in any cultural sense. It follows that business entities, as long as we conceive of them as rational economic actors, can only hold fungible property. It cannot matter to the entity which assets it holds, because by definition it is "willing" to trade off any of its assets at any time for other assets (including money) that will lower its costs or otherwise raise its profits.

This goes for a corporation's land as well as for any other tangible and intangible assets. Under the market ideology, we cannot think that the corporation has become *attached* in some noneconomic sense to the land or the plant it has long been using, for example. Theoretically a corporation would sell its plant as soon as it became cheaper to operate it somewhere else, no matter how long it had been there. (Practically, of course, transaction costs may make moves too expensive.) Controversies over plant closings make clear that sometimes groups (employees, or whole communities) are "attached" in some sense to the old holdings. These groups may represent conflicting economic interests, desiring to maximize their profits instead of the corporation's. But they may also represent noneconomic interests—a noneconomic attachment to a certain job, a certain group of co-workers, a certain community character. These noneconomic interests may fare better in the legal and political arena once it is made explicit that they are up against merely a fungible interest of the business entity, and that this fungible interest does not carry the full weight of the standard ideology of property.[13]

In my essays I did not explore the issues of substantive communitarian property holdings, such as property constitutive of group identity. My project, in a sense, was to see how far I could get by reconsidering the classical liberal ideology, since I do not think attempts to dislodge it in favor of full-fledged communitarianism will get very far. But it cannot be denied that to accept as a starting point the traditional ideology of property is to grant individualism more mythological force than it deserves. Often things that are held in common are the most precious to us. It would be good to have a theory that could help us see that better. Certain groups other than business entities (churches, Indian tribes, clubs, schools, nations) might claim their group's substantive existence as a group is bound up with property (land, buildings, cultural artifacts). Even business entities might, under some communitarian theory in opposition to traditional liberalism, claim to be bound up with some of their property. For those who are outraged by the way the Supreme Court found nothing to oppose desecration of Native American sacred sites, a substantive communitarian theory of property seems to be needed.[14]

Constitutive relationships that are and are not property. Other things besides property can be "personal" in the sense of being related to self-constitution. Indeed, some of them, like the interest in bodily integrity, can be too personal even to be thought of as "property" without arousing great discomfort. My concentration on the distinction between personal and fungible *property* has the potential drawback of making it more difficult to consider together all things socially requisite for self-constitution, whether or not we conventionally think of them as property. For example, an employee's interest in not having her long-term association with a particular workplace terminated may be analogous with a tenant's interest in not having her long-term association with a particular place of residence terminated. Workplace tenure rights may belong to the same debate as residential tenure rights. Yet we are not accustomed to thinking of jobs as property the way we think of property in a leasehold. My categorization, it may be thought, does not help us bring them together; and, it may be thought, they *should* be brought together.

Although focusing on the personal/fungible distinction may thus have the drawback of dividing rights associated with personhood in a way that ultimately may not be the most useful approach, it does have the advantage, as I mentioned earlier, of disaggregating what was previously a blanket extension of the word "property." It did not seem useful at the time I was writing these essays to try to detach from the category "property" the personal category of person-thing relationships and simultaneously integrate the personal category with some broader category of personal rights such as "civil rights" or "welfare rights." The existence of welfare rights is not well accepted in our legal/moral culture, and civil rights are rather narrowly circumscribed in that culture.

In a sense my analysis goes against the grain of our legal culture by suggesting that even though they are "property," fungible property rights are not entitled to so much weight merely by virtue of being conventionally recognized as property. Having disaggregated the concept of property, I sought to assimilate the fungible category with the category of money. People have certain rights to keep their money, of course, but the point is that there is no special mystique about it. Those of us who are not radical libertarians readily accept that people can be taxed from time to time, and asked to accept certain other diminutions in their holdings for the benefit of the polity. This analysis is at the heart of the way I address the "takings" issue, and particularly the problem of "regulatory takings."

In our legal/moral culture, rights that are considered "property" are taken more seriously than any general rights to "liberty." This is even more true today than it was a decade ago. The American Supreme Court goes out of its way to protect people against what it perceives as threatened government invasion when the issue is property rights, yet often goes out of its way to side with the government against the claimant when the issue is liberty.

In light of the importance of "property" in our legal culture, claimants and their supporters often engage in rhetorical gerrymandering. Charles Reich suggested "the new property," for example, to extend the preferred status of property to certain kinds of government licenses and largess.[15] This strategy ultimately largely backfired. The Supreme Court came to hold that "new property" rights did not have the same scope of rights attached to them that presumptively came with traditional property, but rather encompassed just whatever limited scope of rights the government chose to grant.

Recently, Bruce Ackerman has suggested a similar rhetorical strategy. He would have us characterize as a property right, for example, the right of Michael Hardwick to engage in homosexual acts with his lover in private.[16] I predict that this strategy will not be successful; Ackerman will not succeed in altering the general contemporary language so that we conceive of such personal rights as property rights. But even if it succeeded in altering the language, I am afraid the strategy would ultimately backfire. These "property" rights that describe personal interactions rather than the classic picture of landholding will turn out to be second-class "property" rights (just as "new property" rights did).

Moreover, if the language really becomes altered in this way, then we will be out of the frying pan and into the fire. When personal interactions come to be conceived of and perspicuously described as transactions of property, then we have progressed very far indeed toward a commodified world view. Things which we previously conceived of as intrinsic to the person, or attributes of personhood, come to be conceived of, and socially constructed as, separable alienable objects. As I began to discuss in "The Rhetoric of Alienation" (chapter 7), universal commodification is not a desirable development for human flourishing. Today's deep division over "the body as property" makes clear the stakes in this debate. Do we "own" our sexuality, our kidneys, or our reproductive capacities so that we may sell them as we sell books?

Commodification has been helped in its progress, at least intellectually, by the advent of economic analysis of law. One important locution in economic analysis characterizes as a "property" right anything that cannot be divested without the holder's consent.[17] Many economic theorists conceive of all rights of persons, no matter to what they pertain, as property rights. Richard Posner, who argued that the purpose of criminal punishment of rape is protecting property rights in women's persons, is only one of the theorists who popularized this approach.[18] Now he is a federal judge, one of a growing number who find economic analysis congenial. At present it is unclear how judges who lean toward this approach can both say that all rights are "property" and that property rights (meaning those that were traditionally conceived of as property) are more important than other kinds of rights. At least it is ironic that left-liberals like Ackerman find themselves trying to gerrymander the rhetoric of property in much the same way as right-wing economists do.

Because of the very strong hold traditional property still has on our imagination, and because of the association of traditional property with "free" alienation in "free" markets, my instinct at the moment would be to try to curtail rather than expand its scope. That is what my strategy of disaggregation ultimately amounts to. The alternative is to try to metamorphose the dominant mythological meaning of property prevailing in our legal/moral culture. I think whoever tries to do this faces a steep uphill battle.

Rigidity of categories. In "Property and Personhood" I gave the example of a wedding ring. It is fungible when owned by a jewelry store for resale, but it may be personal when owned by someone who feels it has symbolic emotional significance. Perhaps this kind of example unduly risks reification, as if the description "personal" is characterizing the thing itself, rather than the connection between person and thing. Then it appears mysterious how the "thing" changes character.

In reality people's connections with their accustomed surroundings are complex and variable. The categories of personal and fungible, applied to those parts of our accustomed surroundings which are already understood as property, may be an oversimplification. All categorizations are simplifications; but if they are the right ones in their context, we need them to advance our understanding. I was careful to note when I gave examples like the wedding ring that its connection with the owner could change over time. It could become personal over time (its emotional significance could grow); or it could become abruptly depersonalized, perhaps reverting to fungible, if the relationship with which it was associated suddenly became a source of resentment or betrayal.

I should also have noted that the same person in the same time frame can experience the connection as personal in some contexts and fungible in others. When the owner seeks an appraisal of the ring, to obtain insurance for example, she has no trouble understanding it as a fungible market commodity separate from herself. She doesn't tell the agent that it is "priceless" and that she is insulted by having the appraiser put a dollar value on it. Nor does this fungible understanding vis-à-vis obtaining insurance undermine the personal understanding vis-à-vis her spouse.

The fact that in different contexts we experience different relationships with things (or different aspects of a relationship with a thing) does not appear to complicate the issue too much with wedding rings or homeownership. It becomes most important, I think, in the debate over "the body as property."[19] Suppose that people, in one context, conceive of and experience their blood or organs as internal to themselves (perhaps too integral with the self to be comfortably thought of as property at all, even the personal kind). Suppose that in the same time frame but in a different immediate context, people can also conceive of and experience their blood or organs as severable fungible commodities. Then perhaps an objection to markets in organs or blood will be harder to make out on personhood grounds. Suppose that women, in one context, conceive of and experience their sexuality as integral with the self (not property at all). Suppose that in the same time frame but in a different context, women can also conceive of and experience their sexuality as a severable fungible commodity. Then perhaps an objection to markets in sex (prostitution) will be harder to make out on personhood grounds. An analogous argument can be constructed for markets in reproductive capacity (babyselling).

The way we construct our conceptions and experiences (and they construct us) in these cases is complex. My present view is that many of our personal endowments and capacities associated with the body stubbornly resist conventional description as property. They remain "properties" only in the sense of attributes, that is, and do not become "property" in the sense of severable objects. (Of course, this may change if the law and economics movement—or more realistically, if widespread commodification—makes deep enough shifts in our language.) While this situation prevails, the categories of personal and fungible property are not in danger of imposing rigidity in this particular debate, because the personal property category is not applicable. Perhaps as commodification progresses we will tend to think more readily of bodily organs, endowments and capacities as property. If so, maybe the category of personal property would then come into play to help hold the line against complete fungibility of all human attributes.

Institutional appropriateness. Even if a distinction between personal and fungible property holding is recognized as part of our ordinary culture of property, there may be problems with setting about deliberately to write it into our legal institutions. Do we want to encourage legislatures to draw distinctions based upon their understanding of the nature of property claims? Do we want to encourage judges to draw these distinctions?

My thesis is that legislatures and judges are already doing these things. It is just that they are doing them tacitly and without directly focusing on the issues. Legislatures grant special rights to homeowners or to long-term tenants. Judges employ distinctions like commercial versus noncommercial, or irreparable harm versus harm compensable by monetary damages. So the question becomes whether it is better to go on in this unfocused way or better to make the issue explicit. I cannot see any advantage to keeping the issue covert. On the other hand, making it overt might result in better policies. For example, grassroots property tax limitation measures enacted to protect resident homeowners could have excluded commercial holdings.

It is understandable that someone would blanch at the notion of giving a judge power to decide whether her jewelry or paintings are personal or fungible. But the issue whether or not something is appropriately considered personal property is not "subjective," and therefore does not call in general for this kind of case-specific judgment. Whether or not something is appropriately considered personal instead depends upon whether our cultural commitments surrounding property and personhood make it justifiable for persons and a particular category of thing to be treated as connected.

Courts are not called upon to decide case-by-case whether the claimant actually experiences connection with her property, but rather to decide in general which types of cases involve personal property. If the courts make explicit the preferred status of homeownership, for example, that may have repercussions in the law of residential tenancy and in other fields as well, from zoning to eminent domain to taxation. But it will not call upon the court to decide in any particular case whether a resident owner really cares enough about his or her home. Courts make similar general decisions about the cultural commitments of property in nuisance and takings law. They routinely have to decide what activities are "reasonable" for landowners to engage in, even if they annoy the neighbors, and what kinds of yielding of expected rights represent acceptable obligations of citizenship, even if the government takes them without paying.

V

Partly due to my pragmatic frame of mind, it was important to me in these essays to connect theories with practice, with legal property doctrines as they now function. As it turned out, most of my efforts focused on the rights of residential tenants and on the Fifth Amendment takings clause. "Property and Personhood" included a "selective survey" of the implicit distinction between personal and fungible property rights in various fields of legal doctrine: privacy in the home, residential tenancy, searches and seizures of homes and cars, takings, inverse condemnation, free speech in shopping centers, trespass and antidiscrimination, and exclusionary zoning.[20] I later considered adverse possession and servitudes (in chapter 3), returned briefly to exclusionary zoning (in chapter 2), and in a more extended way to residential tenancy and takings (in chapters 2, 4, 5, and 6). Except for residential tenancy and takings, all of my treatments were cursory. Readers I hope will understand them as suggestive but incomplete.

Three of my more recent essays deal with the eminent domain clause of the Constitution and the issue of governmental takings of private property for public use without just compensation. It is the field of property law that I have written about the most. Takings law has fascinated me because as a doctrinal field it is in continuing disarray (chapter 5, "Diagnosing the Takings Problem"). It is easy to show that as long as we do not understand corrective justice we will not understand takings either. Takings law has also fascinated me because it is a lens through which to see both traditional property ideology and to reimagine it through the personhood perspective (chapter 4, "The Liberal Conception of Property"). With the emergence of a conservative Supreme Court, the traditional ideology has become more dominant, but the personhood perspective remains as an undercurrent. Takings law has also fascinated me because cultural commitments of property and the role of the judge's theory of politics can readily be understood through it (chapter 6, "Government Interests and Takings"). In order to see something as a taking we must see it as a government action that changes property rights, and this implicates both how we characterize the prior property regime in effect and how we characterize government action.

I will not say more about takings here, because the three essays adequately convey my views in detail. A few words are in order about residential tenancy, however, which I took up in "Residential Rent

Control" (chapter 2), and revisited twice in the context of the essays on takings. My perspective on tenants' rights varied as time went on. In the first essay I focused a good deal on the connection between an individual tenant and her apartment as a home. Part of the reason for the individualist focus is that I wanted to confront head on the received economic analysis of rent control. Rent control is often imposed to alleviate a shortage of affordable housing. The standard economic analysis says that lowering the price causes a worse housing shortage by raising the demand, results in other misallocations, and leads to black markets; thus rent control is an unmitigated evil. So entrenched is this received view that when I presented the essay in draft at a law school workshop, an economist solemnly warned me that if I defended rent control, "No one will read it." In the first part of the essay, at least, I wanted to accept the economic assumption that the issue about rent control can be framed in terms of a single individual renting an apartment.

I argued that regardless of how the economic efficiency calculus comes out (but still more clearly if its outcome is questionable), efficiency is not the only issue. If a tenant stands to lose her home so that the landlord can reap a higher profit, that can be perceived as wrong. Resident homeowners don't have to pay over more and more of their income to the lienholder as the market value increases or as interest rates increase. Even adjustable mortgages are capped in advance. Resident owners have security of tenure as long as they can maintain the level of payment they planned for. My essay made the case for treating similarly situated resident tenants similarly.[21]

The landlord's interest is fungible. The landlord sells residency rights as a commodity. For landlords that are business entities this does not seem very controversial since, as discussed above, liberal market ideology implies that all property of business entities is fungible. Considering the landlord's interest fungible may be more controversial for landlords who are individuals, but that is because of the overinclusive scope of the traditional ideology of property. The fact that a tenant has tenure rights, and the fact that the landlord does not have the freedom to set whatever price she wishes for her commodity, does not mean that the landlord has been personally "invaded" in the sense that the traditional ideology of property prompts us to think.

But in "Residential Rent Control" I did not explore the question how we should consider the landlord who tells the court she "feels" connected to the property she rents out, or who tells the court she is connected to her tenants in a way other than as a mere seller of a commodity. I did bring up the issue in "The Liberal Conception of Property." There I suggested that legislatures could exempt landlords who own small buildings and actually live in them. This would be an instance of explicit provision for our understanding of the distinction between personal and fungible holding, such as I mentioned above. In that essay I repeated, as does the discussion above, that "subjective" feelings cannot by themselves render property personal.

Moreover, I brought up the issue of the communitarian landlord. Some landlords may be communitarian in that they relate to the tenants as members of a community with themselves and not merely as buyers of a fungible commodity. In "The Liberal Conception of Property" I said that it would be morally counterintuitive to accord such landlords "greater control over their commodities, and hence greater power over buyers of them, than we would ethically accord to someone who corresponded to the caricature commodity-holder."[22] Still, the issue remains to be discussed whether legal enactment of tenants' rights is the best way to make progress toward a world in which landlords and tenants are more closely linked in community. As I mention below, critics from the right think the answer is obviously "no," whereas critics from the left think the answer depends upon whether the tenants themselves push for these rights as part of a program for their own empowerment.

This raises the question of the link between tenants' legal rights and tenants' political activity. This is a question I have not treated in depth, although I did raise it in "The Liberal Conception of Property." Rights like rent control and eviction control, in particular, are designed to foster stability and continuity of residential tenure. Tenants' rights are necessary to community formation, and hence to political voice. It is hard to organize as citizens when you can lose your home at any moment. Hence I said, "As the law has developed, the issue of keeping one's home can be seen as inextricably intertwined with the issue of developing and protecting one's political voice."[23]

I considered tenants' rights from another angle in "Government Interests and Takings" (chapter 6). Since it is obvious that in the past two decades the tenant's "bundle of sticks" has gotten larger and the landlord's smaller, why haven't the courts declared these changes to be takings? Perhaps the legal revolution ushering in the New Deal era following the *Lochner* decision has made it too difficult to consider price control a taking of a property right.[24] But it seems that a deeper explanation is that there is no one government "action" that "took" rights from landlords and "gave" them to tenants. Instead, there has been a gradual evolution of the legal package called tenancy, coextensive with a gradual evolution in the cultural commitments surrounding residential occupancy of rental property. This development shows the feedback loop between law and culture: law can both express a set of underlying cultural commitments, and help contribute to changing them.

VI

Conservative property theorists will find my suggestions wrong, silly, or dangerous. Richard Epstein is probably the most prominent conservative legal property theorist. Conservative legal theorists are also influenced by the work of Robert Nozick, perhaps the most prominent of contemporary libertarian philosophers. A few words are in order here about how my theories confront theirs.

I have partially argued my case against Epstein in chapter 3 ("Problems for the Theory of Absolute Property Rights"). Epstein's basic position is that natural private property rights severely limit government in all respects. His position rests on the premise that there exist natural, prepolitical property entitlements in individuals. These natural property rights are defined by the meaning of the word property, as Blackstone understood it, and as Epstein believes we still understand it today, because he believes property has a real, timeless meaning. Property by natural right is acquired by first possession in a state of nature (often called "title by grab" by the irreverent). Although he is committed to natural rights, Epstein's justificatory arguments almost always take the utilitarian form of transaction cost economics.

It has not been my purpose to refute all of Epstein's claims in detail.[25] Three features of his world view especially interest me. One is the perspective by which an observer looks at regulation and sees it as rent-seeking, a topic I discuss in chapter 6. Another is the notion that the conservative ideologue can coherently be both a libertarian and a devotee of economic efficiency, against which I argue in chapter 3. The third is the stubborn implicit commitment to the idea that there exists a unique specific set of formally realizable prepolitical property rights. Against this commitment I argue, in chapter 3 and elsewhere, again and again, that property is a contested concept, that its content depends upon culture, that it evolves, that it is different for personal and fungible rights.

Epstein, Robert C. Ellickson, and other libertarians have of course vigorously disagreed with my views about rent control. Sometimes the arguments are like ships passing in the night. As noted above, many economic theorists argue that price control on residential housing is *always* inefficient. I find the argument too sweeping. Efficiency in practice is an empirical question; in practice markets do not reach equilibrium; in practice it is hard to know the scope of a market (to know what is "internal" to it and what is an "externality"). Surely the efficiency question is not amenable to such blanket armchair analyses. I do join issue with economic theory by arguing that efficiency is not the only consideration, and that dollar value is not the only kind of value at stake.

Some libertarians make an economic argument that does connect with my concerns. This argument says that rent control causes tenants to stay put when otherwise they would move, and that this is consequentially bad. The idea is that tenants who would otherwise move fail to do so because their apartment is cheaper than market forces would have it, and thus they have strong incentives to stay vis-à-vis other uncontrolled markets. Ellickson argues that this can be "stultifying": "mobility constraints may lock in stale households and lock out the fresh entrants the community most needs to retain its vitality."[26]

It is true that my focus on the connection between persons and the things they surround themselves with emphasizes persons' need for a stable context in order to constitute and express themselves as persons. There is another side to the coin, one that I have not focused on in my work. In order to constitute and express themselves as persons, persons also need the ability to change their surroundings and their commitments; they need flexibility of context. Personhood depends *both* on the ability to embed in contexts and on the ability to break out of contexts. (I will return to this paradox of personhood below.)

Ellickson claims that rent control in effect persuades people to stagnate in their old contexts. He implicitly claims that it would be better for their freedom—and their selfhood, and their communities—if they broke free of their old contexts and sought new ones; and that they would do so if only free market incentives were present. The first claim, that breaking free of context would be better for people, is a noneconomic argument, and one based, like mine, on the values of personhood and community. It is not a *libertarian* argument, however, unless Ellickson thinks that people are being *coerced* into staying, when their *free choice* would be to move.[27] Otherwise Ellickson is just saying that mobility should be forced on people because it is better for them than the stagnation that results when they choose to stay in their old neighborhoods.

But as a libertarian argument Ellickson's is implausible. Coercion is a normative issue. Whether we see coercion depends upon the baseline that we think the person is justified in claiming. When a neighborhood of fairly poor tenants is hit by a sudden rise in market prices, people's dominant experience of what happens likely is that the tenants are forced to move because they can no longer afford the rent. The event is readily characterized as coercive. On the other hand, when tenants stay in an apartment whose rent is "too" low, they might be understood by the libertarian as taking advantage of "consumer surplus"—just as do homeowners who fail to sell their houses after a run-up in the real estate market. Or, in my terms, they might be understood as valuing their self-constitution in this context—just as do homeowners who stay. (Ellickson's arguments about stagnation apply equally to such homeowners.) The act of staying is not readily characterized as coercive, but is instead seen as free choice.

In fact a main point of my arguments is that tenants should have the same range of free choice about whether they stay or go as homeowners. They should not have their ability to choose a stable context, if they wish, destroyed merely for the sake of economic rents to the landlord. Whether on the whole our society provides too many opportunities for stability of context (through property doctrines among other things) and not enough opportunities for flexibility and change is a question of social vision that I have not addressed. It is something that greatly interests my critics on the left, as I shall mention below.

The issue of mobility, and the general issue of freedom to alter one's contexts (and thereby alter oneself) relates to the issue of alienability. In fact one could say that "property" is the classical liberal instantiation of the need for stability of contexts, and "freedom of contract" is the classical liberal instantiation of the need for context-flexibility. The mythology of property expresses rootedness, and the mythology of contract expresses mutability. Libertarians like Nozick argue that freedom of alienation is the key to freedom. His "entitlement theory" of justice is very attractive to conservative legal property theorists. Nozick argues that if the world were wholly just, two principles, the principle of justice in acquisition and the principle of just transfer, would cover the whole subject of justice in holdings. Since the world is not wholly just, he adds, a principle of rectification—roughly equivalent to corrective justice—is needed.

It is easy to see why this scheme appeals to conservatives about property. Nozick's terms correspond to the way lawyers (and perhaps lay people) reason in property cases. The principle of justice in acquisition corresponds to root of title, and the principle of just transfer corresponds to chain of title. If they together exhaust justice, then justice is wholly "private"—it is exhausted by the classical liberal scheme of private property plus free contract. Nozick did not argue in the detail needed to arrange a legal scheme, however: he did not tell us what constitutes a correct principle of just acquisition (occupancy? conquest? discovery?), nor what counts as a just transfer (eminent domain? compensation in tort?). Nor did he tell us what to do if we think all property holdings now extant in the actual world do not rest completely on chains of just transfer, but rather are all tainted by past fraud and violence.

These pragmatic questions are real ones, and I think they tell against Nozick's ideal theory. Nevertheless, I have not provided in these essays, nor will I here provide, an extended critique of Nozick's views.[28] I just want to note a difficult theoretical problem for libertarians, at least for those who follow Nozick in being influenced by Kant, relating to how to distinguish persons from their property. The problem involves how we should construct the theoretical self when we are constructing the self as moral reasoner. The difficulty arises, in my view, because the libertarian agenda seeks both a strong theory of natural entitlement, tending to correlate with a "thick" theoretical self, and a strong theory of freedom of alienation, tending to correlate with a "thin" theoretical self.

For a Kantian moral reasoner, persons are undifferentiated moral agents. What makes up the person in moral reasoning (as opposed to what makes up an individual in real life) is just what is essential to being a free and rational being. Kantian moral persons are undifferentiated contentless selves just because Kantian moral theory regards us as equal, that is identical, as free and rational beings. Kantian moral theorists have the problem of deciding exactly how embodied and how pragmatically situated we are to be considered to be for moral purposes. What aspects of the circumstances and limitations of life as we know it should be abstracted out of the picture when we reason about justice, and which of them should be taken as part of the abstract self as moral agent?

To visualize the problem about the scope of personhood, we can think of a dot surrounded by two concentric circles. The dot is the abstract self, the moral agent, in its barest possible version. The next circle takes in the self's endowments and its attributes. The outer circle takes in its products and possessions. In order to arrive at the strongest possible theory of natural entitlement, there is a tendency to assimilate to the self the inner circle (endowments and attributes) and even to some extent the outer circle (products and possessions). This I call a thick theory of the self. On the other hand, in order to arrive at the strongest possible theory of freedom of alienation, there is a tendency to consider the inner and outer circles as being wholly separate from the essential self, the central point, and readily detachable from it. This I call a thin theory of the self.

The problem for a thick theory that wants to arrive at libertarianism as its principle of justice is that it appears that what is integral to self is prima facie inalienable. The more attributes, characteristics, endowments, etc., are taken in and held to be essential to the self, in order to establish firm individual entitlements, the less is prima facie alienable. Nozick complains against Rawls, for example, that Rawls has treated natural endowments as a collective asset (therefore separable from one's self), whereas the thick theory Nozick seems to adopt in this context means that Rawls's treatment disrespects personhood.[29] Nozick seems to say that one's endowments are simply part of one's self.

On the other hand, a thin theory of the self seems more readily to lend itself to the libertarian commitment to maximum alienability. The self as bare contentless free will can sever all of its attributes, characteristics, endowments, etc., without destroying its essential selfhood. The libertarian could argue, as Nozick seems to in this context, that even personhood is alienable voluntarily; one can sell oneself into slavery.[30] (As Hegel noted, this argument has the problem of figuring out what can possibly remain, if personhood is alienated, to be the repository of the will that does the alienating.)

On the whole, libertarian theory seems to favor a thin theory of the self, in which all endowments, attributes, characteristics, etc., can be severed and alienated. But because the strong form of initial entitlement seems to correlate with a thick theory, in which natural endowments are simply part of the self, there is understandably a strong temptation to try to have it both ways—leaning toward a thick theory when entitlement is in issue, otherwise holding fast to a thin theory to undergird maximum alienability.

In contrast to libertarianism, my thesis, as is implied by much of what I said in these essays, is that a thicker theory of the self is a more plausible theory of the person from which to do ethical theory. (A thick theory has its own hazards, as I will note below.)

VII

My suggestions cause discomfort on the left as well as the right. Some critical legal theorists think that the focus of these essays is too individualistic, or that they are too accepting of the status quo. Stephen Schnably, for example, finds a "conservative bias" in my work.[31] His is a good example of criticism from the left, because he criticizes me both for being too consensus-oriented and for failing to elaborate a "theory of transformative social change." These criticisms reflect two separate strands of contemporary critical thought. The critical rhetoric calling for incessant disruption of consensus resonates with the restless methodology of deconstruction, while the critical rhetoric calling for overarching transformative theory resonates with the utopian longing for total and final revolution.[32]

As a pragmatist I have provisionally assumed arguendo much of the traditional ideology of property (the conceptual "status quo," with its "individualist" bias), because I did not judge it now possible to metamorphose that conception in our legal culture. But I have not made the traditional ideology foundational, nor treated it as in any way a permanent cultural feature. I believed when I wrote "Property and Personhood" that the best way to make gains for the less well-off, under the circumstances, was (a) to appeal to the universality of the notion of personhood, and (b) to drive a wedge into the traditional ideological justification of property by showing that only a very small portion of private property rights fits within that justification.

It cannot be denied that this kind of strategic choice, like all of our political choices, involves a potential double bind. Attempting to transcend the deeply entrenched meaning of property might result in no progress, or in only illusory progress, as happened with the "new property." But provisionally accepting the entrenched meaning might further reinforce and entrench that meaning in our culture, and make future evolution even more difficult. I believe these double binds are a defining mark of political life, and I believe that they have no a priori theoretical solution. In practice, we must judge which alternative is better on the whole, and we must keep reconsidering as circumstances change.

Have circumstances changed enough in the decade-plus since I wrote "Property and Personhood" so that another strategy is called for? On the one hand, now that the Supreme Court more clearly than ever favors traditional property rights over individual liberty rights, we need to debate the pragmatic strategy of assimilating more rights into traditional property.[33] On the other hand, as Schnably argues, the entrenchment of the ideology of "the home" creates a double bind.

In accepting that ideology I took hold of one prong of the dilemma. Traditional property ideology makes the home (and privacy therein) central to notions of individuality and freedom, to the extent of using the-home-as-castle as the cornerstone justification for the existence of private property. Along with this traditional property commitment, there is the commitment of traditional liberalism to treat like cases alike (universalism). Thus, to argue that self-constitution as a person can be justifiably linked to the home might result in gains for some groups who are relatively powerless. Tenants might gain entitlements they need and want, because their apartments can be seen as homes just as much as the kind of dwellings that are owned by wealthier people. Homeless people might gain too if both homeless and nonhomeless people come to believe that persons are owed homes merely by virtue of their status as persons.

Schnably takes hold of the other prong of the dilemma. He argues that these moves reinforce the ideology of the home, and that that ideology might have undesirable ramifications in a number of respects. It might reinforce oppressive understandings of women's roles (as homemakers, creators of home as a haven for men from the hurly-burly of the market). It might reinforce the isolation of suburbia and the pervasive patterns of exclusion: it might contribute to discrimination and homelessness. It might divert attention from alienation in the workplace. Tenants might be disempowered if the ideology of the home dissolves their political will and de-emphasizes political community. Homeless people might be harmed if the ideology of the home degrades them or renders them invisible.

In order to deal with this issue, the immediacy of these risks must somehow be assessed. For what it's worth, I don't think any of us can now loosen the cultural entrenchment of private property, the hold it has on our imaginations and our institutions. So I think we cannot avoid the risk of backlash from the ideology of the home even if we decide it is substantial. But if I were writing these essays today I would want to make the double bind more visible.

Critics on the left also frequently object to pragmatism in general. Some consider pragmatism to be inherently conservative, primarily for two reasons. First, if there can be no transcendent transformative theory by which all progress is measured, then (it is argued) the pragmatist meliorist spirit results not in real progress but rather only in ineffectual tinkering. Second, if pragmatism measures the goodness of the law, or of proposals for change, or of theories of social justice, by "coherence" or "fit" with what we already accept, then the more firmly entrenched is the status quo the harder it will be to avoid blindly reaffirming it. Both of these are indeed issues for pragmatists to face, but, although certain pragmatists may be conservative, pragmatism itself is not inherently conservative.

The first reason it is contended by some that pragmatism is conservative raises the issue of how we can tell that a change is progress, rather than just change. If there can be no overarching transcendent theory of what the world should ideally look like, how can we judge any state of affairs as better than any other? A pragmatist does not suggest that all ideal theory is impossible or that we can somehow do without it altogether. Rather, for the pragmatist, theory is immanent and evolving; its development goes hand in hand with practice.

Visions of a better life are part of life; they give us the impetus to try to change things. At the same time, those visions of the ideal are constituted by life as it is now, and they will change as we change our life. Theory—visions of a different and better future—is indeed necessary or there is nothing that we can understand as progress and therefore no way for us to mobilize ourselves to work for progress. The familiar pragmatist metaphor for this process pictures a ship being rebuilt at sea, plank by plank. The activity of rebuilding guides our theory of what the ship ideally should look like just as much as the ideal of what the ship should look like guides the activity of rebuilding.[34] This process is not the kind of guidance a formalist hopes for—measuring our activities against an unchanging plan. Yet is not "no guidance." It is often enough to make us sure (for now) of the difference between progress and tinkering, and that is all the sureness we can have.

The second reason it is contended that pragmatism is conservative raises what I call the problem of bad coherence. Some pragmatists endorse coherence theories of truth or goodness, in which any given proposition or value is judged by how well it hangs together with the whole system of propositions or values to which we are committed. If a pragmatist defines truth or goodness by means of coherence, then how can the pragmatist recognize a system that is coherent but *bad,* such as institutionally coherent and pervasive racism or sexism? Pragmatism can indeed be conservative if mere pervasive institutional instantiation of a conception is enough to conclude that it is the best. But pragmatists who rely on institutional coherence this way are incomplete pragmatists. They are throwing out the other half of the pragmatist spirit—the importance of our critical visions and imaginative recreations of our world. Inconsistent pragmatists are disabled from critique, but consistent pragmatists are not.

The only way the consistent pragmatist is disabled from appropriate critique of existing institutions is if the alternative, better understanding is simply not currently thinkable (not accessible to the human imagination under existing circumstances). This may have been the situation with the institution of slavery in the ancient world, for example; it may have been unthinkable that all humans are fundamentally equal. But nonpragmatists are no less disabled than pragmatists from thinking the unthinkable. In fact, pragmatists, simply by understanding that most understandings of the world that appear immutable are nevertheless provisional, are perhaps better situated to help the unthinkable become thinkable. I consider the feminist practice of consciousness-raising, for example, to be a pragmatist process of reconceptualization. Through this process it became possible to understand such things as marital rape and sexual harassment, whereas previously they were largely unnamed aspects of women's lives.

VIII

I have already alluded to an issue for personhood involving stability versus flexibility of contexts. For example, in the case of rent control the debate about mobility—whether stability or flexibility should be fostered—is part of a general argument about how context-entrenchment should be evaluated. For appropriate self-constitution it appears both that strong attachment to context and strong possibilities for detachment from context are needed. (A nice saying for parents has it that children need to develop both roots and wings.) But these needs seem to oppose each other and thus to coexist paradoxically. This causes problems for theory and contradictory tendencies in practice.

A potential for context-transcendence is clearly a mark of humanity. Humans do need wings. We conceive of the well-developed human person as being capable of breaking free of her bonds with things and other people, to make a new beginning, to make of herself someone else. But if this mark of human freedom and agency is made theoretically primary, it leads to what I called a thin theory of the person. At the limit of thinness, nothing is intrinsic to personhood but bare undifferentiated free will. This leaves everything else—endowments, characteristics, attributes, capacities, relationships, experiences—as alienable objects, "outside" the self, part of the severable context. Such a vanishingly thin theory of the person appears to facilitate assimilating aspects of ourselves to the realm of commodities, and the vanishing of personhood as we know it.

Context-embeddedness is clearly a mark of humanity as well. Humans need roots too. We conceive of the well-developed human person as capable of making bonds with other people and with things, as existing in the continuity of these relationships over time, and indeed as needing these continuing relationships in order to exist continuously as a person. If this mark of human connectedness is made theoretically primary, it leads to what I called a thick theory of the person. At the limit of thickness, everything in the person's context is inseparable from personhood and "inside" the self. Such an indefinitely thick theory of the person would facilitate social construction of fixed status hierarchies, and would also destroy personhood as we know it.

In a sense, my work on property and personhood can be understood as an antidote to a too-thin theory of personhood that has been dominant in traditional liberalism. Traditional liberal theory placed in property ideology (ownership) the aspect of connectedness, and in contract ideology (exchange) the aspect of separability. But because traditional property ideology makes freedom of alienation through contract an essential characteristic of property, the whole ideological system tends toward commodification. As an antidote, my work is one-sided. It runs the risk of being understood as promoting a too-thick theory, because it concentrates on only one (attachment, connectedness) of the two context-relationships necessary to personhood.

Future work, I think, should try to achieve a better understanding of the nature of the paradoxical coexistence of these two aspects of context in self-constitution. A pragmatic way of doing this would be to investigate the trouble they make in practice. I will close with an example of this kind of trouble, in the field of marital property.

Should the law treat increased earning power of one partner gained during marriage as a marital asset to be part of the estate divisible between the two partners at divorce? Is the increased earning power appropriately treated as a separable object whose monetary value can then be split between the parties? The "object" in question might be a professional degree, involving education and training that was "added" to talent; or it might be the goodwill of a business or practice. Theoretically, although courts have not gone so far in practice, it might be any added increment of earning power—for example, accruing to a good bank executive or a good truck driver.

Traditionally these things were not counted in the marital estate because they were not considered property. They deviated too much from the standard picture of a tangible alienable object. They were not traded in any market and not included in one's personal financial statement. Nevertheless there is a contemporary trend to include them, primarily because it is thought that doing so will help women who contribute substantially to their husbands' increased earning power during marriage and then receive little or nothing at divorce. Whether or not including these "objects" of increased earning capacity in the marital estate will actually benefit disadvantaged women is a complex empirical question that I will leave aside, though it needs investigation; it involves issues ranging from the effect on litigation strategies in divorces to the possible bad effects of increasing objectification in general. My focus here is the way this issue implicates the contradictory aspects of our understanding of personhood.

One argument for conceiving of these "human capital assets" (the term already commodifies) as divisible objects of marital property is the claim that marriage in the contemporary era is, or should be, no different from an ordinary contract. Recognizing divisible property rights in one's spouse's professional degree is merely fulfilling the parties' expected benefit of the bargain. As a New York court said, in holding that the present value of the increased earning power of a husband's medical degree was subject to equitable distribution, marriage is an economic partnership.[35] This argument rejects the traditional conception of marriage as a sharing of souls, reconceiving it as a standard exchange relationship. It is argued that women achieve equal dignity in a standard exchange relationship, whereas traditional marriage was an unequal status relationship. To step up and claim one's fair share of a piece of property bespeaks a relationship of equal dignity; to have to rely on alimony bespeaks subordination.

Another argument for conceiving of these "human capital assets" as divisible marital property takes the opposite tack, reinscribing the traditional ideal of marriage. The argument is based upon the idea of connectedness and relationship. In this argument, marriage is portrayed as a constitutive relationship for the spouses, so that sharing of even the most personal of the other's capacities and endowments is the norm. According to this argument, couples enter into marriage expecting to share for life and constituting themselves accordingly. Thus if "human capital assets" accrue unequally while the spouses remain married, that will not be experienced as a betrayal of expectations. But if the spouses divorce, the expectations and hopes of future sharing should be metamorphosed into expectations of monetary compensation and divided, rather than frustrating expectations altogether.

Describing marriage as simply a market relationship of exchange is a species of commodification. It may harm rather than help women, if they are largely unable to bargain effectively with men they marry. But reinscribing the traditional ideology of marriage may simply reinforce the subordinated status the broadened marital property policy is trying to correct. To reinscribe the traditional ideology may be to embrace a view of personhood in which the theory of the self is too thick; too little room is given for breaking free of entrenchment in a traditional status relationship.

To make the degree-holding spouse (usually pictured as the husband) compensate his former spouse for the development of his own abilities is problematic for his personhood too. He is at least (symbolically) locked into the career projected at the time of divorce, and indeed locked into the marriage itself in a sense. If the discounted present value of the New York M.D.'s future earnings as a doctor must be substantially shared with his divorced wife, how can he be free to transcend his context, to change himself into someone else, perhaps become a poet? Of course, the law could make him pay her the money, if he had it, and then do whatever he likes. But the symbolic message, backed by powerful economic incentives, is that he is locked for life into the career he chose during marriage, because his ex-wife shares forever the self he was then. That perhaps is too much entrenchment in context to be consistent with personhood as we now conceive it. It is also inconsistent with the very idea of divorce as a wholly new start. What of the sharing that is supposed to take place in a new marriage, should one occur, if the self is still involved with the old marriage?

In short, it appears that the idea of divorce brings with it a theory of fresh start that is connected with the aspect of personhood that requires the possibility of breaking free of one's contexts. If we mean unambivalently to embrace this concept of divorce, how should it play out in property theory? It appears that the idea of treating enhanced earning capacity as a divisible market commodity cuts against the concept of divorce by entrenching the self in the first marriage; it seems an ironic throwback to the era in which death was the only escape from marriage. In this way it expresses an unacceptably thick theory of the self. At the same time, commodifying enhanced earning capacity conceives of one's education, abilities, capacities, skills, and experience as objects that are separable from the self and monetizable. In this way, it also expresses an unacceptably thin theory of the self.

These difficulties are not to be escaped merely by sticking with the traditional system. In this the reformers are correct. Traditional marriage is not an institution conducive to women's self-constitution as persons, and alimony is not an institution conducive to women's fuller self-development after divorce. For the property theorist, these difficulties point up the paradoxes of property and personhood. They are part of a skein that awaits disentangling.

Property and Personhood

This essay explores the relationship between property and personhood, a relationship that has commonly been both ignored and taken for granted in legal thought. The premise underlying the personhood perspective is that to achieve proper self-development—to be a *person*—an individual needs some control over resources in the external environment. The necessary assurances of control take the form of property rights. Although explicit elaboration of this perspective is wanting in modern writing on property, the personhood perspective is often implicit in the connections that courts and commentators find between property and privacy or between property and liberty. In addition to its power to explain certain aspects of existing schemes of property entitlement, the personhood perspective can also serve as an explicit source of values for making moral distinctions in property disputes, and hence for either justifying or criticizing current law.

Almost any theory of private property rights can be referred to some notion of personhood. The theory must address the rights accruing to individual persons, and therefore necessarily implicates the nature of the entity to which they accrue. It is not surprising that personhood has played a part in property theories all along the political spectrum. Conservatives rely on an absolute conception of property as sacred to personal autonomy. Communitarians believe that changing conceptions of property reflect and shape the changing nature of persons and communities. Welfare rights liberals find entitlement to a minimal level of resources necessary to the dignity of persons even when the entitlement must curtail the property rights of others. This essay does not emphasize how the notion of personhood might figure in the most prevalent traditional lines of liberal property theory: the Lockean labor-desert theory, which focuses on individual autonomy, or the utilitarian theory, which focuses on welfare maximization.[1] It rather attempts to clarify a third strand of liberal property theory that focuses on personal embodiment or self-constitution in terms of "things." This "personhood perspective" corresponds to, or is the dominant premise of, the so-called personality theory of property. Two main functions of any property theory are the general justification of property rights and their delineation. My purpose here is to consider these two functions from the perspective of personhood. But since a systematic general justification of property rights involves other concerns not within the scope of this essay, I will concentrate on the latter function: exploring how the personhood perspective can help decide specific disputes between rival claimants. Positive analysis will attempt to demonstrate that the personhood perspective has been reflected in some past legal decisions; normative analysis will attempt to show how some legal decisions are justified in light of the personhood perspective and how some are not.

In what follows I shall discuss the personhood perspective as Hegel developed it in *Philosophy of Right,* trace some of its later permutations and entanglements with other perspectives on property, and try to develop a contemporary view useful in the context of the American legal system. Section I presents an intuitive philosophical outline of the personhood perspective and how it figures in the justification of property rights. Section II presents various positions on the appropriate definition of a "person." Section III then distinguishes Hegel's concept of persons from the intuitive view discussed in section I, but identifies some of his insights as useful in developing the idea of property for personhood. Section IV shows that the personhood perspective provides a moral basis for protecting some rights more stringently than others in the context of a legal system. Section V surveys a range of legal problems from the viewpoint of property for personhood. Of particular interest is the way that the personhood property perspective cuts across many different fields of law as seemingly disparate as criminal procedure and freedom of expression. Section VI concludes that a right to property for personhood should be recognized.

I. PROPERTY FOR PERSONHOOD: AN INTUITIVE VIEW

Most people possess certain objects they feel are almost part of themselves. These objects are closely bound up with personhood because they are part of the way we constitute ourselves as continuing personal entities in the world. They may be as different as people are different, but some common examples might be a wedding ring, a portrait, an heirloom, or a house.

One may gauge the strength or significance of someone's relationship with an object by the kind of pain that would be occasioned by its loss. On this view, an object is closely related to one's personhood if its loss causes pain that cannot be relieved by the object's replacement.[2] If so, that particular object is bound up with the holder. For instance, if a wedding ring is stolen from a jeweler, insurance proceeds can reimburse the jeweler, but if a wedding ring is stolen from a loving wearer, the price of a replacement will not restore the status quo—perhaps no amount of money can do so.

The opposite of holding an object that has become a part of oneself is holding an object that is perfectly replaceable with other goods of equal market value. One holds such an object for purely instrumental reasons. The archetype of such a good is, of course, money, which is almost always held only to buy other things. A dollar is worth no more than what one chooses to buy with it, and one dollar bill is as good as another. Other examples are the wedding ring in the hands of the jeweler, the automobile in the hands of the dealer, the land in the hands of the developer, or the apartment in the hands of the commercial landlord. I shall call these theoretical opposites—property that is bound up with a person and property that is held purely instrumentally—personal property and fungible property respectively.[3]

Why refer these intuitions to personhood at all? It may appear that the category I call personal property could be described as simply a category of property for personal autonomy or liberty. Property for personal autonomy or liberty might be a class of objects or resources necessary to be a person or whose absence would hinder the autonomy or liberty attributed to a person. But there is something more in an affirmative notion of an individual being bound up with an external "thing." If autonomy is understood as abstract rationality and responsibility attributed to an individual, it fails to convey this sense of connection with the external world. Neither does liberty, if understood in the bare sense of freedom from interference by others with autonomous choices regarding control of one's external environment.

Once we admit that a person can be bound up with an external "thing" in some constitutive sense, we can argue that by virtue of this connection the person should be accorded broad liberty with respect to control over that "thing." But here liberty follows from property for personhood; personhood is the basic concept, not liberty. Of course, if liberty is viewed not as freedom from interference, or "negative freedom," but rather as some positive will that by acting on the external

world is constitutive of the person, then liberty comes closer to captur-
ing the idea of the self being intimately bound up with things in the
external world.[4]

It intuitively appears that there is such a thing as property for personhood because people become bound up with "things." But this intuitive
view does not compel the conclusion that property for personhood deserves moral recognition or legal protection, because arguably there is
bad as well as good in being bound up with external objects. If there is
a traditional understanding that a well-developed person must invest
herself to some extent in external objects, there is no less a traditional
understanding that one should not invest oneself *in the wrong way* or *to
too great an extent* in external objects. Property is damnation as well as
salvation, object-fetishism as well as moral groundwork. In this view,
the relationship between the shoe fetishist and his shoe will not be respected like that between the spouse and her wedding ring. At the extreme, anyone who lives only for material objects is considered not to
be a well-developed person, but rather to be lacking some important
attribute of humanity.

II. THE ROLE OF THE CONCEPT OF PERSON

The intuitive view of property for personhood just stated is wholly subjective: self-identification through objects varies from person to person.
But if property for personhood cannot be viewed as other than arbitrary
and subjective, then personal objects merely represent strong preferences, and to argue for their recognition by the legal system might collapse to a simple utilitarian preference summing. To avoid this collapse
requires objective criteria differentiating good from bad identification
with objects in order to identify a realm of personal property deserving
recognition. The necessary objective criteria might be sought by appeal
to extrinsic moral reality, to scientific truths of psychology, or to the
concept of person itself. Taking the last route, this section approaches
the problem of developing a standard for recognizing claims to personal
property by referring to the concept of "person" itself. If that concept
necessarily includes certain features, then those features can determine
what personal property is while still avoiding ethical subjectivism.

A. Theories of the Person

The polymorphous nature of the word "person" inevitably creates problems for a moral thesis about property built upon notions of person-

hood. "Person" stems from the Latin *persona,* meaning, among other things, a theatrical role. In Roman law, persona came to mean simply an entity possessing legal rights and duties. Today it commonly signifies any human being. But for philosophers the nature of a person has never been reduced to a generally accepted theory.[5] An overview of their continuing debate suggests four main lines of theory.

Perhaps closest to the persona of Roman law, the first conception is of the person as rights-holder. For Kant, the person is a free and rational agent whose existence is an end in itself.[6] I shall call Kantian the view of person focusing on universal abstract rationality. In this view, personhood has no component of individual human differences, but rather by definition excludes the tastes, talents, and individual histories that differentiate one from another.[7]

Another classical view of the person makes its essential attributes self-consciousness and memory. Locke defines a person as "a thinking intelligent being, that has reason and reflection, and can consider itself as itself, the same thinking thing in different times and places."[8] For Locke, memory signifies this continuous self-consciousness. Locke's theory still holds great appeal for those who puzzle over the mysteries of personal identity.[9]

These two classical views are compatible with thinking of persons as disembodied minds or immaterial essences.[10] In contrast is the view that persons are human bodies.[11] The sophisticated version is that continuous embodiment is a necessary but not sufficient condition of personhood. To recognize something as a person is, among other things, to attribute bodily continuity to it.[12] Indeed, Wittgenstein says that the best picture of the human soul is the human body.[13]

Last, some theorists find these traditional views too pale, and suggest that the individual's ability to project a continuing life plan into the future is as important as memory or continuing consciousness. Allied with this is the view that what counts in recognizing something as a person is a consistent character structure.[14] Persons are what they are in virtue of their past and future integrated by their character.

Other ways of thinking about persons may not fall within these four rough categories.[15] The thorough empiricist or metaphysical skeptic may say there is no such "thing" as a person. To that end, Hume argues that a person is "nothing but a bundle or collection of different perceptions," and that the feeling of self-identity over time is merely a persistent illusion.[16] The behavioral psychologist might say that the self is nothing separate from the body's processes and activity in the environment. In a similarly empirical and skeptical vein, a positive economist might conceive of a person as nothing but a bundle or collection of tastes and desires, conventionally recognized as a unit; but the economist must borrow enough of the Kantian view to attribute instrumental rationality to this aggregate.[17] Alternatively, nonbehavioral psychologists may think of the person as a self, a subject of mental states. This conception relates both to the Lockean self-consciousness theory of the person and to the theory of character structure. Still, the structural postulates of Freudian theory may perhaps be considered a separate theory of the person.[18]

A communitarian would find all of these concepts of personhood wrongheaded because they all derive from the individualistic worldview that flowered in Western society with the industrial revolution. In a society in which the only human entity recognized in social intercourse is some aggregate like the family or clan, there could not be such intense philosophical attention to the biological individual and its ontological, psychological, moral and political status. In view of the individualist roots of these theories of the person, it comes as no surprise that thinkers who wish to progress from an individualist to a communitarian worldview are impatient with them. Communitarians see the myth of the self-contained "man" in a state of nature as politically misleading and dangerous. Persons are embedded in language, history, and culture, which are social creations;[19] there can be no such thing as a person without society.

For the sake of simplicity, I shall initially confine my inquiry to the types of the person posited by the more traditional, individual-oriented theories. But the communitarian critique reminds us that the idea of the person in the abstract should not be pushed beyond its usefulness. In what follows I shall on occasion attempt to pay attention to the role of groups both as constituted by persons and as constitutive of persons.

B. Property and Theories of the Person

Bypassing for the moment Kantian rationality and Lockean memory, let us begin with the person conceived as bodily continuity. Locke says that "every Man has a *Property* in his own *Person*," from which it immediately follows that "[t]he *Labour* of his Body, and the *Work* of his hands . . . are properly his."[20] Though we have seen Locke elsewhere considers the person as reflective consciousness and memory, he may well mean here that one literally owns one's limbs and hence must own their product.[21] If not, perhaps property in one's person should be understood to mean simply that an individual has an entitlement to be a person or to be treated as a person. This would probably include the right to self-preservation on which Locke bases the right to appropriate.[22]

If it makes sense to say that one owns one's body, then on the embodiment theory of personhood the body is quintessentially personal property, because it is literally constitutive of one's personhood. If the body is property, then objectively it is property for personhood. This line of thinking leads to a property theory for the tort of assault and battery: Interference with my body is interference with my personal property. Certain external things, for example the shirt off my back, may also be considered personal property if they are closely enough connected with the body.[23]

The idea of property in one's body presents some interesting paradoxes. In some cases, bodily parts can become fungible commodities just as other personal property can become fungible with a change in its relationship with the owner: blood can be withdrawn and used in a transfusion; hair can be cut off and used by a wigmaker; organs can be transplanted. On the other hand, bodily parts may be too "personal" to be property at all. We have an intuition that property necessarily refers to something in the outside world, separate from oneself. Though the general idea of property for personhood means that the boundary between person and thing cannot be a bright line, still the idea of property seems to require some perceptible boundary, at least insofar as property requires the notion of thing, and the notion of thing requires separation from self. This intuition makes it seem appropriate to call parts of the body property only after they have been removed from the system.[24]

Another paradox is whether replacing any of my body parts with fungible plastic makes me a different person, and whether the plastic parts once inserted should be considered personal property or something else.[25] The plastic parts question represents the converse of the problem concerning the sale of natural organs. The natural organ becomes fungible property when removed from the body but remains purely personal, thus seemingly not property, while it is still inside the body. Conversely, plastic parts are fungible when sold to the hospital, but once inserted they are no longer fungible, and should be considered as the natural organs they replace, hence perhaps no longer property at all.

Next, let us consider the person as individual rationality, the Kantian person. If persons are bare abstract rational agents, there is no necessary connection between persons and property. Therefore, Kantian rationality cannot yield an objective theory of personal property. One might introduce external objects to a population of Kantian persons in the state of nature or in Rawls's original position[26] to see how they divide things among themselves (and so it might be hard to think of justice among these persons without property), but object-relationships are still not a necessary corollary to the concept of personhood in this view.[27]

In Locke's view of persons as continuing self-consciousness characterized by memory, the external world may enter the concept of person. Memory is made of relationships with other people and the world of objects. Much of the property we unhesitatingly consider personal—for example family albums, diaries, photographs, heirlooms, and the home—is connected with memory and the continuity of self through memory. But the pure Lockean conception of personhood does not necessarily imply that object-relations (and the expected continuity of those relations that property gives) are essential to the constitution of persons, because that conception is disembodied enough not to stress our differentiation from one another. It is possible to hold the Lockean conception and still believe that memory is part of an immaterial essence of the person that has no inherent connection to the material world. But in a neo-Lockean view rejecting such dualism and making self-differentiation important, it seems object-relations are necessary and central to self-constitution.[28]

Finally, let us consider the view that what is important in personhood is a continuing character structure encompassing future projects or plans, as well as past events and feelings. The general idea of expressing one's character through property is quite familiar. It is frequently remarked that dogs resemble their masters; the attributes of many material goods, such as cars and clothes, can proclaim character traits of their owners. Of course, many would say that becoming too enthralled with property takes away time and energy needed to develop other faculties constitutive of personhood. But, for example, if you express your generosity by giving away fruits that grow in your orchard, then if the orchard ceases to be your property, you are no longer able to express your character.[29] This at least suggests that property may have an important relationship to certain character traits that partly constitute a person.

This view of personhood also gives us insight into why protecting people's "expectations" of continuing control over objects seems so important. If an object you now control is bound up in your future plans or in your anticipation of your future self, and it is partly these plans for your own continuity that make you a person, then your personhood depends on the realization of these expectations. This turn to expectations might seem to send property theory back toward Bentham, who declared that "the idea of property consists in an established expectation."[30] But this justification for honoring expectations is far from Benthamite, because it applies only to personal property. In order to conclude that an object figuring into someone's expectations is personal, we must conclude both that the person is bound up with the object to a great enough extent, and that the relationship belongs to the class of "good" rather than "bad" object-relations. Hence we are forced to face the problem of fetishism, or "bad" object-relations.

C. The Problem of Fetishism

We must construct sufficiently objective criteria to identify close object-relations that should be excluded from recognition as personal property because the particular nature of the relationship works to hinder rather than to support healthy self-constitution. A key to distinguishing these cases is "healthy." We can tell the difference between personal property and fetishism the same way we can tell the difference between a healthy person and a sick person, or between a sane person and an insane person.[31] In fact, the concepts of sanity and personhood are intertwined: at some point we question whether the insane person is a person at all.[32] Using the word "we" here, however, implies that a consensus exists and can be discerned. Because I seek a source of objective judgments about property for personhood, but do not wish to rely on natural law or simple moral realism, consensus must be a sufficient source of objective moral criteria—and I believe it can be, sometimes, without destroying the meaning of objectivity.[33] In the context of property for personhood, then, a "thing" that someone claims to be bound up with nevertheless should not be treated as personal vis-à-vis other people's claimed rights and interests when there is an objective moral consensus that to be bound up with that category of "thing" is inconsistent with personhood or healthy self-constitution.

Judgments of insanity or fetishism are both made on the basis of the minimum indicia it takes to recognize an individual as one of us.[34] There does not seem to be the same reason to restrain a private fetishist as there is to restrain an insane person prone to violence against others.

But the restraint of denying the fetishist's property special recognition as personal is less severe than that imposed on someone deemed violently insane. To refuse on moral grounds to call fetishist property personal is not to refuse to call it property at all. The immediate consequence of denying personal status to something is merely to treat that thing as fungible property, and hence to deny only those claims that might rely on a preferred status of personal property.

A broader aspect of the problem of fetishism is suggested by Marx's "fetishism of commodities."[35] Marx attributed power in a market society to the commodities that form the market. He believed that people become subordinate in their relations to these commodities. In other words, under capitalism property itself is anti-personhood.

Even if one does not accept that all capitalist market relations with objects destroy personhood, it is probably true that most people view the caricature capitalist with distaste. Most people might consider her lacking in some essential attribute of personhood, such as the capacity to respect other people or the environment. If there is some moral cutoff point, beyond which one is attached too much or in the wrong way to property, the extent to which someone may emulate the caricature capitalist and still claim property for personhood is not clear, but is not unlimited. Although the caricature capitalist cannot express her nature without control over a vast quantity of things and other people, her exercise of this control to constitute herself as the complete capitalist could not objectively be recognized as personal property because at some point there is an objective moral consensus that such control is destroying personhood rather than fostering it.[36]

III. HEGEL, PROPERTY, AND PERSONHOOD
A. Hegel's *Philosophy of Right*

The property theory of Hegel's *Philosophy of Right*,[37] although based on a conception of persons, does not immediately invoke the intuitive personhood perspective. Hegel's person is the same as Kant's—simply an abstract autonomous entity capable of holding rights, a device for abstracting universal principles and hence by definition devoid of individuating characteristics.[38] In postulating persons as rights holders, Hegel thus initially assumes away those characteristics that render individuals unique beings—particular commitments and character traits, particular memories and future plans, particular relationships with other people and with the world of external objects. In contrast, the intuitive perspective assumes that persons are not persons except by virtue of those particulars, and therefore sees the person as the developed, individual human being in the context of the external world. Personal property is important precisely because its holder could not be the particular person she is without it.

Hegel's property theory is only the first part of a logical and historical progression from abstract units of autonomy to developed individuals in the context of a developed community. Hence, Hegel's theory may function to take the person from the abstract realm of rights into the world of concrete individuals having the attributes of personhood as we commonly conceive them. Thus, even though Hegel does not use the word person for the entity described as the person in the theory of personal property, Hegel's theory can be seen as consistent with the idea of personal property. Whereas the theory of personal property begins with the notion that human individuality is inseparable from object-relations of some kind, Hegel makes object-relations the first step on his road from abstract autonomy to full development of the individual in the context of the family and the state.

Because the person in Hegel's conception is merely an abstract unit of free will or autonomy, it has no concrete existence until that will acts on the external world. "[T]he person must give its freedom an external sphere in order to exist as Idea."[39] At this level of particularization, the external sphere "capable of embodying [the person's] freedom" consists of the rest of the world, everything that is distinct from the person.[40]

From the need to embody the person's will to take free will from the abstract realm to the actual, Hegel concludes that the person becomes a real self only by engaging in a property relationship with something external.[41] Such a relationship is the *goal* of the person. In perhaps the best-known passage from this book, Hegel says: "The person has for its substantive end the right of placing its will in any and every thing, which thing is thereby mine; [and] because that thing has no such end in itself, its destiny and soul take on my will. [This constitutes] mankind's absolute right of appropriation over all things."[42] Hence, "property is the first embodiment of freedom and so is in itself a substantive end."[43]

Hegel's property theory is an occupancy theory; the owner's will must be present in the object.[44] Unlike Locke's theory of appropriation from the state of nature, occupancy in Hegel's view does not give rise to an initial entitlement which then has a permanent validity. Rather, continuous occupation is necessary to maintain a property relationship between a person and any particular external thing, because "the will to possess something must express itself."[45] As the autonomous will to possess comes and goes over time, so property must come and go.[46]

Hegel's argument about property in the realm of abstract right mostly reaffirms the liberal positions on property.[47] But because Hegel believes the rights he describes there concern only the Kantian "abstract personality,"[48] he treats them as both logically and developmentally prior to any relationships of right arising from the person's interaction with others in society. Subsequent sections of his book introduce other, more particular property relationships that arise from the nature of groups—the family and the state—rather than from individual autonomy alone.[49] In Hegel's scheme of progress from abstract units of will to the final ideal unity of individuals and the state, these other kinds of property relationships are higher and more advanced. Hegel departs from classical liberalism in discussing these other kinds of property relationships. For Hegel, individuals could not become fully developed outside such relationships. They are important in comparing Hegel's theory to a theory of personal property, because the concept of person in the theory of personal property refers to the fully developed individual.

Hegel derives family property from the personhood of the family unit. When personality or "immediate exclusive individuality" enters into marriage, it "surrenders itself to it," and the parties become one person, or a single autonomous unit.[50] It follows that there must be family property wherein "the family, as person, has its real external existence."[51] Family property must therefore be common property by nature.[52]

Hegel seems to make property "private" on the same level as the unit of autonomy that is embodying its will by holding it. He argues that property is private to individuals when discussing it in the context of the autonomous individual will, and that it is essentially common within a family when discussing it in the context of the autonomous family unit. He does not make the leap to state property, however, even though his theory of the state might suggest it. For Hegel, the properly developed state (in contrast to civil society) is an organic moral entity, "the actuality of the ethical Idea,"[53] and individuals within the state are subsumed into its community morality.[54]

Hegel's theory of the state thus carries the seeds of destruction of all liberal rights attaching to individuals (because in the state particular arbitrary will passes over into willing the universal).[55] Hence, there is in

Hegel's theory a foundation for the communitarian claim that each community is an organic entity in which private property ownership does not make sense. Hegel does not make this claim, perhaps because he is too firmly rooted in his own time. He thought his theory of the state required that the state must take the form of a constitutional monarchy, in which the monarch and the landed aristocracy "attain their position by birth" and "possess a will which rests on itself alone."[56] Hegel at least clearly makes the claim that a human being can only become properly developed—actualize her freedom—in the context of a community of others. Thus, though he speaks of the person in the sphere of abstract right only in the Kantian sense of abstract rationality, he implicitly claims that personhood in the richer sense of self-development and differentiation presupposes the context of human community. If accepted, this claim has important ramifications for a theory of personal property which does rely on that richer sense of personhood.

B. Hegel and Property for Personhood

The intuitive personhood perspective on property is not equivalent to Hegelian personality theory, because that perspective incorporates the attributes of personhood that Hegel initially assumes away. Nevertheless, a theory of personal property can build upon some of Hegel's insights. First, the notion that the will is embodied in things suggests that the entity we know as a person cannot come to exist without both differentiating itself from the physical environment and yet maintaining relationships with portions of that environment. The idea of embodied will, cut loose from Hegel's grand scheme of absolute mind, reminds us that people and things have ongoing relationships which have their own ebb and flow, and that these relationships can be very close to a person's center and sanity. If these relationships justify ownership, or at least contribute to its justification, Hegel's notion that ownership requires continuous embodiment of the will is appealing.

Second, Hegel's incompletely developed notion that property is held by the unit to which one attributes autonomy has powerful implications for the concept of group development and group rights. Hegel thought that freedom (rational self-determination) was only possible in the context of a group (the properly organized and fully developed state). Without accepting this role for the state, one may still conclude that in a given social context certain groups are likely to be constitutive of their members in the sense that the members find self-determination only within the groups. This might have political consequences for claims of the group on certain resources of the external world (i.e., property).

Third, there may be an echo of Hegel's notion of an objective community morality in the intuition that certain kinds of property relationships can be presumed to bear close bonds to personhood. If property in one's body is not too close to personhood to be considered property at all, then it is the clearest case of property for personhood. The property/privacy nexus of the home is also a relatively clear case in our particular history and culture.

IV. TWO KINDS OF PROPERTY: THE DICHOTOMY AS CRITIQUE

One element of the intuitive personhood perspective is that property for personhood gives rise to a stronger moral claim than other property. This division of property resembles a recurrent kind of critique of real-world property arrangements.[57] The underlying insight of the many dualist property theories seems to be that some property is accorded more stringent legal protection than other property, or is otherwise deemed more important than other property by social consensus. To the extent these theories are normative, the claim is that some property is worthier of protection than other property.

If the areas of greater and lesser protection under the various dualist theories coincide to any extent, then there is room for a new and more precise theory of the areas of weaker and stronger property. I suggest that the common thread in these theories relates the stronger property claims to recognized indicia of personhood. The personhood perspective can thus provide a dichotomy that captures this critical intuition explicitly and accurately.

The premise of this form of critique is that any dichotomy in property significantly affects the justification of property rights in the real world. Liberal property theories have traditionally justified a property rights scheme by relying on some paradigm case.[58] But if the paradigm case only applies to a subset of all the things called property, then only that subset is justified, and a dichotomy is established between that subset and forms of property that fall outside the purview of the justification. Locke, for instance, justifies property with a theory of just acquisition, in which the basic assumption is the person in the state of nature. In a heroic inferential leap, he concludes that if property is justified under those conditions, then it is ipso facto justified in the capitalist market society with money and wage-labor.[59] The leap may lead to incoherence if it ignores limitations implied in the premises. Thus, if Locke's claim is that property is justified because it is a condition necessary to produce or sustain free individuals, his theory carries the inherent limitation that any form of property incompatible with free individuals is not justified.[60]

A. Marx and Hobhouse

Marx's distinction between property resting on one's own labor and property resting on the labor of others is an example of this kind of critique.[61] In the *Communist Manifesto,* Marx and Engels allude to a discontinuity in justification based on this distinction:

> The distinguishing feature of Communism is not the abolition of property generally, but the abolition of bourgeois property . . . .
> . . . .
> We Communists have been reproached with the desire of abolishing the right of personally acquiring property as the fruit of a man's own labour, which property is alleged to be the ground work of all personal freedom, activity and independence . . . .
> . . . Do you mean the property of the petty artisan and of the small peasant, a form of property that preceded the bourgeois form? There is no need to abolish that; the development of industry has to a great extent already destroyed it, and is still destroying it daily.[62]

In this passage, Marx and Engels implicitly criticize liberal theories based on personality or on labor-desert as being inapplicable to capitalism. Property in the means of production is not the type of property that forms the basis for personal freedom.

A similar criticism of the classical liberal justification of property is expressed in the dichotomy between property for use and property for power, introduced early in this century by L. T. Hobhouse. Hobhouse distinguishes "use" and "power" as two "social aspects of property" and implies that the classical theory justifies property for use, but not property for "control of persons through things."[63]

> In a developed society a man's property is not merely something which he controls and enjoys, which he can make the basis of his labour and the scene of his ordered activities, but something whereby he can control another man and make it the basis of that man's labour and the scene of activities ordered by himself. The abstract right of property is apt to ignore these trifling distinctions . . . .

> Now these two functions of property, the control of things,
> which gives freedom and security, and the control of persons
> through things, which gives power to the owner, are very different.
> In some respects they are radically opposed . . . . [64]

This passage implies that while "control of things" might be justified by the classical theory, "control of persons through things" cannot be so justified. Hobhouse went on to assert that "modern economic conditions have virtually abolished property *for use*—apart from furniture, clothing, etc.," while bringing about "the accumulation of vast masses of property *for power* in the hands of a relatively narrow class."[65]

This argument has in common with Marx two important features. First, both critiques assume that human individuality and autonomy bear some relation to one's freedom to use, work on, and form expectations about the resources of the external environment. This implies that there is some core of insight, however distorted, in the classical liberal theories of property.[66] Second, both formulate a dichotomy in property in terms of the purposes of the person exercising control over it. While the first feature reflects the persistent insight that the concept of personhood necessarily includes some kinds of continuing relationships with the external environment, the second focuses on the effect of certain types of property arrangements on personal expression and development, that is, on the personhood which is supposed to be their raison d'être.

In the Marxist dichotomy, one can clearly distinguish between ownership of something one has labored on and ownership of things others have labored on. Marx asserts that private ownership of things labored on by others is unjustified, but does not assert that private ownership of things labored on by oneself is necessarily justified. Perhaps Marx would accept the idea that some solidity of expectations based on the freedom to fuse oneself by one's efforts with the external environment is justified because that act is bound up with autonomy and individuality in a way not historically determined by capitalist relations of production, even though he was not willing to extract what he called the property of the artisan from its historical period.[67] In his early writings he spoke of alienated labor as a perversion of man's nature as a laborer at one with his environment, which was man's "species being."[68] Although the laborer who is not alienated has an integrated relationship with the environment, it would not follow that everything worked on could thereby legitimately become property.

Though Marx introduced no element of subjective intent, one might wish to distinguish between laboring on resources that are intended to remain bound up with one's own life and laboring on resources that one intends to use to make exchanges with others.[69] If one has a personhood perspective and feels that a relationship between person and thing is stronger when resources are bound up with the individual than when they are free to be traded or held for trade, then one could more easily justify ownership where resources are to be bound up with one's own life. To put this roughly in Marxist terminology, in a market society this perspective would provide a stronger justification for property held for "use value" than property held for "exchange value."[70]

Perhaps Hobhouse's dichotomy is meant to capture this kind of intuition. But Hobhouse's distinction between property for use and property for power remains vague.[71] It is not clear whether the status of the property holder as producer or nonproducer is the only relevant distinction, or whether the intent of the holder also counts. Is the dichotomy meant to be between property valued by an individual producing it only for its "use value" and all other property? Or is it between property held by the individual producing it and all other property?

Intent may be irrelevant for Hobhouse as it is for Marx. Hobhouse seems to associate property for use simply with that produced by one's own labor and property for power simply with that produced by the labor of others. If this is all that Hobhouse means, then it is Marx's dichotomy minus Marx's assertion that the two types of property could not historically coexist. Apparently this is the way subsequent writers interpret the distinction between property for use and property for power.[72] Yet in Hobhouse there are traces of the intuition which I likened to the distinction between "use value" and "exchange value." In associating property for use with something one can make "the scene of his ordered activities," Hobhouse seems to contemplate the continuing control and continuity of expectation with regard to some resource in the external environment. That is, he seems to associate property for use with personal property. If the foundation of Hobhouse's dichotomy was a concern that a justification of property that purports to rest on individual freedom could not extend to cover instances of property that restrict individual freedom, then he would have had to consider the intent with which an individual values something.

B. A Utilitarian Dichotomy

In apparent contrast to these assertions that certain property claims are stronger than others, some utilitarians might claim that since there is only one social goal, maximization of welfare, so there is only one kind of property—that which results in maximization of welfare. In this utilitarian scheme, there will also be no reason for distinctions between property entitlements and other kinds of individual entitlements except for deference to linguistic tradition. Posner's position represents this view: Efficiency will be maximized only when anything that is scarce in the relevant human society during the relevant time period (thus, a "good" and not merely an undifferentiated attribute of the environment) is the subject of an entitlement.[73]

Yet those who espouse utilitarianism in the form of instrumental economics have elaborated a hierarchy of remedies. The Calabresi-Melamed distinction between protecting entitlements with "property rules" or "liability rules" is now a widely recognized tool of economic analysis.[74] An entitlement is protected by a property rule if B can obtain it from A only by paying whatever price A sets as a willing seller, or if A can obtain an injunction to prevent B's interference. An entitlement is protected by a liability rule if B can obtain it from A by paying some extrinsically determined price (such as the "market" price), even if A is not a willing seller, or if A can obtain only damages on account of B's interference. To some extent, this system does not correspond to the ordinary meaning of property.[75] Most rights traditionally called property are protected against the government only by a liability rule. On the other hand, some rights not traditionally called property, like freedom from bodily intrusion, are protected by property rules.[76]

Calabresi and Melamed sketch some efficiency considerations for making the choice between property and liability rules, and others have investigated the problem in more depth.[77] Without attempting to outline their effect or interaction with efficiency concerns, Calabresi and Melamed also recognize that "distributional" considerations may be relevant to such a choice. Here I merely want to reemphasize that the problem of levels of entitlements is very much a live issue, and the thought persists, for whatever reasons, that some kinds of entitlements are more worthy of protection than others.

The distinction between property and liability rules is different from the others mentioned, not just because it is ostensibly about remedies and not the initial setting of entitlements, but also because it is formulated merely as a statement that different levels of protection do exist, without telling us which items deserve which levels. Writers of the allocative efficiency school suggest that the criterion for a lesser level of protection is the presence of any condition that might block market transactions from achieving the efficient outcome, such as information costs, or free-rider or holdout problems. I am interested in developing a nonutilitarian, moral theory which would provide an alternative explanation for the observed hierarchy of protection, as well as help us to critique it where it goes wrong. It should be possible to give moral reasons why some claims are or should be subject to greater protection (either inalienability or property rules) than others (either liability rules or no entitlement), either as between individuals or between individuals and the government.[78] Though much might be said about the other distinctions, especially the criteria for inalienability, discussion here will be confined primarily to property rules versus liability rules.[79]

C. The Personhood Dichotomy

The personhood dichotomy comes about in the following way: A general justification of property entitlements in terms of their relationship to personhood could hold that the rights that come within the general justification form a continuum from fungible to personal. It then might hold that those rights near one end of the continuum—fungible property rights—can be overridden in some cases in which those near the other—personal property rights—cannot be. This is to argue not that fungible property rights are unrelated to personhood, but simply that distinctions are sometimes warranted depending upon the character or strength of the connection. Thus, the personhood perspective generates a hierarchy of entitlements: The more closely connected with personhood, the stronger the entitlement.

Does it make sense to speak of two levels of property, personal and fungible? I think the answer is yes in many situations, no in many others. Since the personhood perspective depends partly on the subjective nature of the relationships between person and thing, it makes more sense to think of a continuum that ranges from a thing indispensable to someone's being to a thing wholly interchangeable with money. Many relationships between persons and things will fall somewhere in the middle of this continuum. Perhaps the entrepreneur factory owner has ownership of a particular factory and its machines bound up with her being to some degree. If a dichotomy telescoping this continuum to two endpoints is to be useful, it must be because within a given social context certain types of person-thing relationships are understood to fall close to one end or the other of the continuum, so that decision makers within that social context can use the dichotomy as a guide to determine which property is worthier of protection. For example, in our social context a house that is owned by someone who resides there is generally understood to be toward the personal end of the continuum.[80] There is both a positive sense that people are bound up with their homes and a normative sense that this is not fetishistic.

Though they all derive from a common central insight, the personhood hierarchy is different from the property dichotomies I cited earlier. It differs from the Marxist distinction between property resting on the labor of others and property resting on one's own labor because it focuses on where a commodity ends up, not where and how it starts out. In addition, it focuses on the person with whom it ends up—on an internal quality in the holder or a subjective relationship between the holder and the thing, and not on the objective arrangements surrounding production of the thing. The same claim can change from fungible to personal depending on who holds it. The wedding ring is fungible to the artisan who made it and now holds it for exchange even though it is property resting on the artisan's own labor. Conversely, the same item can change from fungible to personal over time without changing hands. People and things become intertwined gradually.

The personhood hierarchy also does not correspond to the implicit Marxist distinction between "use value" and "exchange value," since some things held for "use value" are still not bound up with personhood. Since Hobhouse's "use/power" distinction seems to be merely an ambiguous amalgam of the two Marxist distinctions just mentioned, it too would not correspond to the personhood dichotomy.

The Calabresi-Melamed distinction between property rules and liability rules is initially positivist; it merely recognizes that some entitlements are harder to extinguish than others. In order to make it take on a moral function, there would be a nice simplicity in hypothesizing that personal property should be protected by property rules and that fungible property should be protected by liability rules. If that were true, much that is now protected by a property rule—for example, property held only for investment—is overprotected. In that respect the claim would be truly revolutionary.[81] Yet it would not be revolutionary enough for those who think fungible property should not always be protected even by liability rules—for example, when fungible claims of the rich deprive the poor of meaningful opportunities for personhood. But although the problem does not reduce to such nice simplicity, one might claim that at least personal property should be protected by property rules.

D. Welfare Rights and a Dichotomy in Property

The personhood dichotomy in property, by focusing attention on the importance of certain property to self-constitution, can avoid some distortions that might result from justifications in which all entitlements are considered alike.[82]

It might be argued, however, that what a personhood perspective dictates is a dichotomy in entitlements, not a dichotomy in property. A welfare rights theory might derive from the needs of personhood a set of core entitlements encompassing both property interests, such as shelter, and other interests, such as free speech, employment and health care.[83] In such a scheme, the distinction between property and other rights breaks down.[84] There would be room for a personhood dichotomy but it would not be related to interests traditionally called property. The general task of such a welfare theory would be to carve out for protection a core containing both property interests and other interests.

Whether or not the personhood dichotomy in property is useful in such a theory depends on whether it makes sense, in the context of a larger personhood dichotomy in entitlements, to maintain a distinction between property and nonproperty rights.[85] I think that it does make sense. In the real world, the categories of ordinary language and culture seem reason enough to maintain the distinction. The ordinary connotations of property as external objects reflect our perception of the world in terms of certain aggregations of stimuli. To carve out of all personhood rights a subcategory of personal property suggests that to say that property is a property of persons may be more than just wordplay. The attachment to "things" may be different from other necessities of personhood, and it may be worth noticing the difference sometimes, even though, by itself, it would not determine questions of just distribution.[86]

A welfare rights or minimal entitlement theory of just distribution might hold that a government that respects personhood must guarantee citizens all entitlements necessary for personhood. If the personhood dichotomy in property is taken as the source of a distributive mandate as part of such a general theory, it would suggest that government should make it possible for all citizens to have whatever property is necessary for personhood. But a welfare rights theory incorporating property for personhood would suggest not only that government distribute largess in order to make it possible for people to buy property in which to constitute themselves,[87] but would further suggest that government should rearrange property rights so that fungible property of some people does not overwhelm the opportunities of the rest to constitute themselves in property. That is, rather than simply tell the government to dole out resources, a welfare rights theory incorporating the right to personal property would tell the government to cease allowing one person to impinge on the personhood of another by means of her control over tangible resources.[88]

Curtailing fungible property rights that impinge on others' opportunities for self-constitution may seem a more radical sort of reform than wealth redistribution through taxation. But purely fungible property is just like any other form of wealth. If a welfare rights theory of distribution makes personhood interests take precedence over some claims to wealth, permitting taxation to provide largess for the poor, it may equally permit curtailing fungible property rights that impinge on the poor, unless doing so only for the holders of certain assets would under the circumstances violate accepted norms of equality.

V. Two Kinds of Property: A Selective Survey

This section surveys a number of disparate legal issues from the viewpoint of property for personhood. These issues represent types of cases in which the rough dichotomy between personal and fungible property approximates the world well enough to be useful. Although such a survey does not amount to a systematic critique of the current allocation of property rights, it nonetheless demonstrates both how the personhood perspective is implicit in our law and how its explicit application can help resolve some recurrent problems.

A. The Sanctity of the Home
1. Liberty and Privacy

The idea of the sanctity of the home is a rich field for examining property for personhood in the positive law. The home is a moral nexus between liberty, privacy, and freedom of association. A clear example of the nexus is *Stanley v. Georgia,*[89] with its mixture of First Amendment, privacy, and sanctity-of-the-home reasoning. In *Stanley*, the Supreme Court held that a state may not prosecute a person for possessing obscene materials in her home. Although the Court rested its holding on the "philosophy of the First Amendment," it is apparent that the Court was influenced by an appreciation of our society's traditional connection between one's home and one's sense of autonomy and personhood.[90]

One reason the government should not prescribe what one may do in one's home is liberty; such government prescription is an infringement of an aspect of personhood in the Kantian sense of autonomy or arbitrary will. But if liberty is the reason for limiting the government in such a case, then the rationale has nothing to do with where the actor is when she tries to exercise her will. The liberty rationale can be bent into a privacy rationale by considering the limitations on liberty set by the presence and activities of other people. The argument would be that people do not have sufficient liberty unless they have some realm shut off from the interference of others. Further reasoning is needed to get from the privacy rationale to a "sanctity-of-the-home" rationale. Social convention and people's normal expectations make the home a logical place to consider the arbitrary will least limited; we can readily see that this is where to set off the necessary private sanctuary.[91]

There is more to the rationale based on sanctity of the home; it contains a strand of property for personhood. It is not just that liberty needs some sanctuary and the home is a logical one to choose because of social consensus. There is also the feeling that it would be an insult for the state to invade one's home, because it is the scene of one's history and future, one's life and growth. In other words, one embodies or constitutes oneself there. The home is affirmatively part of oneself—property for personhood—and not just the agreed-on locale for protection from outside interference.

2. Residential Tenancy as Property for Personhood

One problem is that someone's home may not be exclusively her property; it may simultaneously be a landlord's property too. The sanctity of the home as an aspect of the personhood perspective seems to be at work in the modern development of the law of landlord and tenant. Courts frequently picture the residential lease transaction as taking place between a poor or middle-class tenant acquiring a home and a business enterprise owning and leasing residential property.[92] This is one basis for the revolution in tenants' rights. Courts began to view the rights in question as more closely related to the personhood of the tenant than to that of the landlord, and accordingly moved to protect the leasehold as the tenant's home. Many state legislatures followed suit.[93] Of course, this picture of the transaction is overgeneralized. Some landlords live in one half of a duplex and rent the other half, or rent the remodeled basement or attic of their home. Some tenants rent an apartment so that members of their firm will have a place to conduct confidential business. The picture of a poor tenant and commercial landlord may have been a fair generalization for residential tenancies in Washington, D.C., where the revolution in the common law began, but it may be an entirely unwarranted generalization for other communities in diverse states that have adopted the same rationales.

Viewing the leasehold as personal property recognizes a claim in all apartment dwellers, not just poor ones. The common law revolution in tenants' rights, to the extent it relies only on landlords being rich and tenants being poor, could reflect merely a conviction about wealth redistribution.[94] But it is my thesis that the intuition that the leasehold is personal is also at work in the recent common law development. New tenants' rights are granted to all tenants, even where the result is to redistribute wealth to tenants who are wealthier than their landlords. Viewing the leasehold as personal would tend to influence courts and legislatures to grant to all tenants entitlements intended to make an apartment a comfortable home—a perpetual and nonwaivable guarantee of habitability.[95]

The notion that the law should grant permanent tenure to tenants during good behavior, regardless of what the lease contract says about the term, is a more direct instance of the personhood perspective applied to residential tenancies. Consider a hypothetical statute (of a kind often proposed by tenants' rights advocates) providing that a tenancy cannot be terminated except for specified reasons, such as waste, after the tenant has been there for a year.[96] This kind of statute works a profound change in property law, at least in form, since it renders the landlord's reversion conditional and thus in effect changes the time-honored meaning of fee simple absolute. Such a statute supposes that the tenant has put roots into the place (which explains the one-year waiting period). It also incorporates the normative judgment that tenants should be allowed to become attached to places and that the legal system should encourage them to do so.

These judgments are based on two assumptions. First, that in today's society a tenant makes an apartment her home in the sense of a sanctuary needed for personhood. Second, that the old rule under which the landlord could evict a tenant without cause at the expiration of the tenancy—a rule that might have been related to the autonomy and individuality of the landlord—is of lesser importance or less clearly implicated in the typical case today.[97] Once such a statute is viewed as an instance of the personhood perspective at work, then the extraordinary development of the doctrine of retaliatory eviction[98]—under which a landlord may evict for any reason or no reason, so long as it is not the wrong reason—may be seen as a way station along the path toward making the landlord's reversion conditional, because it is fungible, and the leasehold permanent (though defeasible), because it is personal.

The attempt to assure poor tenants of decent housing by imposing implied warranties of habitability may also be understood in light of the personhood perspective, although the argument is less direct. In an article that defends imposing habitability obligations on landlords, Ackerman suggests that decent housing should become a right based upon the tenant's "dignity as a person."[99] He argues further that it is fair to charge some of the costs to landlords rather than to tax society as a whole, because "in a society in which wealth is unjustly distributed it is fair to impose a requirement of decency upon those in the relatively privileged classes who engage in long-lasting relationships with the impoverished."[100] This may be a species of welfare rights or "just wants" argument based on personhood, but it is not simply a conventional argument for wealth redistribution. Instead, it appears to be closer to the argument that private law should cease allowing some people's fungible property rights to deprive other people of important opportunities for personhood. While Ackerman did not elaborate this argument, considering residential tenancies as personal property helps complete the moral underpinning that he considered tentative and sketchy.[101] The argument would justify charging habitability costs to landlords whenever landlords' fungible property rights are prohibiting tenants from establishing or maintaining the kind of personal relationship in the home that our culture considers the basis of individuality.

3. The Fourth Amendment: Homes and Cars

Preventing eviction and imposing warranties of habitability protect possession of the home and the quality of physical comfort it affords. Another aspect of the sanctity of the home, as mentioned earlier, is privacy—home is a place where intimate things are kept from prying eyes, and intimate relationships are carried on away from prying ears. So in a general way, the sanctity of the home also has much to do with the path the Supreme Court has taken in interpreting the Fourth Amendment's protection against unreasonable searches and seizures and its warrant requirement.

The Supreme Court recently held, in *Payton v. New York,* that while warrantless arrests in public are constitutional, warrantless arrests in the home are not.[102] In declaring felony arrests with probable cause to be unconstitutional if carried out in the suspect's home, the Court rejected a well-established practice.[103] The majority based its opinion on a firm distinction between the home and all other places where citizens or their effects may be found.[104] Yet, in other circumstances the Court is quite scornful of such a dichotomy, reminding us that the Fourth Amendment "protects people, not places."[105] The theoretical difficulty of explaining what protecting the core of personal autonomy from the government has to do with the sanctity of the home or of one's property helps to explain the difficulties the Court has had in delineating the scope of the Fourth Amendment.

The Fourth Amendment historically was thought of in terms of protecting property. The Lockean form of this rationale is elaborated in *Boyd v. United States.*[106] In *Boyd,* the Court reasoned that an individual's most personal thoughts as manifested in private papers deserved stringent protections. Intrusions are not to be tolerated unless state interests of the highest order are at stake. *Boyd* quoted extensively from the opinion of Lord Camden in *Entick v. Carrington,* an action in trespass for "entering the plaintiff's dwelling-house . . . and breaking open his desks, boxes, etc., and searching and examining his papers."[107] Lord Camden had said: "Papers are the owner's goods and chattels; they are his dearest property; and are so far from enduring a seizure, that they will hardly bear an inspection; . . . yet where private papers are removed and carried away the secret nature of those goods will be an aggravation of the trespass . . . ."[108] This property theory of the Fourth Amendment required a defeasing argument to justify any seizures. In the case of stolen goods, the property argument is defeased because the goods do not belong to the holder; the government seizes them as agent of the true owner.[109] With respect to possession of contraband, or fruits or instrumentalities of crime, the property argument is defeased because it is illegal to own the objects in question. The property theory had awkward results in the case law, particularly in the early eavesdropping cases where the legality of the intrusion might depend upon the technicalities of state trespass law.[110] It also did not provide a rationale for the seizure of "mere evidence," because of the absence of a justification defeasing the holder's property rights in the evidentiary object. Dissatisfied with what it considered the anomalous results of a musty old doctrine, the Court in *Warden v. Hayden*[111] and *Katz v. United States*[112] decided that privacy, not property, is the philosophical bedrock of the Fourth Amendment.

In *Warden v. Hayden,* the Court interred the "mere evidence" rule. As it was to do later in the *Payton* case,[113] the Court quoted *Boyd's* statement that the Fourth Amendment was intended to protect "the sanctity of a man's home and the privacies of life."[114] But, whereas in *Payton* the Court would again emphasize the first half of that phrase, in *Hayden* it took up the second: "We have recognized that the principal object of the Fourth Amendment is the protection of privacy rather than property, and have increasingly discarded fictional and procedural barriers rested on property concepts."[115] And in *Katz v. United States* the Court made its famous announcement that "the Fourth Amendment protects people, not places."[116] Mr. Katz could not constitutionally be spied upon (absent a warrant) in a bugged telephone booth to obtain evidence against him. The intrusion was a "search" for Fourth Amendment purposes because, even though there was no trespass against Mr. Katz, he had a legitimate expectation of privacy (in his conversation) when he entered the booth. Even outside the sanctity of the home, this was one of the privacies of life that deserved protection.

Justice Harlan's concurrence in *Katz* made clear that the test for whether someone has a legitimate expectation of privacy in a given setting has two prongs, both of which are positivist. First, "a person [must] have exhibited an actual (subjective) expectation of privacy" and, second, the expectation must be one that society is prepared to recognize as reasonable.[117] This positivism quickly got the Court into difficulty. For example, if the government announced that the police may search a citizen's bedroom with impunity, well-informed citizens could no longer reasonably expect privacy in their bedrooms. The Court now recognizes that a "normative inquiry" is needed in such a case.[118] So far the Court has not acknowledged that if a "normative inquiry" is relevant to such a case, it is relevant to all cases. It has thus been able to duck the question of exactly how that normative inquiry would proceed. Homes should be private, the court implies, regardless of what the government might say. And the Court has indicated that the personhood perspective on property (the sanctity of the home) sometimes provides its moral background by the way it draws the line at warrantless arrests in the home.

If homes should be private, regardless of what the Court says, should cars be private, regardless of what the Court says? When automobile searches first became common, the Court treated cars as presumptively private. Warrantless automobile searches on probable cause were permitted only where the vehicle's mobility threatened that it might elude the officers' grasp, and the "automobile exception" to the warrant requirement was impliedly limited to instances where mobility was a worry.[119] But the Court broadened this exception by holding that cars impounded by police may be searched without a warrant if they could have been searched without a warrant while they were still on the road.[120] Furthermore, by applying the *Katz* "expectation of privacy" test to the situation where cars are impounded for reasons not connected with criminal investigation, the Court entirely eliminated Fourth Amendment protections with regard to a large category of searches by finding that there was little expectation of privacy in cars.[121] In doing so, the Court in essence declared that cars are generally not considered private.[122]

The personhood perspective can give us two avenues of approach in deciding the normative question whether cars ought to be a strong enough sanctuary against government intrusion that they should not be penetrated without a warrant. First, if in our society cars are in the general case likely to be personal, then it is as much an intrusion to invade a car as it is an intrusion to invade a home. Are cars likely to be personal? Some cars express one's personal taste and style, and are the recipients of tender loving care. Other cars are simply part of a company's sales fleet. But the reverence for cars in the popular culture might suggest they are toward the personal end of the continuum. Cars are the repository of personal effects, and cars form the backdrop for carrying on private thoughts or intimate relationships, just as homes do. Accordingly, cars should be treated as personal, at least to the extent of narrowing exceptions to the Fourth Amendment's warrant requirement. The error risked by doing so (costs to the government) seems less important than the risk of moral error against personhood inherent in some of the present rules. Second, if private enclaves are needed for personhood to develop and flourish, and if our society is now one in which many people's homes are not that sort of enclave (because of overcrowding, for example), then a liberal government that must respect personhood may be required to make it possible for people to treat their cars as such enclaves. The argument may also hold for a society in which most people do have homes but spend a great deal of time in their cars.

It is too simplistic for the Court to say that the Fourth Amendment excludes property considerations and focuses exclusively on privacy. Property and privacy are intimately intertwined. The Fourth Amendment is worded not in terms of privacy but rather in terms of protecting people's "persons" and people's relationships with certain aspects of their external environment (their "houses, papers and effects"). It has a great deal to do with property, insofar as property is about the relationship between people and things. If through social analysis and normative inquiry one can delineate categories of personal property, then this inquiry also identifies certain interests protected by the Fourth Amendment.

This theory has the advantage of being somewhat congruent with the historical approach to the Fourth Amendment. It is also consistent with an approach that treats the Bill of Rights as a list of enumerated interests indicating that government must respect personhood. Of course, this perspective of property for personhood fails to give us a complete theory of the Fourth Amendment because, first, that amendment grants security to one's "person" as well as one's house, papers and effects, and, second, the perspective of property for personhood does not exhaust the moral perspectives relevant to the relationships between persons and things.[123]

B. Aspects of the Takings Problem

The whole question of government regulation and "taking" of private property is the most difficult yet most promising area for applying the personhood dichotomy. The personhood perspective cannot generate a comprehensive theory of property rights vis-à-vis the government; it can only add another moral inquiry that helps clarify some cases. But this is a field in which a unified theory has not been forthcoming[124]—even the Supreme Court admits that it has no coherent explanation that will cover all of its cases, and that its decisions are largely ad hoc.[125]

1. Object Loss versus Wealth Loss

Ackerman argues that stronger claims attach to items that are property in ordinary language—that is, to discrete units or "bundles of rights" that ordinarily come packaged together in our society.[126] He claims he can thus explain the results which have mystified economists: for example, why is it that six-figure losses imposed by zoning regulations will go uncompensated, while seizure of a one-acre plot of unused gravel patch will be compensated, though perhaps not much monetary loss can be measured? In order for Ackerman's ordinary language explanation to be welfare-maximizing, it would have to be true that people think of their assets in discrete units, or traditional bundles of rights (e.g., my car, my piano, my sofa), rather than thinking habitually about their entire net worth.[127] If this were so, then there might be a special demoralization about losing one of these discrete units that presumably deprived a person of more utility than losing a larger dollar value from some other lessening of net worth that left the number of discrete units relatively intact.

The divergent results Ackerman seeks to explain might also be defended on moral grounds if those grounds establish a right to keep discrete units intact. In the positivist interpretation of why we should focus upon discrete units rather than only upon the size of the wealth loss, the personhood theory may explain the postulated special demoralization. Similarly, in the normative interpretation, the personhood theory helps us understand the nature of the right dictating that discrete units ought to be protected.

An argument that discrete units are more important than total assets takes the following form. A person cannot be fully a person without a sense of continuity of self over time. To maintain that sense of continuity over time and to exercise one's liberty or autonomy, one must have an ongoing relationship with the external environment, consisting of both "things" and other people. One perceives the ongoing relationship to the environment as a set of individual relationships, corresponding to the way our perception separates the world into distinct "things." Some things must remain stationary if anything is to move; some points of reference must be constant, or thought and action are not possible. In order to lead a normal life, there must be some continuity in relating to "things." One's expectations crystallize around certain "things," the loss of which causes more disruption and disorientation than does a simple decrease in aggregate wealth. For example, if someone returns home to find her sofa has disappeared, that is more disorienting than to discover that her house has decreased in market value by five percent. If, by magic, her white sofa were instantly replaced by a blue one of equal market value, it would cause no loss in net worth but would still cause some disruption in her life.

This argument assumes that all discrete units one owns and perceives as part of her continuing environment are to some degree personal. If the white sofa were totally fungible, then magically replacing it with a blue one would cause no disruption. In fact, neither would replacing it with money.

Ackerman's ordinary language analysis may help account for the courts' tendency to protect discrete objects more than general net worth: the ordinary meaning of property is tied up with ordinary patterns of object perception. But this alone does not fully explain why courts are likely to consider object loss more important than wealth loss. Mere ease of categorization may complete the explanation: granting relief for object loss permits line drawing. Courts can perceive whether or not an object has been taken, but cannot in the same way discern whether "too much" wealth has been taken. But the argument above suggests that another element in the explanation is courts' understanding of the necessity of object-relations in ordinary life. Object loss is more important than wealth loss because object loss is specially related to personhood in a way that wealth loss is not. The cases economists find mysterious are mysterious just because economists generally treat property as fungible and those cases treat it as personal.

2. Object Loss: Fungible versus Personal

But the theory of personal property suggests that not all object loss is equally important. Some objects may approach the fungible end of the continuum so that the justification for protecting them as specially related to persons disappears. They might just as well be treated by whatever general moral rules govern wealth loss at the hands of the government. If the moral rules governing wealth loss correspond to Michelman's utilitarian suggestion—government may take whatever wealth is necessary to generate higher welfare in which the individual can confidently expect to share[128]—then the government could take some fungible items without compensation. In general, the moral inquiry for whether fungible property could be taken would be the same as the moral inquiry for whether it is fair to impose a tax on this particular person.

On the other hand, a few objects may be so close to the personal end of the continuum that no compensation could be "just." That is, hypothetically, if some object were so bound up with me that I would cease to be "myself" if it were taken, then a government that must respect persons ought not to take it.[129] If my kidney may be called my property, it is not property subject to condemnation for the general public welfare. Hence, in the context of a legal system, one might expect to find the characteristic use of standards of review and burdens of proof designed to shift risk of error away from protected interests in personal property. For instance, if there were reason to suspect that some object were close to the personal end of the continuum, there might be a prima facie case against taking it. That prima facie case might be rebutted if the government could show that the object is not personal, or perhaps that the object is not "too" personal compared with the importance to the government of acquiring that particular object for social purposes.

This suggests that if the personhood perspective is expressed in law, one might expect to find an implied limitation on the eminent domain power.[130] That is, one might expect to find that a special class of property like a family home is protected against the government by a "property rule" and not just a "liability rule." Or one might expect to find that a special class of property is protected against taking unless the government shows a "compelling state interest" and that taking it is the "least intrusive alternative."

This general limitation has not developed.[131] Perhaps the personhood perspective is not strong enough to outweigh other concerns, especially the government's need to appear evenhanded and the lower administrative costs associated with simpler rules. For example, perhaps we are unwilling to presume that all single-family homes are personal because many houses are held only for investment, and a subjective inquiry into each case slows down government too much. On the other hand, perhaps the personhood perspective is so deeply embedded that, without focusing on the problem, we expect that the condemning authority will take fungible property where possible. We may simply take for granted that the government will not take homesteads when parking lots will do. Still, it seems anomalous that the personhood perspective has not surfaced to give family homes some explicit protection, such as strict scrutiny, from government taking.

Although the personhood perspective has not yielded a general limitation on eminent domain, some fragmentary evidence suggests that *group* property rights, if connected with group autonomy or association, are given enhanced protection. For example, one state court held that a condemnor could not take a parcel sacred to a religious sect unless it could show no adequate alternative.[132] The most interesting area in this connection may be the evolving stance of federal and state governments toward Native American group claims to their ancestral territory.[133]

3. Inverse Condemnation

The earlier discussion suggested that uncompensated "mere" regulation, even if more costly, is more easily sustained by courts than taking of discrete items, because it is seen as wealth loss rather than object loss. As Michelman and Ackerman both point out, the "diminution of value" test found in the case law is really used to test whether so great a proportion of an object was taken as to be assimilable to object loss.[134] If so, then the offending regulation would effectuate a taking, and compensation might be sought in "inverse condemnation."[135]

The personhood perspective may give us further insight into the vicissitudes of the "diminution of value" test. It seems likely that courts would protect one's home to a far greater extent than one's commercial plans, even if the result, in purely monetary terms, seems irrational. For example, in *Just v. Marinette County*[136] the Wisconsin court held that waterfront land was not taken by the county wetlands act which prohibited the filling and subsequent development of the land. The court concluded that a supervening legislative act to require an owner to keep the land in its natural state was not a taking. Its application of the "harm/benefit" test is easily dismissed by those who reason in terms of expectation and market value. But it is possible to infer that a court is more willing to let the legislature destroy the expectation of gain from fungible development rights than it would be to let the legislature destroy the personality ties someone had invested in a home or land.[137] The courts' broad deference to land-use regulations that cause large decreases in market value of land may also reflect the fact that inverse condemnation actions are almost always brought by those who hold land for investment. In addition to the presumption that their property is fungible, investors in this field can be presumed to know their risks—even in the way of a certain probability of "unexpected" changes in the law—and hence already to have monetized them.[138]

C. Fungible Property Rights versus Nonproperty Interests in Personhood

As suggested earlier, a theory of just distribution based upon personhood may be structured so that property for personhood is merely a subcategory of entitlements for personhood. The elaboration of the relationship of the personhood dichotomy in property to theories of justice based on personhood is beyond the scope of this essay, but a glance at some disputes involving nonproperty interests in personhood will help place the personhood dichotomy in a larger context. While I have argued that personal property should be specially recognized, I do not argue that there is no personhood interest even in fungible property. Nevertheless, it is important to realize that in a larger scheme that accords special recognition to core personhood interests in general, some personhood interests not embodied in property will take precedence over claims to fungible property.

The line of cases from *Marsh v. Alabama* through *Hudgens v. NLRB* [139] addressed the problem of people who claimed free speech rights on other people's commercial private property. The Supreme Court ultimately decided that the property owner wins over the speech claimant. [140] In a later case, *PruneYard Shopping Center v. Robins,* [141] the Supreme Court decided that the right to exclude free speech on commercial property is not a federally protected property right. Although the would-be speakers have no First Amendment right to go on private property, it is not a taking for a state to hold that its own constitution does provide access to private commercial shopping centers for speech claimants.

The primary argument on behalf of recognizing a First Amendment right in the speakers was that the types of commercial property in question were quasi-public, and therefore that the owners should treat speech claimants the way the government would have to. But there is a separate argument to be made on behalf of the speech claimants. Shopping center property is not likely to be bound up with the personhood of the shopping center owner, while public speech, especially if considered political, is likely to be tied to the personhood of the speaker. The situation invites balancing, either of the strength of moral rights based on personhood [142] or, to translate into utilitarian terms, of the likely effects on individual and aggregate welfare if speech rights are granted or denied. At least in the moral weighing, the balance would have to consider the speech's content, but only to determine whether the speech is likely to be closely connected to personhood. One might roughly assume that "commercial" speech is not closely enough related to personhood, and "noncommercial" or "political" speech is. One might also consider the importance to personhood of speaking at a particular shopping center rather than some other forum. The result of this rough

weighing is that fungible property rights should yield to others' personhood claims. Large-scale commercial property ownership, which is
likely to be fungible, must be deemed not to contain rights wholly to
exclude noncommercial speakers, especially those that cannot speak effectively elsewhere.[143]

The shopping center demonstration controversy presents only one
manifestation of the larger problem of elaborating the moral limitations
on state trespass law. The general problem is to decide the enforceability
of exclusion—"property"—rights against various categories of claimed
interests in entry. The larger problem so defined bears some relationship
to one form of welfare rights argument discussed earlier. Is the property
owner who seeks to exclude another person using fungible property
rights in a way that significantly curtails the other's set of opportunities
to develop and express personhood in our society? From this perspective
one may decide, for example, that those who deliver basic welfare ser-
vices to farm workers should be able to enter large farms over the objec-
tions of corporate growers.[144]

But the personhood perspective gives better insight into some situations than others. A hard case for making distinctions on the basis of
personhood is *Bell v. Maryland.*[145] The issue in *Bell*—which the Court
was able to avoid deciding because intervening civil rights legislation
obviated the issue[146]—was whether a restaurant owner could invoke a
state trespass law to exclude blacks who demanded service. From the
perspective of personhood, a proprietor could argue that she had her
personhood bound up with being able to exclude blacks, while the
blacks could argue that their personhood is bound up with being served.
The concurring opinions of Justices Goldberg and Douglas suggest that
the property owner's argument should win if she is a homeowner, but
should lose if she runs a commercial establishment where she may be
catering to the prejudices of others to increase profits.[147] In other words,
these opinions find a reason to believe the proprietor's claimed exclusion
right is fungible rather than personal.[148] The case is more difficult from
the perspective of personhood if we imagine a small proprietor whose
prejudice is noncommercial and whose personhood is inseparable from
the business.[149] At this point, other moral arguments, perhaps involving
social obligations toward historically oppressed groups, would have to
be brought forward on behalf of the black claimants.

A difficult case for the personhood perspective arises when groups
claiming to be necessary to their members' self-constitution bring con-

flicting claims. In this kind of case, personhood is involved for the members of each group primarily in the claim of freedom of association whether or not the group's claim involves property. One reason this kind of case is difficult is that we lack a convincing theory of group rights. But as the communitarian critique of the traditional notion of person reminds us, group cohesion may be important or even necessary to personhood.

An example of this kind of case can be constructed by a somewhat free analysis of *Village of Belle Terre v. Boraas.* [150] The seven hundred residents of the village of Belle Terre zoned their town to be open essentially only to nuclear families. Six students living together in a rented house challenged the regulation. This dispute can be seen as involving personhood, in the guise of freedom of association, on both sides. [151] In fact, the case could easily involve property for personhood on both sides if one imagines seven hundred single-family residences governed by a set of restrictive servitudes. Then, the students argue that their leasehold is personal, and the townspeople argue that their benefit under the servitude is personal. It is difficult to choose between these two arguments.

Justice Douglas may have decided for the village because the students' personhood interest seemed weaker, since they had not yet had time to put down roots in the village. He mentioned family values, and the importance of maintaining places where those values could be freely expressed. Yet one may be troubled by that aspect of the case which permits those who represent mainstream majority moral attitudes to exclude dissenters. Those who constitute themselves as members of traditional families presumably have ample opportunities in our culture to reinforce and express that life-style. The personhood perspective can give a clearer answer where one group stands to lose one of its few opportunities to express personhood and the other does not. Thus, if the village residents had represented a minority group or some group outside the mainstream of American culture, their claims would seem stronger because more clearly necessary to their being able to constitute themselves as a group and hence as persons within that group.

VI. CONCLUSION

Just as Warren and Brandeis argued long ago that there was a right to privacy that had not yet been named, [152] this essay may be understood to argue that there is a right to personal property that should be recognized. Concomitantly, I have preliminarily argued that property rights that are *not* personal should not necessarily take precedence over stronger claims related to personhood. Our reverence for the sanctity of the home is rooted in the understanding that the home is inextricably part of the individual, the family, and the fabric of society. Where other kinds of object-relations attain qualitatively similar individual and social importance, they should be treated similarly.

I have not attempted to use the personhood perspective in property to determine a comprehensive structure specifying both a general justification of property and its detailed, institutional working-out. Instead, I have only given a survey of some of its roots, manifestations, and implications.[153] At this stage of knowledge and insight about the roles of the personhood perspective, I suggest, as a starting point for further thought, these propositions:

(1) At least some conventional property interests in society ought to be recognized and preserved as personal.

(2) Where we can ascertain that a given property right is personal, there is a prima facie case that that right should be protected to some extent against invasion by government and against cancellation by conflicting fungible property claims of other people. This case is strongest where without the claimed protection of property as personal the claimants' opportunities to become fully developed persons in the context of our society would be destroyed or significantly lessened, and probably also where the personal property rights are claimed by individuals who are maintaining and expressing their group identity.

(3) Where we can ascertain that a property right is fungible, there is a prima facie case that that right should yield to some extent in the face of conflicting, recognized personhood interests not embodied in property. This case is strongest where without the claimed personhood interest the claimants' opportunities to become fully developed persons in the context of our society would be destroyed or significantly lessened.

Residential Rent Control

Often the stated rationale for imposing residential rent control is that there is a shortage of affordable rental housing. As it stands this is at most a rationale for government subsidies either to housing consumers or suppliers, not price control. It becomes a rationale for price control by inserting the empirical premise that rent ceilings will increase the supply of affordable rental housing. But this implicit premise causes economists to gnash their teeth. It is easy to apply classic price theory to the imposition of rent ceilings. The well-known diagram representing the competitive market in equilibrium and the effects of imposing a price below the market-clearing price portrays the familiar result that the quantity supplied will go down and the quantity demanded will go up.[1] Landlords will use their buildings for something other than rental housing; they will not use vacant land to build more rental housing; tenants will stay put when otherwise they would move; more tenants will want to rent the remaining (cheaper) apartments. The housing shortage will then be even worse than the shortage before the imposition of the rent ceiling, and the "real" market price will be even higher.

The price-theory analysis goes on to suggest that under rent control we will find in operation the classic mechanisms for allocating supply when demand exceeds supply and the nominal price can't be raised, and for adjusting the market to a new equilibrium. That is, one will expect a black market in apartments, and various forms of rationing and queuing. (Queuing means there will be waiting lists for apartments.) The black market may take the form of under-the-table payments to those who can deliver an apartment. One will also expect to see disguised pricing and decreases in quality, both of which raise the real price. Disguised pricing may take the form of a tie-in to an uncontrolled "product" (a hundred dollars extra for the key, fifty dollars extra for the television antenna), or implementation of landlord prejudices. Decreases in quality may take the form of slipshod maintenance, or undesirable nonprice terms in leases, like onerous tenant rules or exculpatory clauses.

In short, classic price theory suggests that imposition of rent control will exacerbate the housing shortage that gave rise to the high rents that gave rise to the imposition of rent control, and at the same time will encourage landlords to supply lower-quality housing. No wonder rent control is anathema to economists who espouse this picture. The cure is not only worse than the disease, it is a worse case of the same disease.

From the predictions of this empirical model, the normative conclusion that there ought not to be rent control seems, for some, to follow as a matter of course. There is a misallocation of resources when landlords take their units off the market to enter some other business which is less preferred, while people who are willing to rent at the market price cannot find apartments to rent and must go elsewhere. Social welfare is not maximized, and therefore the arrangement is bad.

This is clearly a simple kind of utilitarian analysis. It assumes utility maximization is measured by wealth maximization, and it assumes that housing may be treated normatively like any other market commodity. But even for an economist who accepts both assumptions, the conclusion condemning rent control is too sweeping. If the landlords can collude to extract high prices, then rent control may merely bring prices down to the competitive level.[2] Even if the landlords cannot collude, if they are reaping high "rents" in the economic sense,[3] making them lower prices to the competitive level should result in no restriction of supply or other misallocation of resources.

A more complex ethical analysis might question the two assumptions and find the normative conclusion barring rent control not so obvious. Might the level of efficiency losses be outweighed by other gains? Might some right of tenants "trump" the utility analysis? In this article I focus primarily on challenging the second of the assumptions: the idea that housing is appropriately treated as an ordinary market commodity. In doing so I shall explore a nonutilitarian approach.

Because the basic assumptions of the simple economic model may be questioned, I believe that the normative question is complex even if the model is an accurate predictor in every housing market. But that is a big "if." More complexities are introduced to the extent the model is not a perfect fit. Moreover, the specific level of efficiency losses in the context of particular circumstances will, I think, affect the moral analysis. In short, the normative approach to rent control must be an exercise in nonideal theory.

By nonideal theory I mean a normative theory that takes into account the uncertainties and complexities of actual practice;[4] that descends from the realm of neat generality to the realm of messy particulars. The term is also meant to suggest that in my view moral judgment requires attention to particular circumstances in a manner more complex than application of abstract principles ("ideals") to a supposedly canonically described set of facts. Thus I shall argue that no general principles compel either that rent control is always justified or that it never is. I shall suggest that the real purpose of rent control is to make it possible for existing tenants to stay where they are, with roughly the same proportion of their income going to rent as they have become used to, and that in light of this purpose rent control might be justified more readily in some particular circumstances or contexts than in others. Thus the analysis I suggest is an all-things-considered weighing of each situation in light of moral factors relevant to the particular situation.

I. FRAMING SOME NORMATIVE ISSUES

To begin, let us introduce some normative approaches to the justice of rent control. To consider approaches other than the simple allocative efficiency model, we must assume that rent control works to some extent, in the sense that tenants are really paying less money for the same thing (or, possibly, less money for a less luxurious but still habitable and adequately maintained dwelling). If rent control doesn't work, it would be hard to justify it merely for the sake of appearances. Hence, we must assume that accompanying circumstances make it impossible for the landlords to reach a new market equilibrium of no benefit to tenants (unacceptable lower quality for the controlled price; or "real" price higher than the controlled nominal price). This in practice will mean that along with rent control there must be concomitant legal safeguards. They might include enactments such as prohibition of disguised pricing; strict housing code enforcement; legal habitability rights; eviction controls; demolition controls; and limitations on conversions to other uses, such as condominiums. The choice of concomitant safeguards may affect the justification of rent control under the circumstances (more about this later).

Assuming that rent control works, the main normative issue seems to be this: Where rent control lowers rents at the landlord's expense (that is, thereby decreasing the landlord's profit), is that just?[5] Under one market scenario, landlords are a cartel (oligopoly or shared monopoly). The justice of trust-busting is not disputed very much these days by anyone, whether of utilitarian or other ethical persuasion, so I shall pass this as an easy case. That is, I assume it would be just to lower rents from the monopoly price to the competitive price.

The question of economic rents is more interesting. If the market is competitive (not monopolistic), we may assume either (1) that landlords have high economic rents, so that rent control causes a "mere" wealth transfer from landlords to tenants; or (2) that landlords do not have high economic rents, so that there will be some decrease in supply accompanying the wealth transfer. In the second scenario there is an allocative inefficiency; in the first there is not.

A "mere" wealth redistribution between landlords and tenants, if unaccompanied by allocative inefficiencies, should be theoretically acceptable to a "pure" welfare economist, whom I shall call Posnerian.[6] Only the size of the pie matters, not the size of the pieces held by individuals. If we can assume that landlords are relatively richer than tenants, and if we accept the diminishing marginal utility of money, the wealth will in fact yield more welfare in the hands of the tenants, a situation to be preferred by egalitarians as well as Posnerians.

Someone of libertarian views regarding justice in entitlements, however, might find such redistribution unacceptable even if a welfare gain resulted, simply because it represents nonconsensual governmental alteration of the existing entitlement structure. A hypothetical "pure" libertarian, whom I shall call Nozickian,[7] might well condemn rent control across the board. The Nozickian might argue that unconditional choice of transfer terms is inherent in the concept of property ownership.[8] Alienability is a prime attribute of property in the market society. Another way to put this is that the infrastructure of the market society is not just private property, but private property plus free contract. This is expressed by Nozick's claim that justice in holdings results from just acquisition and just transfers; that is, entitlement plus alienability. Hence, the Nozickian might argue that landlords have the right to set the price at which they choose to rent their property—period.[9]

The question of overall efficiency or welfare seems irrelevant to rights-based libertarianism: the landlord either does or does not have an individual right against redistribution. If it seems intuitively plausible that the scenario where no inefficiency results from rent control should be treated differently from the scenario where rent control causes a loss of total welfare, then it is likely that one is either a utilitarian or holds some form of complex metaethic in which general welfare plays some role. I think many of our moral intuitions do relate to such a complex ethics. Accordingly, how some plausible intuitions about rent control might be normatively analyzed in a mixed mode is the main problem I wish to pursue here. In this mixed mode we take into account both concerns for general welfare and concerns about individuals. It is a mode that might be called contextual because of its focus on particular circumstances rather than broad abstract categories.

When rent control is imposed, the benefit of the wealth redistribution goes not to tenants generally but rather to the tenants who already live in a given political subdivision at the time it imposes rent control. These tenants also receive the nonmonetary benefit of being enabled to maintain the same residence. The immediate costs fall not only upon the landlords, but also upon would-be tenants who wish to move into the community and upon tenants who are forced to move out because their landlord withdraws from the market. Lowering the price of rental housing creates a class of would-be tenants who wish to rent at the new prices what they did not wish to (or could not) rent at the old.

Under the market scenario in which landlords merely lose economic rents, causing no losses in total welfare, formal efficiency analysis does not recognize the frustration of these would-be tenants as a cost, although a more sophisticated utilitarianism might do so. Under this scenario no existing tenants are forced to move out. Under the scenario where economic rents cannot offset the redistribution for all landlords, so that some landlords leave the rental housing market, there is a formal efficiency loss as well as frustration. Landlords will be supplying fewer units at the lower price. The existing tenants who occupied the vanished units must leave for less-preferred housing, causing a total welfare loss.[10] The loss is ongoing because would-be tenants for these units must also go to less-preferred alternatives. So a further normative question arises: Ought the government to be permitted to benefit one class of tenants (those already living in the jurisdiction at the time it enacts rent control) at the expense of another (those who do not currently have apartments in the jurisdiction)?

Putting this together with what has been said so far, and sticking to the more complex scenario in which landlords not only lose economic rents but there is also some allocative inefficiency, the problem so far discloses (at least) nine normative aspects to be simultaneously considered where rent control is imposed: (1) the general loss to overall welfare or happiness or wealth; (2) the wealth loss to landlords; (3) the curtailment of their choice in price setting and other aspects of control of their property; (4) the wealth gain to current tenants; (5) the non-monetary benefit to current tenants; (6) the wealth loss to would-be tenants (and their unmonetized frustration); (7) the differential treatment of landlords and tenants; (8) the differential treatment of current tenants and would-be tenants; and (9) the differential treatment of tenants who would be forced out but for rent control and those forced out by rent control.

Of these nine considerations that might cut against rent control, four—(1), (6), (8), and (9)—arguably do not arise under the simpler "mere-transfer-of-wealth" scenario. None of them, except possibly (3), carries the same import if the rental housing market is monopolized or noncompetitive and rent control can be imposed in such a way as to restore or create competitive conditions.

Against these considerations that arise if rent control is imposed are to be weighed the considerations that arise under circumstances of rapidly rising market rents if rent control is not imposed. They include (at least): (10) the wealth loss to tenants as the proportion of their income allocated to rent rises, or (11) the losses to tenants attributable to changing residences in response to high rent levels.[11] They also include, of course, (12) the corresponding wealth gains to landlords and (13) to those who are able to move into the residences vacated by those who are forced to leave. In what follows I shall consider more particularly some portions of this cluster of issues. Primarily, I want to explore what can be said about the circumstances in which (11) is likely to be heavily weighted if rent control is not imposed; hence, also in which (5) is likely to weigh in favor of rent control.

The apparent complexity of this cluster would not trouble a pure utilitarian, because for a pure utilitarian all else is subordinate to issue (1). Once the utilitarian framework is chosen, the justification (or not) of rent control depends on positive factors—market circumstances and people's subjective preferences. My point of view is that nonutilitarian concerns enter in and make the utilitarian analysis seem unsatisfactory, but at the same time positive factors—the circumstances in which rent control is imposed—are normatively relevant.

To elucidate why I think this is so, it is worth noticing that so far this essay has implicitly assumed that residential rent control is somehow a separate topic from rent control generally. This is not something the economic approach would readily assume. The perversity of rent control

from the efficiency point of view is merely a specific instance of a perfectly generalizable point about what happens when a below-equilibrium
price is imposed upon any good whatever. All are commodities; all have
prices; all obey economic laws. Why write about rent control rather than
general price control? An economist *could* try to answer, Because rental
housing markets everywhere exhibit characteristics that distinguish them
from other markets. But I think a more plausible answer is outside the
realm of economic (market) reasoning. To assume the separability of
residential rent control is to question the appropriateness of treating
residential housing as any old market commodity. It is implicitly to place
housing at least partially outside the realm of market reasoning.

More generally, it seems that the separability of residential rent
control cannot be assumed by any theory that fails to make normative distinctions among different kinds of recognized property rights
depending upon the degree to which various kinds of property are appropriately treated as laissez-faire market commodities (subject to regulation only under conditions of market failure). Otherwise there would
be no relevant dividing line between owning housing and owning widgets (for example, carpet-cleaning machines) such that the classes composed of lessors and lessees of such items might form separate categories
for normative analysis. It is a normative distinction between rented residences and other rented and sold things, in other words, that makes it
appropriate to consider residential rent control separately from rent control generally or price control generally. If the appropriateness appears
intuitively obvious, then the normative distinction is embedded in the
framework within which the reader sees the issue. The reader is willing
to see residential housing as incompletely commodified, and thus not
morally equivalent to widgets, in reasoning about justice in holdings and
transfers. The argument in sections II and III will give an account, based
on personhood and community, of why residential rent control is appropriately treated separately; that is, why residential housing is appropriately treated as incompletely commodified.

It is likewise possible to give a utilitarian account of the separability
of residential rent control, by postulating that very high subjective welfare almost always (in our social setting) inheres in being able to maintain the same residence. This postulate would allow us to separate the
utility analysis of rental housing from the general utility analysis of market trading in commodities of all sorts. A similar postulate would allow
separability of any recognizable category thought to be the repository

of high subjective value; for example, "mom-and-pop" grocery stores. I do not rest my conclusions on such a categorized utilitarian approach because I do not wish to treat the value involved as subjective, nor to grant that all commodities bearing (postulated) high subjective values to their holders should be viewed in the same way normatively. To the extent one feels that the subjective welfare of the "compleat capitalist," someone who has immense subjective attachment to an immense empire of property, is not normatively equivalent to that of the tenant, the utilitarian analysis will seem unsatisfactory.

In what follows I approach the cluster of normative questions in two ways, one roughly individualist and one roughly group- or community-oriented. Under the first heading we may consider whether a current tenant as an individual has some claim to continuity of residence at a controlled price that takes priority over various individual claims of landlords and would-be tenants. Under the second heading we may consider whether the current tenants as a group or community have a claim that takes priority over claims of the class of would-be tenants and the class of landlords.

II. THE ARGUMENT FROM THE TENANT AS INDIVIDUAL

Most of us, I think, feel that a tenant's interest in continuing to live in an apartment that she has made home for some time seems somehow a stronger or more exigent claim than a commercial landlord's interest in maintaining the same scope of freedom of choice regarding lease terms and in maintaining a high profit margin. Where rising rents are forcing out tenants and where landlords have significant economic rents, one feels the tenant's claim is stronger than the landlord's.[12] Even where significant economic rents are not present, so that some landlords are forced to leave the business, one may still feel that the tenant's expectation or desire to continue in her home is more important than the commercial landlord's expectation or desire to continue in the landlord business over some other business that will yield a better return. We do not recognize any general right to remain in a specific business such that regulation of the industry would be prohibited if regulation would operate to force some of the less-efficient suppliers out of that market and into others.

The intuitive general rule is that preservation of one's home is a stronger claim than preservation of one's business, or that noncommercial personal use of an apartment as a home is morally entitled to more

weight than purely commercial landlording. I shall discuss shortly a
plausible basis for this rule and elaborate what I mean by the distinction
between personal and purely commercial holding. It will be helpful first
to notice that the exceptions or qualifications that come to mind serve
to prove the rule. One class of exceptions involves situations where the
landlord's claim seems noncommercial and therefore more like the tenant's. For example, perhaps the landlord lives on the premises, or perhaps the building constitutes a long-term family business personally
maintained by its members. Another class of exceptions involves situations where the tenant's claim is not plausibly that of maintaining an
established home; for example, where the tenant is transient. If the landlord appears noncommercial or the tenant's interest is not that of an
established home, then the tenant's claim no longer appears obviously
weightier than the landlord's. Rent-control ordinances usually exempt
transient accommodations and regularly grant special consideration to
noncommercial interests of the landlord, such as her desire to move in a
family member. Such provisions are responsive to the limits of the intuitive general rule.

The intuitive general rule I just mentioned does not apply to would-
be tenants. When we consider people who are tenants elsewhere and
wish to become tenants in the rent-controlled community, we are not
struck with a similar general intuition of a strong claim. If the claims of
would-be tenants seem especially strong, it is likely to be in the situation
where large numbers of people work (or perhaps go to school) in the
jurisdiction but are unable to find housing there. Their desire to live in
the community where they are established in their work (or perhaps
their school, but that seems more transient) may seem to make their
interest more like that of the current tenants. Unfortunately, many of
these people may be losers either way: the vacancies may not exist under
rent control, but under laissez-faire they would be priced too high.[13]

No doubt there is a misallocation of resources when the would-be
tenants are forced to rent in their next-preferred community rather than
the one they would have chosen at the "real" market price if it were
allowed to prevail. This may be significant for the efficiency approach.
To the extent one is swayed by general welfare concerns, the size of this
welfare loss might matter. Furthermore, the fact that the community is
closed to them seems offensive to the political value of free migration
within our nation, which could (although need not) be construed as an
individual right accruing to each would-be tenant. Yet these kinds of

losses do not seem as important as the kind of loss that results when one is forced to move out of one's *home* when the rent, even if what the competitive market will bear, ceases to be within one's budget.

Since the intuition that residential tenants have a better claim than commercial landlords does not extend in full force to would-be residential tenants, the salient distinction is not (or not only) between noncommercial and commercial interests, or even between use as a home versus other uses. The salient point is rather the strength of one's interest in an *established* home versus other interests; at least, those that are not both noncommercial and well established.

Let me refer to the situation where the tenant stands to lose an established home and the landlord is purely commercial as "standard circumstances." To the extent there does exist the intuitive appeal for preserving the tenant's home in standard circumstances that I postulate here, it can be understood in terms of the distinction between personal and fungible property that I elaborated in an earlier essay.[14] Property that is "personal" in this philosophical sense is bound up with one's personhood, and is distinguishable from property that is held merely instrumentally or for investment and exchange and is therefore purely commercial or "fungible." One way to look at this distinction is to say that fungible property is fully commodified, or represents the ideal of the commodity form, whereas personal property is at least partially noncommodified.

Personal property describes specific categories in the external world in which holders can become justifiably self-invested, so that their individuality and selfhood become intertwined with a particular object. The object then cannot be replaced without pain by money or another similar object of equivalent market value; the particular object takes on unique value for the individual. Only a few special objects or categories of objects are personal property. Other property items, which can be replaced by their equivalents or money at no pain to the holder, are merely fungible, that is not bound up with personhood. When a holding is fungible, the value for the holder is the exchange or market value, not the object per se; one dollar bill is as good as another, or the equivalent in stocks or bonds, or any other item with market value. When a holding is personal the specific object matters, and the fact that it matters is justifiable.

The notion that external objects can become bound up with personhood reflects a philosophical view of personhood. In this view persons are not merely abstract, disembodied rational units, but rather concrete selves whose situation in an environment of objects and other persons is constitutive. That is, on this view the external world is integral to personhood. The view is perhaps neo-Hegelian in that it calls to mind Hegel's theory that putting the will into an external object takes the person from abstract to actual.[15] But it blurs or bridges the subject/object dichotomy in a way I believe Hegel did not.[16] It is also related to the view espoused by a number of writers on personal identity, that what is important to personhood is a continuity of memory and anticipation, or a continuing character structure encompassing future projects or plans, as well as past events and feelings. The way this view generates the category of personal property is through the notion of the central importance of certain object-relations in maintaining the kinds of continuity related to personhood. The objects that are in this way important to personhood I describe as bound up with the person, and I denominate personal, as opposed to fungible.

The view that personhood is involved with continuity of context need not be limited to the property or object relations I am discussing here. It could generate other categories of human interactions where continuity is involved with personhood, perhaps most notably in connection with work and the workplace. Partial decommodification both of certain categories of property and of labor may be mandated by this kind of contextual view of personhood. There would be both a general claim that housing and labor be regulated, and a stronger specific claim to stay in a residence or job that one has held for some time.

There are several immediate difficulties with this general view, or points in need of further elucidation. One is that the personal/fungible distinction must actually be a continuum and not a dichotomy. Self-investment in external objects seems to be a matter of degree, not either/or. Another is that the distinction might be regarded as subjective or conventional; that is, dependent only upon a given individual's subjective feelings about an object, or dependent only upon our general social consensus about self-investment in homes, cars, or whatever. Still another point in need of further discussion is the prevailing moral conviction that some kinds of attachments to external objects are destructive of personhood, not constitutive of it. Also, there seems to be slippage on the issue of what is required to be a person or the "same" person versus what is required to be a "well-developed" or "fulfilled" person.

That the personal/fungible distinction is not really a dichotomy is not troubling in the present context. Given that my view of personhood does not endorse a bright-line distinction between persons and objects, it does make more sense to think of a continuum that ranges from a thing central to one's being to a thing wholly interchangeable with something else, rather than to think of a personal/fungible dichotomy. But telescoping the continuum to its two endpoints is useful when referring to situations well accepted as being near one or the other endpoint of the continuum. The "home"—usually conceived of as an owner-occupied single-family residence—seems to be a paradigm case of personal property in our social context. In this essay I wish to suggest that a residential tenancy carries the same moral weight because and insofar as it is the tenant's "home" in the same sense.

The moral conviction that some kinds of self-investment in objects are destructive is a serious philosophical problem for the personhood theory of property insofar as that theory is utilized to delineate categories of property to receive preferred treatment morally or legally. Someone (the "compleat capitalist" I mentioned earlier) might be "bound up with" a vast empire of property, living for nought but to revel in ownership, and we would want to say this is an example of bad or perverted object-relations, to be discouraged, not enshrined as morally central. The "compleat capitalist" problem implicates these difficulties: Is what makes object-relations good or bad wholly subjective? Are we talking about what makes someone the person she is, good or bad, or what might be appropriate for a "good" or "adequate" person? The "compleat capitalist" is particularly a problem for a utilitarian construal of personal property as merely a category in which high subjective welfare can be thought to repose, and is one reason I do not take the utilitarian tack.

Rather, in order to deal with these problems some level of moral objectivity seems to be needed. That is, in seeking to know whether someone's relationship with her property holds the moral status of property for personhood, we look not merely to the subjective aspects of the relationship (its intensity, its centrality in her particular life, and so on) but also to whether the subjective attachment that in fact exists is good or bad.[17] In other words, we are seeking to know about good or acceptable attachments to property. Personal property marks out a category of objects that become justifiably bound up with the person. Such attachments contribute to personal continuity and hence to being a fulfilled person. Because they are justifiable, they contribute as well to being an adequate or well-developed person. The empire of the "compleat capitalist," on the other hand, might contribute to her continuity and to her own sense of fulfillment, but it would not contribute to her being a well-developed person, for the "compleat capitalist" is not well developed; she has embraced an inferior concept of human flourishing.

I do not mean to suggest that one must have property or a home to be a person at all. The homeless are surely persons. The argument here might suggest that by virtue of their personhood they are owed homes, not that our failure to ensure that they have homes renders them nonpersons beyond our concern. Neither are religious ascetics who renounce all property nonpersons. Some of them might be better persons than others who cling to their possessions. I do suggest that the home as a stable context is for many people involved with continuity and personal identity, and that this involvement can be treated as morally appropriate. It is thus appropriate to foster this category of property attachment, though not appropriate to condemn its absence.

Thus, my claim is simply that the private home is a justifiable form of personal property, while a landlord's interest is often fungible. A tenancy, no less than a single-family house, is the sort of property interest in which a person becomes self-invested; and after the self-investment has taken place, retention of the interest becomes a priority claim over curtailment of merely fungible interests of others. To pursue the parallel with homeownership, there the owner's interest is personal and the mortgagee's interest is fungible. That is why it seems right to safeguard the owner from losing her home even if it means some curtailment of the mortgagee's interest. Consider how we take for granted special concessions to homeowners (such as homesteading, exemptions in bankruptcy, redemption rights in foreclosure) to avoid loss of their homes.[18] Similarly, it also seems right to safeguard the tenant from losing her home even if it means some curtailment of the landlord's interest.

Notice that this personhood argument by its terms applies most readily in the case I have called standard circumstances, where the established tenant cannot afford the "real" market price and would in fact lose her home without rent control. Thus, the argument is most appealing if tenants are relatively poor as a class. This is not a difficult assumption to make, for, given the structure of our tax laws, the great majority of those who can muster a down payment will establish their home by buying rather than renting.[19]

In order to apply the argument to nonmarginal tenants, one might say that it is not fair for landlords to be able to make tenants continually pay over their consumer surplus in order to keep the home in which they are self-invested; there are no such continuing levies for a home-owner's consumer surplus. Part of the stability of context associated with the home could be stability of the proportion of one's income required to maintain it. Or one might make the systemic argument: it is important to protect the personhood interest of poor tenants, and where we cannot select them out for special treatment very readily, it is not wrong to benefit others as well. Still, it is evident that the person-hood argument carries most force in situations where long-term tenants are being forced out by rising rents.

We should pause here to consider how the tenants' argument would look different if it were based on welfare rights rather than on personal property. By welfare rights I mean claims as of right to merit wants or minimal entitlements. Suppose that shelter is considered such a merit want. Then all would have rights to shelter, and if tenants as a class cannot afford the free-market price of adequate shelter, the government would be required somehow to intervene to make adequate shelter available to them. Although regulation of housing prices may be one possible government action, this argument does not cut in favor of rent control to the extent the personhood argument does. Under the welfare rights claim the tenant's right is at best to *an* apartment, not to *this particular* apartment; and the claims of existing tenants are not differentiated from the claims of would-be tenants. Furthermore, the argument depends fundamentally on assuming that tenants as a class are absolutely impoverished; government would not be required to intervene unless tenants could not afford adequate shelter. (That is, could not afford adequate shelter without falling below the minimum in other welfare rights such as food and health care.) As we have seen, the tenant's relative poverty also figures in the personhood argument, but its role is different. The apartment the tenant has become established in does not have to be at base subsistence level to merit protection. Finally, since the landlord's property interest is not considered different in kind from the tenant's when arguing merely about shelter as a welfare right, no immediate justification appears why the government should provide this merit want at landlords' expense rather than at the expense of all taxpayers. If we agree that there are tenants' welfare rights to adequate shelter (a habitable apartment), the question remains whether these rights justify charging costs to the landlords. Many welfare rights arguments seem to imply that the government (that is, everyone) should be charged. Perhaps the question remaining could be phrased: Tax everyone, or tax landlords?

The same question arises under the personhood argument: Why not tax everyone, and compensate the landlords for having to yield fungible wealth in favor of tenants' personhood interests? But I think it can be answered more readily. It is plausible to maintain that if government must respect equally the personhood of all, it cannot permit forms of fungible property that make full self-development impossible for one class and are not necessary for the self-development of the holders. If the government has erroneously permitted wrongful fungible property, or wrongful commodification, and acts to correct its error, compensation is not appropriate for reasons analogous to why it is inappropriate to compensate "expropriated" slaveholders or those whose "absolute exclusion" rights were diminished by the 1964 Civil Rights Act. The citizenry as a whole is not required to legitimate (by paying the value of) a benefit that the beneficiary held in error and as a wrong against our ideals of individual worth. Furthermore, if part of the wrong is the fact of commodification, the fact of placing the object in the market realm, then to place a market value on the interest even while decommodifying it seems contradictory or equivocal. If this argument is accepted, there is no corrective justice reason to compensate landlords whose wealth is diminished by rent control. To the extent landlords hold expectations of free-market economic rents for all residential tenancies, they are wrongly held, just as former expectations that property rights always included discrimination rights were wrongly held. And to the extent we do arrive at an understanding that it is wrong to treat certain residential tenancies just like free-market commodities in pricing and other conditions of exchange, it will also appear wrong to treat them as such in meting out corrective justice.

III. The Argument from Tenant Community

The form of personhood argument discussed thus far, as well as the welfare rights argument, is individualistic in flavor. The personhood argument can be seen, however, to have communitarian roots if the necessary objective judgment about the category of personal property has a communitarian basis. Some forms of welfare rights arguments, although individualistic in the sense that the rights accrue to individuals, are group based in that comparative inequalities between classes play a role.

For that matter, simple utilitarianism is communitarian in the sense that only total group welfare counts. Thus it is more accurate to say that the preceding argument has primarily considered tenants as individuals, not that it is wholly individualistic.

A different set of arguments may be added by considering an explicit communitarian basis. That is, we must consider the argument from a tenant community. I mean here the situation in which the tenants in a geographical "community" form also a spiritual "community."

Theoretically we might also consider a community including both landlords and tenants. Although such a world might be far from an ideal world of no inequality or no property, it may nevertheless be one stage closer to the ideal than the usual rent-control situation. In fact rent control with absentee landlords seems intuitively more palatable than rent control with landlords who live on the premises. This could be for individualistic personhood reasons (resident landlords are as personally invested as their tenants), but it could have a communitarian basis as well. I focus primarily on the nonideal case of a tenant community in what I have called the standard circumstances of dealing with commercial landlords, because it seems to accord with much of the current state of the world. Thus I do not treat the more utopian case of landlord-tenant spiritual community.

Consider the idea that a predominantly tenant community is justified in enacting rent control to avoid dispersion of the community to other and cheaper markets. Under what circumstances would this justification hold? To justify control on this ground would seem to require the general condition (1) that real community (in the spiritual sense) may be preserved even at some expense to fungible property interests of others, at least where the group affirms through local political action like rent control that it seeks continuity; and the specific condition (2) that a particular rent-controlled jurisdiction is indeed such a tenant community. In addition, the argument is strengthened if (3) the community will certainly be dispersed unless rent control is imposed. That is, analogous to the argument from personhood, the argument goes through more readily if tenants are poor, an assumption that is plausible because of the tax structure. Analogous to what was said earlier in the context of distinguishing the argument based on personhood from an argument based on welfare rights, the argument does not evaporate if tenants are not down and out. It is perhaps not fair, and harmful to community stability, for the price of community preservation to go up and up;

and—the systemic argument—we should err on the side of community preservation because it is an important value.

To take first the general condition (1), it is possible to argue for community either as a good in itself (a species of corporativism) or as something that is valued by all the participants as individuals. Neocorporativist theory is presently murky,[20] though for many people the notion that some human wholes are greater than the sums of their parts seems obvious. One argument is that persons are (partly) constituted by communities. If communities are so constitutive, they must be a good in themselves or at least not totally derivative from individualist values.[21] To assume that communities are merely of instrumental value to persons seems to contradict this by postulating a person wholly separate from the community, capable of receiving the instrumental benefit. But even sticking with the individualist base, there are utilitarian and nonutilitarian arguments for preserving community which seem strong enough to hold up against some extent of wealth losses from market distortions. The utilitarian argument is straightforward: we suppose from our knowledge of life in the general society of which we are a part that the personal utility attributable to living in an established, close-knit community is very high. The nonutilitarian argument is equally straightforward: we suppose from our knowledge of life in this society that personhood is fostered by living within an established community of other persons.

It is easier to defend long-term rent control by appeal to community than by appeal strictly to the individual interests of present tenants. Relying solely on individual interests seems to imply that rent control is no longer justified when the present tenant dies or moves voluntarily. Communities last beyond the tenure of any one individual. Still, communities too may die of natural causes, so that not even a communitarian-based justification is necessarily permanent in principle.

Assuming that community may be preserved when it exists, at least where the group affirms through local political action like rent control that it seeks continuity, there arises the specific question (2) of when a rent-controlled jurisdiction is in fact such a community. Without a more well-developed theory of community, it is not possible to outline the indicia of community. But it seems there are particular intuitions we can feel fairly confident about, even without a fully developed theory. Sometimes, for example, tenants are primarily members of one ethnic group who interact in ways that form a cohesive and defined group. On the other hand, perhaps a very high turnover rate might convince us we are not dealing with a real community. Sometimes, the case of elderly people on fixed incomes being squeezed out of their long-term homes by younger, wealthier people is especially sympathetic. Of course, the elderly people may have remained strangers to each other during their years of residence, in which case their claims would have to rest on individualism. But it is perhaps more likely that over the years they have developed ties of friendship and support that unite them into a group or community.

There may be many instances where the boundaries of the political jurisdiction are not the same as the boundaries of the spiritual community. Then the normative question becomes whether we may justifiably benefit some nonmembers along with some (or all) members.[22] In addition, there is a "federalism" issue. What circumstances render it appropriate to consider *this* community as the appropriate unit of justice? Political morality might dictate that the appropriate community to preserve is a larger community and not the particular group or locale. If so, we might conclude that the local policy of rent control is causing distortions for the larger community, for example by making it impossible for workers who need to live near their jobs to move into the local jurisdiction. That might render local rent control unjustified. The workers as would-be tenants might have a stronger claim than some of the present tenants. Lacking good theories of what constitutes a community as an entity, it is hard to know how we would choose the size of the unit whose preservation is a good to be pursued. If a normative concern is to integrate the home and workplace in a single (spiritual and geographic) community, then "bedroom communities" would be disfavored. (They would be relatively disfavored for rent control anyway if all tenants in them are relatively well off.)

I wish to turn now to a brief examination of how typical provisions of rent-control legislation might reflect some of the concerns I have discussed. I shall first summarize the position at which the foregoing discussion has arrived. I conclude that there is sometimes a case for rent control because of the importance of the personhood interest in the home and the appropriateness of preserving established communities. If a jurisdiction is such that there is a tenant community to preserve, and if the tenants as a class in that community are relatively poor, then on balance rent control may be justified, especially if landlords appear purely commercial and market factors (especially economic rents to landlords) are such that efficiency losses are relatively low. On the other hand, if it does not make sense to speak of property for personhood or of community with respect to the tenants involved, then on balance rent control may not be justified, especially if most landlords appear noncommercial or efficiency losses are high. As with all practical moral decisions, there can still be undecided hard cases; for example, if efficiency losses are very high, tenants are a poor community that is deeply self-invested, and many landlords are noncommercial while not feeling community solidarity with their tenants. But I think the analysis here can at least help us sort out the hard cases from the easier ones.

IV. SOME PROVISIONS OF RENT-CONTROL LEGISLATION

A survey of rent-control provisions in light of what has been said is now in order.[23] An almost universal companion of rent control is eviction control. The typical rent-control ordinance gives the tenant tantamount to permanent tenure during good behavior. This is in marked contrast to the normal legal rule that periodic tenancies are terminable at will with proper notice, at least if the landlord's motive is not retaliatory.[24] If vacancy decontrol (to be discussed in a moment) is present, eviction control is a necessary safeguard to prevent easy evasion of rent control by landlords. But eviction control represents more than that, as is shown by the fact that it is enacted even without vacancy decontrol. Eviction control demonstrates that rent control is enacted primarily so that tenants may keep their apartments. It is a device to protect the personhood interest of the tenant and the value of community, at least as against commercial landlords. There are almost always exceptions for landlords who wish to move in themselves or their family members,[25] and sometimes for small-scale landlords as well.

Common companions of rent control are condominium-conversion control and demolition control. These prevent landlords from easy exit into another business on the same land; in other words, individual landlords may exit to the widget business by selling their buildings to other landlords, but the number of rental buildings does not decrease. An exception to allow condominium conversion at the instance of tenants themselves might serve the tenants' interest in maintaining their homes.

Two common exemptions in rent-control legislation are vacancy decontrol, permitting the landlord to raise rent to any level she chooses (that is, the "real" price) when a tenant leaves voluntarily or dies, and an exemption for new buildings. The exemption for new buildings may be seen primarily as a method of offsetting the decrease in supply of rental housing that simple price theory predicts. There is no personhood interest to protect in housing that has never been occupied. (Serious problems arise if rent control goes on for a long time and a twenty-year-old building is exempt because it succeeded rent control. Jurisdictions with long-term rent control must adjust such problems from time to time.) Vacancy decontrol seems clearly related to the issue of the individual personhood interest of the established tenant. It is one way of striking a compromise: tenure for a tenant during good behavior, protecting her interest in establishing a home; free choice for the landlord otherwise. Vacancy decontrol seems unresponsive to communitarian concerns, because others of the same spiritual community (for example, adult children of members) may be precluded from moving into the vacancies, so the community may gradually die off as its departing members' decontrolled apartments are filled with (presumably richer) nonmembers. And, of course, vacancy decontrol is terrible for progress toward a better world of landlord-tenant community, since the "rational" landlord will be always hoping her long-term tenants will leave.

Previously I have mentioned in passing the occasional exemptions for small-scale landlords, or landlords who live on the premises, which may be attempts to direct rent control only against landlords whose interest is fungible. There are also sometimes exemptions for rented single-family houses and for "luxury units." The luxury-unit exemption is most readily explained in terms of assumptions about tenants' wealth. As we have seen, the easiest case for rent control is where landlords are reaping high economic rents from tenants who stand to lose their homes. The luxury-unit level may represent the legislators' attempt to draw a line between poor tenants who might lose their homes and wealthy tenants who won't. Furthermore, the interest of wealthy tenants is less likely to be personal. Wealthy tenants perhaps rent an apartment merely as a pied-à-terre, or for a temporary stay by the beach. There are few if any jurisdictions in which wealthy people, who could be owners, establish their homes as long-term renters. The exemption for single-family homes, where it appears, may be a proxy for the luxury-unit exemption. Depending on the circumstances, it may also carve out a renters' community for protection; for example, a portion of town devoted to multi-unit dwellings. It may also reflect the assumption that rent control is more readily justified as against commercial landlords, whose interest is fungible. Those who rent out single-family dwellings or one half of a duplex are less likely to be commercial landlords; their interest may tend to be personal.

It is also important to place rent control within the legal context of tenants' rights generally. To do so one must view residential rent control in its interaction with housing codes and other tenants' entitlements such as the implied warranty of habitability. These entitlements, although enacted for other reasons, function as concomitant safeguards to make rent control work. Moreover, the need for housing codes and habitability rights in general is partly evidence of the existence of a class of low-income tenants who cannot effectively bargain for these rights in the market; and perhaps as well evidence of something about the structure of landownership and housing that gives rise to a continuing rental housing shortage or information problems and transaction costs such that nobody can bargain very well in the normally understood contractual sense. It is time-consuming and difficult to shop for housing; apartments and their environments are not identical, and comparison shopping might seem like comparing apples and oranges; not all salient characteristics of apartments are apparent upon inspection; and once the tenant has moved in it is costly to move out for a better deal. These problems can just as well give rise to price controls as they can to quality controls such as tenants' entitlements to habitability rights. Furthermore, if the imposition of habitability rights such as housing codes and implied warranties is perverse in making rents to poor tenants go up, because the landlords are able under market circumstances to pass on the costs, and/or because some landlords withdraw their product from the market when their costs go up, enabling others to raise prices, then price control is all the more likely. Modern rent control and habitability rights are very closely linked.

In deference to landlords' desire to stay in business, one often finds a statutory or judge-made entitlement to a "fair rent" or a "reasonable rate of return." This constitutes an exemption to the rent-control legislation in cases where it is determined that the controlled price is too low for an individual landlord. Since I think the statutory versions of this entitlement are most likely motivated by the anticipated response of some courts, I shall discuss this exemption in the context of a brief discussion of judicial review of rent control.

V. Judicial Review of Rent Control

Rent control is legally justified if imposed by majority rule of a legislative body unless there is some reason to overturn that legislative judgment. Thus there is a legal prima facie case for rent control once imposed. The reason to overturn a local legislative decision may be a state statute that preempts local law on the subject, or may be that state law prohibits local governments from exercising such regulatory power. Otherwise, the primary way a court may invalidate a legislative act is to invoke the federal or state constitution. The main constitutional claims that come up are taking of the landlord's property without just compensation or violation of substantive due process. In the Constitution these claims stem from Fourteenth Amendment due process limitations on the actions of state and local governments, with the taking claim referring back to the just compensation clause of the Fifth Amendment. State constitutions have various analogous provisions.

Under the current state of constitutional law, the taking claim will fail unless the rent-control ordinance is judged to confiscate the landlord's property rather than merely diminish the returns on her investment. In some circumstances, courts have even held that regulation preventing the landlord from removing the unit from the rental market, either by demolition or by taking up residency, is not a confiscation of the landlord's property.[26] The substantive due process claim will be subject to the so-called rational basis test, which asks only that rent control be shown to be a rational method of achieving a legitimate governmental purpose. Thus, for example, the California Supreme Court held that rent control is constitutional if a housing shortage and its concomitant ill effects really do exist. But that court held it not to be a rational response—in other words unconstitutional—if the rent levels are set "too" low simply because of choosing the wrong standard to set rents, or because of unnecessary procedural delays in allowing landlords to get the rents adjusted. The California court said, as have other courts when faced with the problem, that in order for rent control to be constitutional it must be rationally calculated to eliminate excessive rents *and* at the same time give the landlord a just and reasonable return.[27]

Under some circumstances one cannot both eliminate excessive rents and give the landlord a "just and reasonable" or "fair" return. Of course, if the landlord has high economic rents, one could lower her profits and still consider her return reasonable. But regardless of whether the market is competitive or cartelized, if the landlord has recently bought the building under conditions of rising real estate prices and expected rent increases, the "excessive" rents might in fact just barely cover the landlord's costs. That is, the expected rent increases, whether at a competitive or monopoly level, will be priced into the market value of the building, and the landlord's operating expenses and debt service on her loans will be close to the amount of the "excessive" rents.

Furthermore, there are many uncertainties. What constitutes the constitutionally required reasonable or fair rate of return? It seems circular and contrary to the purposes of rent control to define rent levels with respect to the market value of the building when the market value of the building depends on expected rent levels. It is possible to suggest a standard that would avoid this problem (such as a percentage above net operating costs, not including debt service), but it would not necessarily give a positive return on the landlord's investment or yield a net positive cash flow. Other questions are, what level of vacancy rate constitutes the required shortage which renders rent control rational? (Will rent control be irrational for the purposes of due process if, as classic price theory suggests, in a given jurisdiction it can be empirically shown that rent control will merely exacerbate the shortage?) What will constitute the concomitant serious ill effects of the shortage required to render rent control constitutional?

Yet, even though the language of due process and constitutional law is cumbersome in this context, one might sympathetically read the courts as groping for the kind of all-things-considered analysis I have suggested. The ill effects of high rents and housing shortages may be more serious for real communities and poor tenants. The efficiency losses might be less serious in relatively stable communities where at the same time tenants' personhood interests and community interests are more important. High economic rents to the landlords may exist in communities where most of the buildings have been held by the same landlord for a long time, and lived in by the same tenants; that is, in communities that have been relatively stable, and then hit with a sudden rise in market values. In some of these relatively stable communities the landlords may choose not to reap the economic rents, preferring stability to profit. In that case, perhaps the landlords' interest may not be appropriately treated as fully fungible. In that sort of community, however, perhaps we have made progress toward the better world of landlord-tenant community where landlords value stability as much as the tenants, do not raise rents in keeping with rising market prices, and rent control does not become necessary to protect tenants' continuity interest.

I would go further and suggest that a requirement that every landlord be able to obtain a reasonable return (in the sense of net positive cash flow) is unjustified. If one is an inefficient supplier, or if one bought one's capital plant speculatively in a rising market, and then regulation is imposed upon one's business, there doesn't seem to be any intrinsic right to remain in that business. Insofar as it is fair to consider the landlord a business, and this seems fair in many situations, it does not follow that the landlord is entitled to remain a landlord under all circumstances. Our intuitions should tolerate some efficiency losses (exit of marginal landlords to other businesses) in light of strong personhood claims by tenants, as long as the landlord's interest is fungible.

There may be landlords whose property is personal; and perhaps they should be treated differently. Though there should be no general right that all landlords receive a reasonable rate of return under rent control, at least if that means a right to a certain positive cash flow, perhaps there should be a "substantive due process" personhood exemption to prevent loss of buildings held as personal property by landlords. Rent-control ordinances responsive to this concern might define certain likely categories as exempt from rent control; for example, duplexes in which the landlord resides. They might also create an exemption for a landlord who can show that the circumstances of her particular case give rise to a claim of violation of the interest in personal continuity and self-development if the controlled price level is enforced with respect to her. Of course, as discussed earlier, a claim that I am the "compleat capitalist" and personally "need" absolute dominion over all my investments should not suffice here because this is not an idea of self-development that we should respect, at least as against the tenants' interest.

VI. CONCLUSION: LINE DRAWING FOR PERSONHOOD AND COMMUNITY

Thus rent-control ordinances may justifiably create subcategories of protected landlords (and unprotected tenants). We become understandably nervous when differential treatment is spoken of, because of the risk of error involved.[28] How can we tell the difference between invidious discrimination where we fail to treat relevantly like cases alike, and beneficial discrimination where we treat the relevantly different cases appropriately differently? Yet where defensible distinctions can in fact be made, it is unfair not to. The dilemma is not solved simply by making rules as broad and inclusive as possible. If some but not all tenants hold apartments as personal property, and if some but not all jurisdictions enacting rent control comprise tenant communities, and if some but not all landlords hold buildings as fungible property, and if some but not all landlords reap high economic rents, it does not follow either that rent control is always justified or that it never is, at least if we have means of separating these relevant categories with some degree of confidence. As I hope this essay has made clear, I believe that some lines can be drawn in the case of rent control.

Whether or not rent control is justified in a given jurisdiction will partly depend on whether the legislation draws these lines appropriately. The specific provisions discussed in section IV, among others, must be tailored to local circumstances. For example, it appears that rich tenants are less entitled to the benefits of rent control, since it is less likely that without it they will lose their homes. So it does not seem offensive on this ground for jurisdictions with substantial proportions of wealthy tenants to exempt luxury units from rent control. On the other hand, perhaps in some markets the resulting incentive for landlords to own only luxury units will in fact have prohibited side effects on the poor. In some jurisdictions, landlords who live on their premises, or those who own just one building, and have owned it for a number of years and personally maintained it, might in fact be entitled to a "just and reasonable return" (net positive cash flow) because of their personal claim not to be forced out of this particular business. In other jurisdictions, resident landlords may be newcomers who paid high prices and expect to sell out soon at even higher ones: their interest is fungible. The line drawing should express the underlying values of personhood and community. In general, we shall have made substantial progress in the non-ideal normative analysis of residential rent control once we recognize that the moral claims attached to personal property and community are strong enough to be respected even at some cost to efficiency.

VII. Postscript: Exclusion and Pluralism

Finally, the normative examination of rent control brings up the broader issue of community exclusion. The issue is when it is appropriate for a community to make it hard for others to become members. Here the analogy between growth control (exclusionary zoning and servitudes) and rent control (exclusionary pricing?) is striking. Exclusionary zoning refers to local government regulation of lot sizes, unit sizes, household compositions, etc., that has the effect of excluding certain groups, most frequently the less affluent. The same effect can be achieved by complexes of exclusionary servitudes imposed by developers in order to increase the market value of the housing being sold.

Exclusionary zoning and rent control are both acts by local government that have the effect of keeping out would-be entrants. There appears in each case tension between how far we are to pursue our underlying political value of free migration and how far we are to pursue our underlying political values of stability of individuals' homes and local community continuity. Because of the conflict of values involved, the problems are difficult.

Rent control may be more often justifiable than exclusionary zoning to the extent that rent control protects the homes of poor individuals and communities of poor individuals. In a rising market, a poor person stands to lose her home without rent control (or some other intervention such as an income subsidy offsetting the differential between housing price increases and wage increases). Communities of poor individuals are not likely to be able to regroup elsewhere. Exclusionary zoning, on the other hand, often helps the relatively affluent form enclaves to keep out minority and poor people. They may have an association claim in so doing. But the wealthy do not in general have trouble maintaining their identity, and the poor struggle for a place to form theirs. When those doing the excluding are the mainstream of American society and the middle class, their claims of association and personhood may pale beside the claims of personhood and association of the less mainstream and the less fortunate who seek entry. The case against exclusion on the basis of race, for example, has been easy in liberal political theory.

But the tables may be turned. Consider an incorporated town of several hundred black separatists that wishes to exclude whites; consider an incorporated town of several hundred Orthodox Jews that wishes to exclude those of other religions, or at least to ban those who do not observe certain religious rules. Anyone committed to pluralism and the preservation of minority ways cannot be certain this kind of exclusion should be disallowed.[29] The size of the community, its cohesiveness, and its need for exclusionary practices in order to survive as a community might on balance convince us that exclusion is just in these types of cases. Exclusion—whether effected by rent control or other means—is not per se pro- or antipersonhood or pro- or anticommunity; the evaluation depends upon the circumstances.

THREE

Problems for the Theory of Absolute Property Rights

Among contemporary academic lawyers, the conservative property theorist Richard Epstein is the most forceful ideological adherent of absolute property rights. Here I take him as representative to show two central problems with much of the modern defense of absolute property rights: an uncritical conceptualism, and an overly expedient amalgam of economic and libertarian rhetoric. Epstein supports a complex of property rules reflecting classical liberal ideology of absolute ownership and laissez-faire markets. This complex of rules includes acquisition of title by first possession in a state of nature along with absolute rights of disposition, either by alienation inter vivos or by transmission at death. Sometimes Epstein summarizes his position by saying that property implies absolute rights of possession, disposition, and use.

In his book, *Takings: Private Property and the Power of Eminent Domain,* Epstein defends a radically conservative thesis: "All regulations, all taxes, and all modifications of liability rules are takings of private property prima facie compensable by the state."[1] To this blanket rule he admits only two exceptions: (1) Some regulations are justified by the police power—very narrowly defined to mean nuisance prevention. (Zoning is not within the police power, according to Epstein, and surely not historical or environmental preservation.) (2) Some regulations are permissible because compensation has been given in the form of "implicit in-kind compensation."[2] In addition, although according to Epstein all welfare entitlements like social security are takings, he thinks that perhaps long-term reliance on these rights means that they should not now be canceled.

Epstein characterizes himself as a neo-Lockean. Yet for him government is justified by the welfare gains that can be achieved by cooperation. From this justification it follows that government can force cooperation to produce public goods (benefits to all that otherwise cannot be produced), but it must give compensation pro rata to holders of productive resources, whose claims derive from original prepolitical property entitlements. The first part of this argument accounts for the Fifth Amendment's "public use" requirement: government cannot regulate at all unless regulation results in net total welfare gain. The second part accounts for its "just compensation" requirement: government can regulate if social gain will result, but then it must compensate entitlement holders.

In the case of what Epstein calls "large number partial takings"[3]— taxes, tenants' rights, collective bargaining rights, job security, antidiscrimination rights, etc.—he proposes three tests for when we can assume rent-seeking is the reason for a regulation. If we find rent-seeking to be its reason, then we can assume that the regulation is either not generally welfare-creating or does not provide adequate "implicit in-kind compensation." The common-pool test, involving the tragedy of the commons, invalidates zoning and collective bargaining; the motive test invalidates measures that are designed to help poor people; and the disproportionate impact test invalidates measures that work to shift wealth across classes.[4]

Throughout Epstein's work two central kinds of claims recur, and these kinds of claims are common to many who share his ideological commitments about property. The first kind of claim affirms a conceptualist, formalist methodology. Epstein maintains that property has an essential, prepolitical meaning, and that that meaning is sufficiently precise and detailed to determine legal rules and outcomes in practice. The second kind of claim is about justification. Epstein maintains that the conservative complex of rules about property is justified both by neo-Lockean libertarianism and by neo-Benthamite utilitarianism in the form of transaction cost economics. Thus he claims that deontology and consequentialism converge: the conservative complex of property rights is superjustified.

In what follows, I dispute these central claims of Epstein's. In section I, entitled "The Consequences of Conceptualism," I respond to Epstein's book, *Takings*. I use the advent of antidiscrimination rights, among other things, to argue against the idea that property has a fixed and timeless meaning. In section II, entitled "Time, Possession, and Alienation," I respond to Epstein's article, "Past and Future: The Temporal Dimension in the Law of Property." I use the common law doctrines of adverse possession and restraints on alienation to argue against the idea that one can coherently be a libertarian and a utilitarian at the same time.[5]

I. The Consequences of Conceptualism

For several decades, scholars in many disciplines have been busy persuading us that we completely misunderstand the nature of words and the world when we think that there are rigid, clear concepts applicable to particular circumstances in a self-evident logical manner. In his book, *Takings,* Richard Epstein remains unpersuaded. About property, at least, he is an unabashed conceptualist and formalist.

Epstein is a conceptualist because he thinks there is a concept of property that, in fact, is the right one or the only one. He thinks, that is, that there is *a* conception of property that is *the* concept of property. He is also a formalist (in the sense in which that word is most commonly used in jurisprudence) because he thinks the concept of property can be applied formally, i.e., logically and mechanically, to yield results that should be obvious to readers and legal decision-makers. Epstein's tacit acceptance of conceptualism and formalism goes a long way toward explaining why he seems so blithely to believe that results many readers find breathtakingly wrong are just obvious to rational people. Here I shall leave aside his formalism, or mechanical jurisprudence, because I don't suppose I have anything new to say about what's wrong with it. Instead, I shall observe a few things about his conceptualism and its consequences.

A.

The conception of property that Epstein takes for granted, his one-and-only concept of property, is never stated in detail. Perhaps he thinks it is too obvious to require an explicit defense. It can be inferred, however, that the concept consists of general principles—exclusive possession, use, and disposition—and a list of specific rules that delineate the exact extent or application of these principles; that is, how these principles mechanically decide specific cases. Epstein fails to give us this list of specific rules that delineate *the* concept of property—the institution of property as it ought to be.

At some points Epstein seems to state or imply that property is whatever it was at common law. This raises numerous unanswerable questions. The common law at exactly what date? Could it not be that common law judges were wrong about a few things? Which ones? At other points, particularly in the discussions at the Conference on Takings of Property and the Constitution, Epstein argues that what I and other symposiasts recognized as some Humean law of practical reason prepolitically determines what property is.[6] In his book, Epstein identifies Lockean natural rights as the source of the concept of property, and given his reliance upon the common law, it seems he must have thought that the common law perfectly expressed them. But this Humean move at the conference makes the concept of property prepolitical in only a pragmatic (Hume said "artificial") sense, not in a natural rights sense. In fact, Epstein said that natural rights arguments—like the one in his book, I suppose—are merely the kind of mythology that political theorists were forced to resort to in describing an efficient regime, in the centuries before we learned enough about economics to speak precisely about these matters.[7]

At any rate, whatever its basis or source, Epstein thinks *the* concept of property—consisting of articulated detailed rules—is obvious; and it isn't. None of the proposed sources of the concept (Lockean natural rights, Humean prepolitical artifice, or for that matter, pure law-and-economics utilitarianism) generates the rules Epstein takes for granted as implicit in the concept of property. For example, consider the following, taken from a passage arguing against inheritance taxes:

> The conception of property includes the exclusive rights of possession, use, and disposition. The right of disposition includes dispositions during life, by gift or by sale, and it includes dispositions at death, which are limited only by the status claims of family members protected, for example, by rules relating to dower and forced shares.[8]

Does the concept of property really include all dispositions by sale? The common law recognized a good many inalienabilities.[9] Does the concept of property really include disposition by will? Then we must at least suppose the common law did not work out the concept of property until the Statute of Wills. Why do rules relating, for example, to dower and forced shares limit disposition by will? Forced shares was a nineteenth-century statutory reform prompted by the inequities of the common law when it came to marital property. (Why isn't this reform a taking?) If a particular version of "dower" is part of the concept of property, then is "curtesy" also included?[10] And what portions of the common law of intestacy are part of the concept of property? (Is primogeniture?) Is the whole common law system of future interests part of the concept of property? If so, do we begin before or after the Statute of Uses? Is the common law Rule Against Perpetuities part of the concept of property? (If it is, is the "wait-and-see" rule a taking?) Epstein's conceptualism not only supposes a determinateness the concept of property cannot have, it denies that the concept has evolved over time, and that it is still evolving. That is, Epstein denies not just the problem of vagueness, but also the reality of change. His is a timeless conservative conceptualism.

Not only is property vague and evolving; it is also essentially contested. I don't suppose Epstein means to be ungracious in not telling us what the eternal, formal concept of property, which contains all the rules necessary to solve all our problem cases, actually is. Rather, I imagine he supposes that all he has to do is refer to it obliquely, and all its detail will become clear to the reader. He must suppose, then, that we are monolithically socialized into one culture of property. But this I find astonishing; not only because it is patently not the case, but also because it is quite contrary to the ideology of liberalism to suppose that it should be so. As liberals, we pride ourselves on being pluralist about these things of fundamental political and moral significance. Property is, and probably always will be, a contested concept. While this doesn't mean, necessarily, that there is no "best" conception, it certainly means that that conception has to be argued for.

B.

"The idea of property embraces the absolute right to exclude."[11] Perhaps the most serious consequence of Epstein's timeless conservative conceptualism is a disquieting inference about discrimination. The common law did not preclude discrimination on the basis of race, sex, religion, or national origin. Are discrimination rights part of the exclusion rights inherent in *the* concept of property? Is the Civil Rights Act[12] a taking?

In his book, Epstein does not face up to this disquieting inference. Would he say that the Civil Rights Act is prima facie a taking, but saved somehow either by implicit in-kind compensation or reliance? Unlike social security and welfare, which he deems saved by reliance,[13] the Civil Rights Act has not been around for very long. And it is hard to argue that bigots are "really" benefited when they are forced to accept those they seek to exclude. At the very least, it would be hard for Epstein to argue this while also remaining an advocate of the Hobbesian rent seeking model of politics.[14]

The crucial point is that there is no room in Epstein's theory to admit that certain things formerly called property rights—such as the right to discriminate and the right to own human beings—were wrongly so designated, and wrongly held as against the personhood of others. Under Epstein's theory, it seems we must consider the cancellation of these "rights" to be a taking. If Epstein were to admit that some things have been (and still are?) wrongly thought of as property, his theory would need a great deal of amendment; for some things wrongly called property should not be treated as property interests requiring compensation of those who held them wrongly. That is, if exclusion rights against nonwhites were formerly considered to be part of the bundle of rights called property, they were wrongly so considered; and to correct this wrong against human personhood is not a taking.

Epstein deplores positivism because it seems to make property rights too mutable: what the government giveth, the government taketh away. Yet he flirts with the pitfalls of positivism to the extent he embraces a utilitarian approach to solving property problems. Bentham, of course, met the problem head on and declared: "Property and law are born together, and die together."[15] The "public choice" (rent seeking) model of politics coheres most readily with the positivist, consequentialist model of property. It can be gathered from Epstein's remarks at the Conference on Takings of Property and the Constitution that he thinks the Humean move[16] can give him both nonpositivist immutability and positivist efficiency. That, of course, is open to much dispute;[17] but it is a topic for another book because he did not raise it in this one.

Epstein's timeless conservative conceptualism is not the only alternative to positivism. I agree with Epstein that to treat property rights as mutable at the whim of the government does, sometimes, fail to respect persons and their liberty or autonomy. But I think one could better respect the deep moral significance of some property by becoming a progressive naturalist. A progressive naturalist would say that there is a best conception of property, but we haven't yet reached it. The history of changing property notions is describable as a history of rejecting bad parts of the institution and substituting better ones—a process that can continue indefinitely. This view would allow us to suppose we have reached a point in history when we can recognize that exclusionary rights countenancing discrimination on the basis of race, etc., are wrong, and have always been wrong. In my view, this would be more satisfactory than a positivist, consequentialist justification of the Civil Rights Act (e.g., antidiscrimination laws presently serve efficiency), or Richard Epstein's, if he has one.

C.

Allied to Epstein's conceptualism is his rigidity about what the label "property" confers. For him, property is an all-or-nothing concept; there are no gradations. If something is property, a full panoply of moral force and legal protection attaches to it. Property is property is property. Homes and wedding rings are no different from machine tools and parking lots.

Apparently Epstein does recognize gradations in the category of free speech, for he says that "it is better . . . to create responsible subcategories and rebuttable presumptions than it is to pretend that all speech is of equal importance, when it evidently is not."[18] In my view, it is equally evident that not all property is of equal importance. This requires creating "responsible subcategories" in property as well. Once, Epstein alludes to this notion by mentioning the categories of "commercial" and "personal" property in such a way as to suggest that "personal" property requires higher compensation when the government takes it.[19] Yet he seems quite unaware of the sweeping implication of such a distinction, and it is absent from the rest of his book.

Such subcategories have been part of the discourse about property for a long time, perhaps since Karl Marx[20] distinguished between use value and exchange value, and at least since Morris Cohen[21] distinguished between property for use and property for power. Just as speech directly related to political struggle seems closer to the interests the First Amendment clearly recognizes and protects, so only a subcategory of everything we think of as property seems directly connected to the interest in personal autonomy and self-development that forms the core of the ideology of property. Property that is personal in the sense of being justifiably bound up with the self and its individuality deserves, and in our system often receives, a higher level of respect and protection than property that is not.

Fungible property—that which is held merely for investment or exchange and is not justifiably bound up with the person—is fully interchangeable with its market value in money, while personal property is not. This has many ramifications for a theory of eminent domain which are as yet unexplored. For example: Is there some personal property that government may not take at all? Is there some personal property that can be taken, but only if compensation is greater than the market price? Is there some fungible property that can be taken without compensation, either because doing so is equivalent to taxation, or because the property impinges on more important personal interests of others? Just as Epstein's brand of conceptualism prevents him from adequately dealing with the problem that certain traditional property rules have been wrong, so it also prevents him from seeing more than very dimly that property is neither morally nor legally monolithic.

II. TIME, POSSESSION, AND ALIENATION
A. Time and Property Theory

Epstein's article on the temporal dimension in the law of property begins, "All human interactions, and hence all legal rules, have a temporal dimension."[22] But the temporal dimension of human affairs figures differently in different theories of property that might explain or justify legal rules. In this commentary I want to examine how the varying role of the temporal dimension in different underlying theories of property relates to some of the problems in the law of adverse possession and restraints on alienation. I have selected these from the wide variety of topics Epstein presents because I find them particularly interesting for examining the relationship between legal doctrine and the temporal dimension of theory.

There are three traditional strains in liberal property theory: the Lockean labor-desert theory; the Benthamite utilitarian (and economic) theory; and the Hegelian personality theory. In the Lockean theory, the temporal or dynamic dimension of human affairs seems to be irrelevant, but it plays an important role in the other two.

1. Lockean Entitlement

The reason that the temporal dimension is irrelevant to the Lockean theory of property is that, at least in its classic form, it is only a theory of just acquisition, concerning itself only with the moment in which entitlements come into being. Entitlements come into being through mixing one's labor with an unowned object, or, in Epstein's version, through occupancy or first possession of an unowned object, and thereby are fixed forever. Thus, one moment in time is relevant to entitlement, the moment when nonproperty becomes property; but the temporal dimension of human affairs, our situation in an ongoing stream of time, is irrelevant.

The term "just acquisition" belongs to the prominent neo-Lockean Robert Nozick, who theorizes that justice in holdings ideally consists of whatever results from just acquisition and sequences of just transfers.[23] This corresponds to saying that a holding is just if a valid chain of title and a valid root of title (in original acquisition out of the common) can both be shown. Here a temporal element enters in; the chain of title extends in time from original acquisition to today. Thus, in neo-Lockean theory, there is a temporal element connected with just transfer, but not with initial entitlement itself.

In a nonideal world, there are sometimes rip-offs and frauds instead of just transfers. This makes necessary a third kind of theory in addition to a theory of just acquisition and a theory of just transfer; namely, a corrective justice theory, which Nozick calls a theory of rectification. Because Nozick is engaged mainly in ideal theory, he does not develop a theory of rectification. Whether a neo-Lockean theory of corrective justice would contain temporal elements is therefore unclear, but it seems, at least, that a Nozickian theory of corrective justice would not allow time to diminish the force of old harms.[24] In neo-Lockean, ideal libertarian justice there seems to be no statute of repose. Once the chain is tainted somewhere between original acquisition and today, corrective justice seems to require that titles be redistributed to undo the effect of the oppression or fraud, no matter how long ago. To say less than this would undermine the absolute nature of the Lockean rights of property acquisition and free contract.

2. Utilitarianism

Utilitarian theory is more directly time-bound. In act-utilitarianism, the preferred or justified course of action is to maximize welfare (or utility, or whatever is the maximand) right now. But human interactions and our environment are dynamic, so as time moves on the preferred or justified course of action changes. Furthermore, in determining the preferred course of action the future is what governs. To judge an act by its consequences for utility is, from the standpoint of the time of making the decision, to rest rightness on prediction.

In rule-utilitarianism, the preferred or justified course of action is to maximize welfare (or whatever) in "the long run" in contradistinction to right now. Hence, the dynamic nature of human affairs is more directly implicated in the preferred course of action. One consequence of this is that in rule-utilitarianism we are always cognizant of systemic concerns: How will any given choice affect the entire system of entitlements and expectations as it produces and maintains welfare over time? Thus, time is embedded at the heart of rule-utilitarianism. Indeed, its temporal heart harbors its deepest puzzles. How long is the long run? Does it include future generations? If so, how do we attribute utility (or whatever) to them, and how do we compare it with the utility of people alive today? Is the utility of people who are not alive today but were alive yesterday of any relevance? If so, at what point does the utility of the dead cease to count? In order to maximize utility, should we (in light of the principle of decreasing marginal utility) maximize population until everyone is at a bare subsistence level? And so forth.

3. Property and Personhood

Time is also at the heart of the personality theory, but in a different way. In the Hegelian theory, ownership is accomplished by placing one's will into an object. A modern extrapolation of this idea suggests that the claim to an owned object grows stronger as, over time, the holder becomes bound up with the object. Conversely, the claim to an object grows weaker as the will (or personhood) is withdrawn. In other words, in personality theory the strength of property claims is itself dynamic because over time the bond between persons and objects can wax and wane.

Because personality theory concerns individual rights and not general welfare, it does not harbor the same temporal puzzles as rule-utilitarianism. Since it places entitlement in the present state of the relationship between person and object and not in some aboriginal appropriation, it also avoids the major problem of the Lockean individual rights theory. Personality theory must struggle instead with how to construe the notion of personhood and the notion of relationships between persons and objects. In coherence and contextualist philosophical views, these central notions themselves are developing through history; that is, they have a temporal dimension.

B. Adverse Possession

In this section I shall comment on two aspects of Epstein's treatment of adverse possession, suggesting that his lack of clear focus on the varying role of the temporal element in the different theories of property results

in some distortions. First, Epstein sees a tension between Lockean entitlement theory, which he refers to as "principle," and what appears to
be a form of rule-utilitarianism, which he refers to as "pragmatic."[25]
With respect to this opposition of principle and pragmatics, I suggest
that Epstein himself is in tension with regard to the extent of his commitment to Lockean entitlement or rule-utilitarianism as his primary
normative theory. Second, Epstein ignores personality theory. This
might mean that he finds it wholly implausible as an explanatory/justifi-
catory theory, and if so I differ with him. I think it sheds interesting
light on some aspects of the problem of adverse possession.[26]

1. Entitlement and Utilitarianism: Principle versus Pragmatics?

First, let us consider the tension between Lockeanism and rule-
utilitarianism with regard to adverse possession; that is, with regard to
awarding title to present possession of sufficient length rather than trac-
ing title to first possession. "As a matter of high principle," Epstein says,
"what comes first is best; as a matter of evidence and proof, however,
what comes last is more reliable and certain."[27] But why is it important
to be reliable and certain, rather than simply pursuing what is best, let-
ting the chips fall where they may? If entitlement is a matter of natural
right, superior to all manipulations of the state in the interest of social
welfare, why isn't this a matter of *fiat justitia, ruat cælum*? For Epstein,
at least, it is important to be reliable and certain because that will maximize the general gain.[28] This is implicitly a species of rule-utilitarianism
known as transaction-costs economics.

But now we are prompted to ask, if rule-utilitarianism governs entitlements *now*, why doesn't it govern entitlements *then*? That is, why
doesn't Epstein simply argue that it is efficiency, suitably construed as
"long run" or dynamic, that governs entitlements? If efficiency governs
entitlements, then there is no tension between "high principle" and the
merely "pragmatic," there is just the problem of what really is efficient,
given the dynamic nature of the system. Certainly the principle of first
possession could be reconstrued in rule-utilitarian terms: it makes utilitarian sense to get things out of the common and into the control of a
single decision-maker, and the principle of first possession is (the argument would run) cheaper to agree upon than others that might present
themselves. The problem for a utilitarian who is trying to be a libertarian at the same time is rather that the thoroughgoing rule-utilitarian

approach to entitlement seems not to be absolute; it seems, in fact, to require redistribution of entitlements under certain circumstances.[29]

In other words, under thoroughgoing rule-utilitarianism, rearrangement of entitlements over time through means other than transfer by contract between individuals cannot be confined to adverse possession. Whatever assumptions we choose about the long run and the role of the utility of future generations, etc., it is hard to construct a utilitarian argument concluding that an entitlement gained through first possession is fixed for all time. Utilitarianism is too empirical for such absolutes. For utilitarianism, "pragmatics" is "high principle." All we have is some giant balance weighing the welfare gain from certainty of planning and transacting, and from not disturbing the "subjective" value of developed expectations of continued control over resources,[30] against the welfare losses from holdouts against land reform, or implementation of new technology, or the demoralization of the have-nots vis-à-vis the haves, etc. The advantage of Lockean (and Nozickian) natural rights theory is that it seems proof against noncontractual redistribution.[31] The disadvantage is that it cannot account for adverse possession, which it appears the functioning legal system—the enforcer of those "absolute" entitlements—cannot do without.[32] Hence Epstein's tension. Does he intend to defend a pluralist metaethic? (Are absolute natural rights somehow involved in a paradoxical coexistence with utility maximization as the sole good?) Or does he intend to abandon natural rights theory and face the difficulties of utilitarian ethics? Epstein has not yet squarely faced this problem.

2. Property Theory and Adverse Possession

Now let me complicate the question by throwing another "ethic" into the hopper. For personality theory, adverse possession is easy, at least if one is envisioning possession by natural persons who successively occupy land. The title follows the will, or investment of personhood. If the old titleholder has withdrawn her will, and the new possessor has entered, a new title follows. Title is temporal because the state of relations between wills and objects changes.[33] The result of this theory is to attach normative force, and not merely practical significance, to the bond developing between adverse possessor and object over time; and to attach normative force, as well, to the "laches" of the titleholder who allows this to happen.

To suggest how the problem of adverse possession might be further illuminated through explicit attention to theories of property, I shall now consider how the three "ethics" map onto the problem. In order to talk about this, I would like to introduce two categories that I think are helpful in organizing discussion of adverse possession. One category involves differentiating among three paradigm cases of adverse possession; the other involves the shifting role in legal doctrine and practice of the adverse possessor's state of mind.

First, the cases in which adverse possession comes up can usefully be divided into three paradigms, which I call "color of title," "boundaries," and "squatters." These are subsets that might well refine Epstein's treatment of the problem. While the layperson may picture adverse possession as applying to the situation where aggressive trespassers take over a plot of ground and treat it as their own, and while some theoretical treatments of adverse possession, pro and con, may seem to have this "squatters" paradigm in mind,[34] most legal cases involve the other two paradigms. In the "color of title" case, the possessor holds an invalid document of title and eventually has to defend against the "true owner" or someone claiming under her. This happens, for example, where a grantor fraudulently grants the same parcel twice and the second grantee takes possession.[35] In the "boundaries" case, the boundary line observed by neighboring property owners in practice does not correspond with what their documents say; eventually one of them litigates to correct the discrepancy.[36]

Second, I think it is useful to take note of the disagreement, both in legal doctrine and practice,[37] regarding the role of the adverse possessor's state of mind. There are three positions that have existed in legal doctrine: (1) state of mind is irrelevant; (2) the required state of mind is, "I thought I owned it"; and (3) the required state of mind is, "I thought I did *not* own it [and intended to take it]."[38] These can roughly be thought of as the objective standard, the good-faith standard, and the aggressive-trespass standard.

Utilitarianism. The utilitarian argument is often stated as requiring simply that titles must be cleared to facilitate transactions now (i.e., for the immediate future). In this form at least, the utilitarian argument seems to favor the objective standard making state of mind evidence irrelevant. State of mind evidence is one more cost of litigation, and presumably will result in fewer titles being cleared.

Utilitarianism can countenance all three paradigms, and does not privilege the "color of title" case over the case of the aggressive, productive trespasser.[39] But the "boundary" case seems unclear. Once the discrepancy between the record books and the lived boundaries is discovered, does it maximize the gain for the system as a whole to change the records to reflect the lived boundaries or to change the lived boundaries to correspond with the records?[40]

The utilitarian argument, at least in its simple form, strongly favors "tacking." On the side of the possessor, it creates a new chain of title in the adverse possessor. To allow "tacking" on the other side presumably reflects that anyone who buys from a titleholder out of possession is the best cost-avoider of losses due to adverse possession. The utilitarian argument also favors clearing title as against future interest holders at the same time the adverse possessor acquires the present estate.[41] In addition, it favors an objective interpretation of the notice requirement ("open and notorious") that does not depend upon whether the titleholder knew of the adverse possession or even reasonably could have known.[42] "Disabilities" on the side of the old titleholder are difficult for utilitarianism, for the losses to titleholders who are children, insane, etc.,[43] and unable to bring suit must be weighed against the costs to the system of having a possible "disability" lurking behind every case where there may be unknown persons on the side of the old titleholder, which greatly prolongs clouds on the title.

Personhood. If one assumes, contrary to Hegel, that placing one's will into an object, in the sense of having it become bound up with personhood, is a process that does not take place overnight, then the personality theory is as follows: The possessor's interest, initially fungible, becomes more and more personal[44] as time passes. At the same time, the titleholder's interest fades from personal to fungible and finally to nothingness. At what point is the titleholder detached enough and the adverse possessor attached enough to make the switch? This is not a statute of limitations, but a moral judgment. Should this judgment be made case-by-case or approximated by a blanket rule? A blanket rule (such as a number) would be chosen if that choice entailed less risk of moral error against embodied personhood than other choices. If a number is chosen, that number would be based upon the socially acceptable or "right" time it takes to become attached/detached.[45]

Personality theory might seem to favor an explicit "good-faith" standard on the issue of the adverse possessor's state of mind, because it is unclear how one's personhood can become bound up with ownership of something unless she thinks she owns it. This may be its salient applicable intuition to modern law. If one of the things adverse possession does is protect developed expectations, in the sense of bonds between persons and things, it is hard to see how these bonds can be as strong in the case of people who know the object is not theirs. So, it seems personality theory is more comfortable with the "color of title" case than with "squatters." In the "boundary" case, it would recommend, more clearly than would utilitarianism, that the boundaries as they are lived should after a while supersede the boundaries on paper.

The personality theory would seem to disfavor tacking on the side of the adverse possessor. If the statute of limitations represents the time it takes for the adverse possessor to become sufficiently bound up with the property, then it appears that adverse possession has to be accomplished by one person. On the other hand, personality theory does not seem to yield an objection to tacking on the side of the old titleholder, since each owner voluntarily severs the bonds.

Personality theory does not have anything to say about adverse possession by corporations. Nor does it address the problem of future interest holders since they have not yet had a chance to become self-invested in the property. But since we need either voluntary transfers or true "laches" in order to remove the bonds on the side of the old titleholder, I imagine the issue of "disabilities" looms larger than it does in a utilitarian view. (But there are many problems here: Has an insane person removed herself from involvement with her property?)

Lockean entitlement. As already discussed, the pure Lockean theory does not countenance adverse possession. But perhaps it colors the theory of adverse possession anyway by lending some sympathy to "squatters." After all, if property is acquired from the common by a nonowner simply by taking it and using it, can we not sympathize with someone who does likewise with owned but unused property, especially if she does not know it is owned?

C. Restraints upon Alienation

The topic of inalienability and restraints upon alienation is a much broader one than the topic of adverse possession, but so far has been insufficiently studied.[46] The legal infrastructure of capitalism—that is, what is necessary in order for a laissez-faire market system to operate—comprises not merely private property, but private property plus free contract. That is, in order for the exchange system to operate to allocate resources, there must be both private entitlement to resources and permission to transfer entitlements at will to other private owners. One of the ways liberal theory has sometimes reflected this necessity is by claiming that free alienability is inherent in the concept of property.[47] (Liberal theory could equally well claim, of course, and sometimes does, that private entitlement is implicit in the concept of freedom of contract.) The result has been that the ideal picture of property is perfect alienability, perfect fungibility.

Because of its centrality to the market society infrastructure, alienability is one of the most important liberal indicia of property. The whole maze of fees tail, defeasible fees, and future interests, as well as the common law marital property scheme, can be seen as restraints upon alienation in the sense of deviating from the idealized model of the unrestricted fee simple absolute, as can the various servitude doctrines. The holder of a fee tail could never alienate a fee simple. The holder of a defeasible fee cannot transfer it free of the defeasing conditions, just as the modern freeholder cannot transfer free of running covenants and servitudes. Hence the land is in practice inalienable (nontransferrable) to those who would violate the conditions.

The common law developed various doctrines limiting restraints upon alienation imposed by grantors.[48] Fees tail became relatively easy to evade, and now are disallowed by various statutes that reconstrue an attempted fee tail as another (more alienable) interest. Permissible servitudes were (and are) limited by the requirement that they "touch and concern" land, among others. Although the common law did not develop workable limits on future interests remaining in the grantor (possibilities of reverter and rights of entry), there is a trend in modern law to limit them, primarily by marketable title acts.

1. Free Contract and Utilitarianism:
Another Case of Principle versus Pragmatics?

Epstein is puzzled by the limits on restraints upon alienation in the common law. In turn, I am puzzled by his puzzlement.[49] He seems to think that utilitarian (and Lockean?) reasoning would lead to total freedom in grantors to create whatever restraints they wish.[50] There is the same puzzle in the common law limitations on servitudes. Epstein seems to think there is no utilitarian or Lockean reason for limiting the kinds and durations of servitudes that landowners can create. In other words, whatever restrictions the grantor-developer inserts in the deed and manages to sell would be at the same time efficient, an expression of total dominion or liberty with respect to property, and an expression of absolute freedom of contract. I shall argue, however, that rather than finding this harmony, Epstein should find here the same tension between absolute rights and rule-utilitarianism that he finds in the law of adverse possession.

The common law limits on restraints on alienation suggest that there may have to be some limits on market transactions now in order to ensure that there will still be a market in the future. This can be perfectly rationalized in utilitarian terms, as can the common law rule that "a man cannot create a new kind of inheritance."[51] Assuming that it is efficient to maintain a market with a large scope forever (the long run), then it is efficient to impose enough restraints now to prevent grantors from tying up resources for the future in ways that seriously reduce the scope of the free market. And it seems prima facie cost-effective to disallow endless proliferation of different "bundles of sticks" which would cause a great amount of uncertainty and transaction costs; although, of course, the grantors' welfare in imposing their whims would have to be weighed against this, and whims are hard to weigh.

Epstein is not unaware of the problem of the future market versus the present liberty of contract, of course, but I suggest that it needs deeper treatment than he has so far accorded it. In his paper, it is dismissed in one rather opaque paragraph:

> The attack against absolute ownership is not only based upon a concern for dynamics of wealth disposition within the family. In part, the criticism derives from an extensive social concern with inter-generational fairness, where it has two dimensions. The first arises from the fact that no future person can own property today. The second derives from a concern with income redistribution, which taken in its extreme form holds that initial financial endowments of any individual should not depend upon the wealth of his parents. Often these concerns are offered as reasons to limit the rights of present owners to dispose of property as they will. But the concern is misplaced. Even if members of the present generation have absolute control over their own material wealth, they cannot deny to members of the next generation their right to their own labor—rights that will be worth more to them in an open and

prosperous society. Efforts at confiscation are likely to produce defensive measures that will dissipate the overall stock of wealth, and short of a violent disruption of the family, they cannot reach the wide range of implicit and explicit transfers that take place when children live in the family household. Far from taking coercive steps to promote a set of equal economic endowments for the unborn, the better strategy is to develop institutional arrangements that insure that all members of the next generation will be able to develop their own talents without having to pay (say, in the form of higher taxes) for the extravagances of the previous one, and without being subject to various restrictions (e.g., the minimum wage) that work to entrench the established interests.[52]

I shall do no more than sketch several reasons why this is unsatisfactory. First, if in Epstein's view the market is absolutely or conceptually necessary for liberty, and liberty is an absolute right, then the idea of intergenerational fairness, if it conjures up some balancing between present and future satisfactions, does not adequately capture the absolute necessity, inherent in the notion of liberty, that the market remain available. Second, I do not think the future market in labor alone satisfies this intrinsic necessity of liberal theory, to keep the market available for the future. At minimum it is clearly not the case, as Epstein suggests, that preserving only the right to sell one's labor would allow for more valuable opportunities (over the alternative of permitting government limits on grantors' freedom to restrain alienation of land for the future) for exploitation of one's talents.

To take an extreme hypothetical, suppose that all land and other natural resources used as capital are entailed or otherwise nontransferable. The situation would frustrate laborers because, no matter how "valuable" their labor, they could not acquire these kinds of capital in order to maximize their wealth. Capitalists also would be frustrated because, no matter how "valuable" their capital, they could not invade it to acquire the labor necessary to maximize their wealth. Under these circumstances, it hardly makes sense to say that labor has "value," much less that its "value" is maximized. Unless the worker is creating things for her own consumption, her labor (under a capitalist system, at any rate) has no value in the absence of a buyer. Similarly, unless many classes of widgets (other productive goods and inventions) could be produced without using these tied-up and unreplenishable resources, the market could not exist.[53]

Thus, to "develop institutional arrangements that insure that all members of the next generation will be able to develop their own talents" involves imposing the type of institutional restraints on grantors' freedom that will insure both that the members of the next generation can sell their labor to capitalists who are free to trade for it and that they can acquire capital of their own. Finally, of course, this concern is by no means a concern about "equal economic endowments for the unborn." It is rather a concern about the meaning of the absolute value of liberty and how it should be thought of in respect of the unborn, and a concern about what is required to maximize wealth over time.

Even if the conceptual position that free alienability is inherent in the concept of property accurately characterizes the common law, Epstein misunderstands it. I view the common law position on the free alienability of property as a position in aid of there being free markets in whatever resources are deemed capable of being property. To argue further in a conceptual vein, as Epstein seems to,[54] that the power to make something inalienable for the future is logically included in the property owner's full alienability at present, does not further free markets as time goes on. Hence it would seem to be in contradiction to the ideal of alienability that Epstein tries to derive it from, once the ideal of alienability is seen in a dynamic dimension. This is true both from a utilitarian and a libertarian point of view. For the utilitarian, open markets for the future are necessary for the long-run maximization of welfare. For the libertarian, market liberty now cannot be construed so as to foreclose significant market liberty for those who will come later. Freedom of contract contains the same temporal tension as does entitlement.

2. Temporality and the Servitude Problem

I would like to consider this temporal tension in slightly more detail with respect to easements, covenants, and servitudes, which I refer to generically as servitudes. Although Epstein's view seems to be that a grantor-developer can create whatever servitudes she desires, and, if the lots are sold, make them "run" forever unless all parties subject to them can get together to strike a new bargain, I think both the libertarian and the economic or rule-utilitarian view of servitudes must be much more complicated. In view of the need for alienability in a dynamic sense if there is to be a free market in the long run, I believe more needs to be said than that we should not permit any restraints upon present owners to burden land for the future, because to do so "denies the original parties their contractual freedom by subordinating their desires to the interests of future third parties, who by definition have no proprietary claim to the subject property."[55] Otherwise Epstein's theory of how to deal with the temporal dimension of human affairs when considering liberty (of all "future third parties") boils down to a version of *après moi, le déluge*.

A rule-utilitarian theory of servitudes is likewise a complex problem, especially in light of the fact that whole tracts are covered by packages of servitudes ("residential private governments"). First, as commentators often note,[56] it is hard to end servitudes by bargaining because of familiar transaction-costs problems and strategic behavior (holding out against those who attempt to negotiate; free riding on those who litigate). The common law "changed conditions" doctrine is a kind of "sunset" doctrine which can be construed as recognizing this. Marketable title acts, to the extent they apply to servitudes, are even more clearly "sunset laws." Does Epstein oppose marketable title acts? Does he favor them only as a default provision that grantor-developers can disclaim? If so, how will he square this with the imperative he finds in adverse possession, that property as it is treated in real life must periodically be brought into conformity with the record books?

Second, it is not clear that the nature of the land market and the residential housing market is such (or everywhere such) that developers will be forced by competition to create optimal servitude packages. To the extent that market failure is present, optimal results will not be achieved through laissez-faire. If liberty or Lockean dominion nevertheless requires total freedom of servitude creation, with respect to duration as well as form, then Epstein will have to face a trade-off of efficiency for liberty.

Third, in order to decide whether a package of servitudes is welfare-maximizing, we must consider whether we are trying to maximize only the welfare of those in the tract covered by the servitudes, or the welfare of the suburb in which the tract is located, or the welfare of the whole city or region, etc. In other words, in order to know whether a servitude package is optimal, one of the things we have to know is whether it creates significant externalities, and in order to know what are to count as externalities we have to know the "jurisdiction" over which we are maximizing welfare. If we are maximizing welfare merely within the tract itself, we do not mind that its requirement that all houses be painted sky-blue pink casts significant costs onto neighboring tracts, whereas if our welfare "jurisdiction" is the entire suburb, sky-blue pink becomes a cost that must be taken into account.[57] To make matters worse, the optimal jurisdiction is likely to vary over time, and there is no reason to suppose that it will be coextensive with political boundaries, still less with the extent of land owned by any given grantor-developer imposing servitudes. To my knowledge, commentators on the servitude problem, while often pointing to the externality-creating potential, have ignored this problem.

Time creates complexities in the servitude problem from the point of view of personality theory also. I shall conclude by taking note of some of them. A community that either by local zoning legislation or by "residential private government" excludes certain kinds of people, for example by age, gender, class, or race, or even certain kinds of architecture, is creating a social environment for itself. The community might be desirable to purchasers for the very reason that it is "exclusionary" in this sense. These physical and social characteristics of a community can become bound up over time with the personhood of individual residents and with the group's existence as a community. In other words, these restrictions create long-term status relationships that resist alteration by contract. Since this is so, it is misleading to think of servitudes as only contractual, even though they begin by original buyers voluntarily (or nominally voluntarily) signing on to them.

In my present thinking on this subject, one cannot judge in the abstract whether this kind of status creation is good or bad. It might be bad if those in the mainstream of American culture and economic life, who are not having difficulty living out their culture and beliefs, create monolithic exclusions that make it impossible for minorities and dissenters to form communities and live out their alternative visions. It might be good if it instead enables minorities and dissenters to form communities and live out their alternative visions. Be that as it may, unless we are sure that wealth distribution is such, and the housing market is such, that those who live under servitudes can freely go elsewhere if they find them onerous, it does not sit well in liberal ideology for someone to be stuck with a status forever, even if she has "chosen" it originally, and still less does it sit well with liberal ideology for successors in title to be stuck with it forever.[58] The progress from status to contract, from feudalism to the free market, is viewed as progress in freedom to make of oneself what one will, with flexibility to develop and change in the course of one's lifetime.

This whole debate is often couched in terms of trying to breathe life into the common law touch-and-concern requirement.[59] It might be better for us just to say there are moral limitations on servitudes. Allowing people to get stuck in statuses that are anti-personhood is contrary to the liberal ideal of self-development, while allowing them to create enduring statuses that are pro-personhood is an expression of the liberal ideal. For personality theory, the degree of attachment to the servitude would be relevant, as well as whether it creates a status that persons *should* become attached to in expressing personhood or freedom.[60] What counts as a pro-personhood status is in my view also contextual; that is, it evolves through time.

III. Conclusion

As I argued in section I, Epstein's conceptualism about property precludes his taking account either of how property is always a contested concept or of how it changes over time. As I argued in section II, his affinity for formalist modes of thought likewise leads him to believe, in spite of a tension between "principle" and "pragmatics," that Lockean and utilitarian reasoning converge upon a unique set of "natural" rules. His formalist affinity also precludes him from seeing that the problem of maintaining freedom over time and throughout a legal and political system is not the same problem theoretically as exercising freedom at the moment.[61] In his general treatment of restraints upon alienation he has focused on the formal freedom of individual grantors and creators of servitudes, without taking fully into account what role the resulting restraints play in enhancing or inhibiting freedom or personhood systematically and over time. The tension engendered by this issue is analogous to the tension in normative theories of property that Epstein has noticed, but not taken sufficiently seriously, in his treatment of adverse possession. Epstein shakes together libertarian and utilitarian rhetoric, but the mixture still separates.

The Liberal Conception of Property: Crosscurrents in the Jurisprudence of Takings

The classical liberal conception of property embraces a number of broad aspects or indicia, often condensed to three: the exclusive rights to possession, use, and disposition. This essay considers the question whether the liberal conception should be understood to be embodied in our Constitution. The question has both normative and positive aspects. On the positive side, to what extent has our Constitution in fact been interpreted to protect—or to require—the liberal conception of property? On the normative side, to what extent *should* the Constitution be so interpreted?

After a glance at a neoconservative theory that normatively urges the classical liberal conception of property, section I offers observations on the Supreme Court's recent "takings" jurisprudence to show that the liberal conception is only incompletely embodied in our constitutional practice, although I think a trend in that practice now favors the liberal conception. In the course of my discussion I shall consider the significance of the struggle between conceptualism and pragmatism in that practice, in particular the significance of what I shall call conceptual severance. Section II then proceeds to more visionary thoughts on our constitutional practice of property. What if the evident tensions in our current constitutional practice were to issue in an ideological reorientation that understood the distinction between personal and fungible property to be of constitutional significance? I shall offer some preliminary suggestions about how such a reorientation might be reflected in practice, ranging through a rethinking of our constitutional treatment of possession, disposition, and use. For example, I believe the strength of the right of exclusion must vary depending upon whether property is personal or fungible, and hence a per se rule against physical occupation cannot be the talisman the Court now considers it to be. Another of my suggestions is that the strength of the interest of individuals in personal property should generate limits on the eminent domain power. I shall suggest finally that we must consider the relative political strength of various groups of claimants in weighing the decision to label government rearrangement of property rights a taking.

I. THE LIBERAL CONCEPTION OF PROPERTY
AND THE JURISPRUDENCE OF TAKINGS

This section seeks to encapsulate what I am calling the liberal conception of property, and then to inquire to what extent it is embodied in recent constitutional practice; that is, in the Supreme Court's jurisprudence of takings. In my discussion I shall use a shorthand term, "constitutional property," to mean either the set of property rights that are thought to be of constitutional status, or the practice by which the Supreme Court attempts to protect those rights. I shall first contrast two views of constitutional property, a neoconservative view exemplified by Richard Epstein, and the Court's, paying attention to the role of conceptualism as a conservative strategy of interpretation. After a review of some recent takings jurisprudence, I shall reflect on the significance of the opposing tendencies of conceptualism and pragmatism.

A. A Neoconservative View of Property
1. The Liberal Triad: Exclusive Control Over Possession, Use, and Disposition

A strain of neoconservative argument vigorously maintains that the liberal conception of property—lock, stock and barrel—is part of our Constitution. Its best-known recent advocate is Richard Epstein.[1] Epstein holds that the Constitution immunizes against change those liberal indicia of property existing in the legal and political status quo. Moreover—this is his radical side—Epstein holds essentially that the Constitution requires us to change the status quo insofar as it does not embody the liberal indicia. The Epstein model thus constitutionalizes a classical liberal conception of private property.

Epstein succinctly expresses the classical liberal view when he states that "[t]he conception of property includes the exclusive rights of possession, use, and disposition."[2] Elaborating on possession, he says that "[t]he idea of property embraces the absolute right to exclude."[3] Elaborating on use, he implies that property includes the right to choose any use or nonuse so long as it is not a nuisance.[4] Elaborating on disposition, he stresses alienation. This is the most important liberal subcategory of disposition, the right of one owner to transfer entitlement to another. Alienation in this sense underlies freedom of contract and hence is at the heart of the market order.[5]

For Epstein, *any* legislative curtailment of one of these broad "exclusive rights" to possession, use, and disposition is a prima facie taking under the eminent domain clause. The only limitation appears to be a version of the harm principle: the concept or idea of property does not include the right to invade or harm the persons or property of others; rather, it includes the right to fend off those who attempt to invade you.[6] Once a government action is a prima facie taking, compensation is due, unless the action can be defended in one of two ways. Compensation is not required if the government action can be seen to result in "implicit in-kind compensation,"[7] or—possibly, in extreme cases—if the action has caused widespread and long-term reliance.[8] Thus for Epstein, taxation is a prima facie taking, and so are all required welfare contributions, including social security. Price control—and any other regulation of the free market—is a prima facie taking. All forms of zoning restrictions or restrictions on development, unless they are antinuisance measures, are prima facie takings. And so on.

2. *The Conceptualist Strategy of Interpretation*

Critical to the neoconservative view of constitutional property is the process of interpretation neoconservatives employ to find "in" the Constitution the rights to possession, use, and disposition, including alienation in a laissez-faire market. For Richard Epstein, who I believe is rather typical in this regard, the process is clearly a kind of naive conceptualism. Epstein finds the meaning of the word "property" in the Fifth and Fourteenth amendments to be obvious.[9] The entire classical liberal conception of property is the obvious, objective meaning of the word "property." Epstein's conceptualism about property is coupled with a literalism or semantic reductionism in constitutional interpretation. It is the words of the document we are to obey, not the intent of its framers,[10] or the result of any kind of value inquiry.[11] Thus, in applying the Fifth and Fourteenth amendments we can rely on objective timeless meaning[12] and need not grapple with subjective historical mental states or evanescent values. Articulated, detailed rules that can mechanically decide individual cases are part of the obvious meaning of the word "property." Hence, according to Epstein, the application of the constitutional provisions to the vast majority of concrete cases is apparent from a reading of the document together with our knowledge of the concept of property.

Why does Epstein not at least admit that the meaning of the word "property" can change over time? That would raise for him the dilemma of whether, for purposes of understanding the Constitution, we should use the late eighteenth-century meaning or the meaning of today. He avoids the dilemma simply by assuming the meaning is constant, that "stable and unique meanings are possible in principle and usually obtainable in fact."[13] Consequently, he is able to say that "[t]he community of understanding that lends meaning to the Constitution comes of necessity from outside the text, in the way these words are used in ordinary discourse by persons who are educated in the normal social and cultural discourse of their own time,"[14] (the interpreter's time? the framers' time?) while also maintaining that "Blackstone's account of private property explains what the term means in the eminent domain clause."[15]

It is unclear from Epstein's remarks on constitutional interpretation whether he thinks that Blackstone sets forth some philosophically "real" delineation of property, or whether he thinks that it simply happens to be empirically the case that we are monolithically socialized into a conventional Blackstonian view. Most of the time he seems to be operating as if there is a "real" Platonic form of property: the "proposition which the eminent domain clause asserts" is that "there is some natural and unique set of entitlements that are protected under a system of private property."[16]

B. Constitutional Property in Recent Takings Decisions

Unlike Richard Epstein, our Supreme Court has not fully constitutionalized (that is, found "in" the Constitution) the classical liberal conception of property. The questions to ask are to what extent the Court has done so, and whether there is now a trend under way to constitutionalize the liberal conception further. A brief review of some salient cases shows that the Court has not done so to a very great extent, although perhaps Chief Justice Rehnquist spearheads such a trend.

1. Incomplete Constitutionalization of the Liberal Indicia of Property: The Focus on Exclusion

In the 1979 case *Kaiser Aetna v. United States,*[17] the Court decided that the government took private property when it asserted that a private marina, created when a corporate developer dredged a pond and removed a barrier beach separating it from the Pacific Ocean, was subject to public access through the navigation servitude of the United States. In his opinion for the majority, Justice Rehnquist stated that certain "expectancies" are "embodied in the concept of 'property,'" which, "if sufficiently important," cannot be curtailed by the government without condemnation and compensation.[18]

What are these "expectancies"? In *Kaiser Aetna*, Rehnquist focused on the "'right to exclude,' so universally held to be a fundamental element of the property right."[19] This avowed fundamentalness of the "right to exclude" plays a central role in the jurisprudence of takings, and especially in the recent developments I am exploring here. Most important, in 1982 Justice Marshall referred to this passage in *Kaiser Aetna* in his majority opinion in *Loretto v. Teleprompter Manhattan CATV Corp.*,[20] a case whose interpretation of the constitutional meaning of the fundamental right to exclude is pivotal for later developments in the treatment of physical invasion in the jurisprudence of takings. In *Loretto,* the majority held it was a taking for a statute to permit a cable television operator to install a cable on a building without the owner's permission, even if the operator paid the owner a nominal fee and indemnified her for damages. The *Loretto* opinion reiterated the liberal triad—possession, use, disposition[21]—but focused on exclusion, declaring that "[t]he power to exclude has traditionally been considered one of the most treasured strands in an owner's bundle of property rights."[22]

Loretto was a flashback to earlier takings jurisprudence in which physical occupation was the talisman. In *Loretto* the Court said that "permanent physical occupation" of property is per se a taking, because it "effectively destroys *each*" of the rights in the liberal bundle.[23] But in *Loretto* there was a new twist on the traditional emphasis on physical occupation: the physical occupation was what we would ordinarily call a mere easement or servitude rather than complete dispossession. *Loretto* not only revives the old rule; it expands its scope.[24]

Thus the reinvigorated physical occupation test of *Loretto* became a per se rule exception to the prevailing "multi-factor balancing test" of *Penn Central Transportation Co. v. City of New York.*[25] In *Penn Central* the Court had decided that New York's landmark preservation law did not take Penn Central's property by prohibiting construction of an office tower on top of Grand Central Terminal. In contrast to the conceptualism of the per se rule, the balancing test is pragmatic, requiring a case-by-case particularist analysis. Under the balancing test, whether or not the government action can be characterized as a physical invasion is only one of the significant factors to be weighed.[26] The *Loretto* majority explained that it did not need to use the balancing test of *Penn Central* because when physical invasion is permanent that factor becomes per se dispositive of the taking issue. The Court also thought this rule "avoids otherwise difficult line-drawing problems."[27]

Loretto exacerbates the well-known paradox of takings jurisprudence: owners may suffer large pecuniary losses—as in *Penn Central,*[28] or for that matter as in the classic *Euclid* case[29]—without a court's finding a taking requiring compensation, whereas if the court decides to characterize the government action as a physical occupation, a taking will be found even if the loss or inconvenience to the owner is minuscule. Epstein would eliminate this paradox by making loss of expected monetary gain just as compensable as "physical invasion."[30] Unlike Epstein, the Court still focuses primarily on exclusion, not on expected monetary gain from market transactions.

Does the Supreme Court's trend toward constitutionalization of the liberal conception of property extend past exclusion toward the aspect of market transfer? For the Court to treat freedom of market alienation as sacred would be radical indeed, because then any regulatory deviation from a laissez-faire regime would be a prima facie taking. So far, to the contrary, the Court has not even held that complete market-inalienability—a ban on sales—is necessarily a taking. In *Andrus v. Allard,*[31] with no dissent, the Court held that it was not a taking for Congress to declare eagle feathers and other bird artifacts nonsalable pursuant to a conservation statute.

The liberal aspect of market alienability, though it is a pillar of the notion of private property in a capitalist society, has not received the solicitude accorded to the aspect of exclusive physical occupation. Neo-conservative dismay over cases like *Andrus* has not yet moved the Court.[32] Yet it may have begun to move some of its members. In *Hodel v. Irving,*[33] Chief Justice Rehnquist and Justices Scalia and Powell thought *Andrus* must now be limited "to its facts,"[34] implying that they think that market-alienability is generally of constitutional stature. In *Irving,* Justice O'Connor's opinion for the majority declared that another strand of the liberal bundle of rights, disposition at death, could not be abrogated, seemingly because its traditional importance is analogous to the right to exclude others that the Court had already found to be fundamental in *Kaiser Aetna.*[35]

At this point, however, even Chief Justice Rehnquist has so far not tried directly to constitutionalize alienability. He is certainly willing to push the notion of physical occupation to (or beyond) its extremes. In doing so, he may sweep in some aspects of alienability under the guise of physical occupation. In *Kaiser Aetna,* Rehnquist stretched the notion of physical occupation, saying that nonexclusive physical "invasion" (government's using "only an easement" in one's property) requires just compensation.[36] He has since said that a regulation preventing a land-lord from demolishing a rent-controlled apartment building is perma-nent physical occupation by the government, hence a taking requiring compensation.[37] The latter case, especially, is more readily understood as a restraint upon alienation: under certain circumstances, the regula-tion withdrew the landlord's supposed right to rent or not to rent as the landlord saw fit.

At a minimum, Rehnquist's statements go further than *Loretto,* which based its per se rule on the idea that permanent physical occupation "effectively destroys *each*" of the rights in the liberal bundle.[38] When "occupation" is nonexclusive or merely constructive, the government ac-tion does not effectively destroy all rights in the bundle. It merely cur-tails some of them. Thus, Rehnquist is closer to Epstein's position than is the Court as a whole, though he is still not as radical as Epstein. For Epstein, any curtailment of one of the liberal indicia is a prima facie taking, whereas for Rehnquist it appears that the curtailment must be deemed significant.

2. Conceptual Severance

In 1987 the Supreme Court held, per Chief Justice Rehnquist, that if regulatory legislation is ultimately determined to work a taking, compen-sation is due for the period from the imposition of the legislation until its judicial invalidation. In *First English Evangelical Lutheran Church v. County of Los Angeles,*[39] the church was rendered temporarily unable to use its campground by an interim flood control ordinance that prohib-ited construction or reconstruction in a flood area pending a county study of permanent flood control measures. Although there was some doubt, Rehnquist construed the church's complaint as alleging a tak-ing.[40] He then held that if a taking is found, invalidation of the ordi-nance is not a constitutionally sufficient remedy. Rehnquist also declared that "'temporary' takings . . . are not different in kind from permanent takings."[41] As a formal matter, this statement is dictum for the present case, because the courts had not yet passed on the church's taking claim. But it seems destined to come back as holding. Does the *First English* case herald a turn toward more rigid constitutional protection of the liberal indicia of property?

One thing to be observed is that, from the viewpoint of previous substantive law, if the decision finding invalidation of the offending ordinance to be a constitutionally inadequate remedy rests on the per se rule against physical occupation, it seems to harbor a logical error.[42] The substantive decision that any legislation is per se a taking, according to the majority view of *Loretto,* supposedly rests on the notion of "permanent" and complete physical occupation.[43] By hypothesis, in a case like *First English* the "occupation" is not permanent, because it ceases when the ordinance is declared invalid. How can a taking in the same sense as *Loretto* ever be found so as to raise the question whether California's remedy is constitutionally adequate?

If a taking per se cannot be found, the outcome would depend on the balancing test on the underlying substantive issue of whether the government action "takes" property. If one were to accept this reasoning, all "temporary" takings would have to be decided under the much less stringent multi-factor balancing test. To this argument Chief Justice Rehnquist might reply that temporary "occupations" rise to the level of per se constitutional injury, just as in his view do nonexclusive "occupations"—such as the navigational servitude—or merely constructive "occupations"—such as giving tenants tenure rights against landlords. In the important dictum quoted earlier, he seemed to make this reply, by saying that "temporary" takings have the same constitutional status as permanent ones. This statement does seem to submerge the question of how—if at all—the temporariness is to figure in the decision to call an action a taking. Would Rehnquist find a three-month moratorium on development to be a per se taking? Moreover, the line of reasoning of this proposed reply seems capable of expanding to prohibit all government actions that alter entitlements in any way, thus arriving at the Epstein position. If Rehnquist limits it with a proviso to the effect that the alteration must be "significant," then we are back to some form of balancing test.

In order to avoid these difficulties, Rehnquist might reply instead that the "occupation" in *First English* was indeed permanent and complete—it was a permanent, complete taking of an estate for years. This strategy I shall call "conceptual severance." To apply conceptual severance one delineates a property interest consisting of just what the government action has removed from the owner, and then asserts that that particular whole thing has been permanently taken. Thus, this strategy hypothetically or conceptually "severs" from the whole bundle of rights just those strands that are interfered with by the regulation, and then hypothetically or conceptually construes those strands in the aggregate as a separate whole thing.

In *First English,* Rehnquist did not stress conceptual severance, though he did analogize to the complete taking of a leasehold.[44] In *Penn Central,* however, Rehnquist in dissent explicitly relied on the conceptual severance strategy. He argued that depriving Penn Central of the right to develop an office building over Grand Central Terminal was a complete taking—of its air rights.[45] The whole thing taken, in other words, was a particular negative servitude precluding building into the airspace above the existing building.

The Court as a whole so far has been less willing than Rehnquist to find takings by conceptual severance. The majority opinion in *Penn Central* declared that "'[t]aking' jurisprudence does not divide a single parcel into discrete segments and attempt to determine whether rights in a particular segment have been entirely abrogated"; rather, it focuses on "the parcel as a whole."[46] Nevertheless, *Loretto* moves away from that position and toward conceptual severance. In order to find that placing a cable on a building "effectively destroys *each*" of the liberal rights, one must first decide that one is talking about fee simple absolute not in the building as a whole, but rather in the space occupied by the cable. And in the 1987 case of *Nollan v. California Coastal Commission,*[47] the Court—per Justice Scalia—again engaged in conceptual severance by construing a public access easement as a complete thing taken, separate from the parcel as a whole.

In *Nollan* the Court decided that even if, pursuant to California's Coastal Act of 1976,[48] the Coastal Commission could have denied entirely the Nollans' application to develop their beachfront property, the Commission could not constitutionally adopt the seemingly less restrictive alternative of conditioning its grant of the permit upon the Nollans' dedication of a right of public access—which may indeed already have been owned by the public[49]—through their property beyond their seawall. Justice Scalia reasoned that the condition was not closely enough connected to the admittedly legitimate government purposes served by limiting beachfront development. He found conceptual severance to be the only rational way to construe the situation:

> To say that the appropriation of a public easement across a lan-
> downer's premises does not constitute the taking of a property in-
> terest but rather . . . "a mere restriction on its use" [as the dissenters
> and the court below had done in applying the multi-factor balanc-
> ing test to the parcel as a whole] is to use words in a manner that
> deprives them of all their ordinary meaning.[50]

Contrary to Scalia's view, the Court has traditionally understood the ordinary meaning of property to be the owner's parcel as a whole. Thus, in order for the Court to find that "something" has been completely taken, the severance—the division of the fee into various discrete sub-packages—must have existed prior to the government's action. In the famous *Pennsylvania Coal*[51] case, legislation that de facto prevented coal mining "took" a coal company's mining rights, but mining rights were all that the company owned; whereas in the equally famous *Goldblatt*[52] case, the would-be quarry operator owned the fee, and the loss of the quarry rights was not deemed a taking. This traditional reluctance to use conceptual severance is usually chalked up to crystallized expectations or ordinary language and culture.[53] That is, the appropriate understanding of what constitutes a "parcel as a whole"—and hence the owner's "prop-erty"—is previous real-life treatment of the resource, not the conceptual possibilities property law holds available.

Be that as it may, we must observe that as soon as one adopts concep-tual severance, as it seems the Court did in *Loretto* and *Nollan,* there is a steep slippery slope to the radical Epstein position. Every curtailment of any of the liberal indicia of property, every regulation of any portion of an owner's "bundle of sticks," is a taking of the whole of that particular portion considered separately.[54] Price regulations "take" that particu-lar servitude curtailing free alienability, building restrictions "take" a particular negative easement curtailing control over development, and so on.

Thus, one way to consider whether the *First English* and *Nollan* cases presage greater constitutionalization of the liberal conception of prop-erty is to consider whether they will lead to more acceptance of concep-tual severance. As we have seen, looking back on the Court's recent takings jurisprudence, a trend toward conceptual severance is already in progress. The interest taken by the legislation at issue in *Loretto* should—according to crystallized expectations or our ordinary language and culture of property—be characterized not as a permanent, complete physical invasion of the owner's parcel, but rather as an easement to run a cable; the interest taken by the government's action in *Kaiser Aetna* is likewise most readily characterized as an easement or servitude. Moreover, the taking of easements or servitudes cannot be ipso facto a taking of an owner's entire parcel, for all curtailments of property rights can be conceptually characterized as easements or servitudes.

3. Exclusion and Negative Liberty

What we must now notice, however, is that even if there is a general trend toward conceptual severance, it relates only to the issue of *exclusion*. The Court's solicitude for exclusion may correspond to the picture, at the core of liberal ideology, of the individual's right to use property to express her individual liberty, which means using property to fend off intruders into her space. As Charles Reich put this ideological picture, property is supposed to provide "a small but sovereign island of [one's] own."[55] The boats of strangers physically entered Kaiser Aetna's water; the cables of another were physically placed on Loretto's building; other people walked on the beach owned by the Nollans. Ideologically, these are incursions into the owner's "island." In his *Penn Central* dissent,[56] Rehnquist went beyond this ideological picture. By preventing Penn Central from using its air rights, New York had sent no physical object into Penn Central's space. Even though conservatives think it obvious that Justice Rehnquist was right in *Penn Central*, the Court has not yet joined him. The Court engages in conceptual severance only for curtailments of property rights that can be characterized as affirmative easements or servitudes, not for those that are negative.[57]

The idea that property is a "sovereign island" that one can use to defend her arbitrary freedom of action seems to be an aspect of the liberal ideology of negative liberty. Inside your "sovereign island" your freedom consists in doing anything you want, no matter how irrational or antisocial, as long as you do not harm others—in whatever sense the harm principle is to be construed.

It is true that negative servitudes also restrict an owner's arbitrary freedom of action: Penn Central's inability to build an office building indeed seems like a more serious restriction than Loretto's inability to rip the offending cable off her apartment building. Yet affirmative incursion seems to make more explicit and immediate the fact that the owner is not alone in control of a "sovereign island." The forced sharing of space brings home the forced coexistence with other people in the world and the forced sharing of decision-making power. Affirmative incursions, in other words, conflict more sharply than do negative restrictions with the ideology of individualism that underlies the liberal conception of liberty. Affirmative incursions must be anathema to anyone who accepts Blackstone's declaration that property is "that sole and despotic dominion which one man claims and exercises over the external things of the world, in total exclusion of the right of any other individual in the universe."[58]

Thus, a commitment to negative liberty with a consequent constitutionalization of the "sovereign island" picture may be the reason for the centrality of the idea of "physical invasion" in the constitutional jurisprudence of property. If so, the Court has constitutionalized the "sovereign island" picture in a conservative and not very thoughtful way. The Court has applied this ideological picture only to traditional property interests,[59] and has not taken into account the difference in the ethical case for a "sovereign island" depending upon whether the property holder is a person or a corporation.[60]

Nevertheless, we should not fail to notice that there are vast reaches of the liberal conception of property that are not constitutionalized. Perhaps the most weighty aspect of the liberal conception of property involves exclusive management decisions and unfettered choice about exchange. These aspects of property relating to the laissez-faire market are not constitutionalized in the modern era. Since the rejection of *Lochner*,[61] the state is not forestalled from regulation of the terms and conditions under which things are produced and sold. Industrial health and safety regulations, environmental protection regulations, minimum wage regulations, price control, and other restrictions on the laissez-faire market restrict the conditions under which things may be produced and exchanged but are not deemed "takings" of owners' property rights. Our practice with respect to constitutional property evidences only an incomplete commitment to the liberal conception of property.

4. Pragmatism in the Jurisprudence of Takings: A Problem for the Rule of Law?

In contrast to Epstein's conceptualism, the Supreme Court has so far not based its limited constitutionalization of the liberal indicia of property on semantic assertions about the meaning of the word "property."[62] As Justice Brennan candidly admitted in *Penn Central*: "[T]his Court, quite simply, has been unable to develop any 'set formula' for determining when 'justice and fairness' require that economic injuries caused by public action be compensated by the government"; rather, whether or not a government action is a taking "depends largely 'upon the particular circumstances in that case.'"[63] The Court must engage in "essentially ad hoc, factual inquiries."[64]

But is anything wrong with "essentially ad hoc, factual inquiries"? That is simply one way of expressing a pragmatic approach to decision making. Pragmatism is essentially particularist, essentially context-bound and holistic; each decision is an all-things-considered intuitive weighing. Pragmatism is indeed "essentially" ad hoc. There is a great philosophical tradition of pragmatism, currently enjoying a renaissance,[65] and there is much to recommend a view that legal decision making and legal practice is best understood as pragmatic.[66] Yet pragmatism is much feared because of its particularism, because of its wholehearted embrace of the contextuality of everything.

The fear of "essentially ad hoc" inquiries—the fear of pragmatism—is a fear of arbitrariness. How can we achieve consistency—or at least perceived consistency—and fairness by deciding like cases alike, unless some general rule by force of its own formulation can carve out a whole category of cases that we can be sure fall together under the rule? How can we give citizens notice of what they may or may not do under the law if we cannot lay down hard-and-fast rules?

When put this way, we can see that the dialectic in takings jurisprudence that I have been discussing—between the per se rule of *Loretto* and the balancing test of *Penn Central*—is simply an instance of what has been called the dialectic of rules and standards.[67] In this dialectic, the "rule" pole is associated with conceptualism and per se rules and the "standards" pole is associated with pragmatism and balancing tests. When we put the problem this way, we can also see, as Frank Michelman points out,[68] that deeply at work in takings jurisprudence—as indeed in all jurisprudence—is the question whether pragmatism and balancing tests can be faithful to the ideal of the Rule of Law. All of the questions of consistency and like treatment under the law, and the preexistence and knowability of law necessary for notice and compliance, reflect the elements of the ideal of the Rule of Law.[69] The fear of arbitrariness is thus rooted in fears about undermining the Rule of Law.

Michelman raises complex issues when he says that because the Court's turn to conceptualism is likely rooted in fears about the Rule of Law, I need not conjecture that the turn to conceptualism also signifies movement of our constitutional property practice in a conservative ideological direction.[70] If Michelman means merely that the conservative trend is not likely to move very far past the Court's focus on the supposed fundamentalness of the right of exclusion toward reinstitution of *Lochner,* and that the Court as a whole is not likely fully to adopt Epstein's views, I agree with him. In turn, I am sure that he agrees with me that indeed the Court is more conservative now than it was in the recent past. The complexity comes when we consider to what extent the interpretation of the Rule of Law which insists that law must consist of hard-and-fast preexisting rules is itself a conservative—that is, classical liberal—conception of the Rule of Law which is in fact intertwined with a conservative—that is, classical liberal—conception of property. This issue will require some elaboration.

I suggest that the search for conceptual bright lines and per se rules signifies a conservative trend both on the broad level of the nature of law generally—it must consist of rules—and on the narrower level of property—the extension of the word, the instances that the term will comprehend, must be definite and known by preexisting rules.[71] That is, there is a conservative connection between the rule-like view of law and the rule-like view of property. I suggest, moreover, that not only is there a deep connection between the rule-like view of law generally and the rule-like view of property; there is also a deep connection between the rule-like view of law and the specific rules in the liberal conception of property. That is, there is a connection between thinking that law must consist of rules and thinking that property must consist of rules about exclusive rights to control over possession, use, and disposition of resources. If the Court is committed to the conservative view of the Rule of Law, an inference that it finds the whole conservative conception of property congenial is appropriate, even if the Court is not prepared to follow this path to its *Lochner*-like conclusion.

To understand why the inference connecting the rule-like view of law with the liberal conception of property is appropriate, we must recall that both views rest on the same underlying premises. The model of rules is a conservative interpretation of the Rule of Law, or at least congenial to conservatives, because it ties in so well with the Hobbesian view of politics.[72] If majority rule is a shifting coalition of rent seekers, then democratic government is a Leviathan to be restrained. But if majoritarian bargains can be dissolved by unelected judges whose decisions do not even represent fulfillment of interest-group bargaining, then judges are even more in need of restraint than legislatures. Unless judges can be so completely restrained as to be rendered mere tools of implementation of the real social contract—without which citizens cannot be expected to yield their arbitrary powers against others—citizens are caught between the predations of the majority and the predations of the judiciary, and the social contract dissolves. The only way the conservative can see to tie judges down this way is to employ formal rules with self-evident applications. In other words, unless law consists of rules that tie judges' hands, government is unjustified.[73]

One who accepts a Hobbesian model of politics requiring law as the model of rules also accepts an underlying Hobbesian model of human nature. In this model of human nature, limitless self-interest and the consequent urgent need for self-defense require the most expansive possible notion of private property, indeed, the classical liberal conception of property. Nothing will get produced unless people are guaranteed the permanent internalization of the benefits of their labor; nobody will restrain herself from predation against others unless all are restrained from predation against her. It is no accident that those who think of politics and human nature in a Hobbesian—or for that matter Humean or Benthamite—way also tend to think of property the way Hobbes, Hume, and Bentham did. Those thinkers, after all, did a good job of *deriving* the liberal conception of property from their assumptions.[74] The modern economic "spin" on the Hobbesian model of human nature makes it even more clear that exclusive control by individuals over all aspects of decision making about the utilization of identifiable scarce resources is the necessary conception of property to correlate with the model's assumptions about human capacities, needs, interests, and motives—at least if we can assume that a major purpose of the postulated social contract is welfare maximization, and hence that pursuit of efficiency plays a major role in whether or not government action is justified.[75] Thus, those who tend toward Hobbesian views, in particular many who find the economic view of law congenial—for example, Richard Epstein and Justice Scalia—tend toward both the formalist model of rules and the liberal conception of property.

We can now understand more clearly why neoconservatives think that if takings jurisprudence cannot be reduced to formal rules—a "set formula" such as the *Loretto* per se rule—it must violate the Rule of Law. Nevertheless, I think instead that this is a field in which pragmatic judgment under a standard—an explicit balancing approach—is better. The pragmatic ethical issue defies reduction to formal rules. When the

Court's takings jurisprudence has not been conclusory, it has usually attempted to address in a practical way an underlying issue of political and moral theory: is it appropriate to make this particular person bear the cost of this particular government action for the benefit of this particular community? Such is the burden of the *Penn Central* multi-factor balancing test,[76] created under the salutary influence of Frank Michelman's famous article.[77] For all but true believers in the Platonic form of property, squarely facing the ethical/political issue in this way is far superior to any mediation through per se rules or conceptualism.

Yet now a per se exception to the multi-factor balancing test has been declared for "permanent physical occupations"; now a majority has endorsed the statement, albeit in dictum, that temporary takings are not different in kind from permanent takings; and now the "right to exclude" has been held to be embodied in the concept of property, and so fundamental that its loss must always give rise to compensation. So perhaps we have the beginning of a trend toward conceptualism, both on the grand level of seeing a Platonic form of property, and on the strategic level of willingness to engage in conceptual severance. If so, the trend is just beginning.

II. Toward a Postliberal Reinterpretation of Constitutional Property

This section points out two deep tensions in our constitutional property practice. First, our apparent commitment to treat all property as fungible, expressed in the modern scope of the eminent domain power, conflicts with our abiding tendency to treat some property as personal. Second, our commitment to individual security and self-protection as the moral basis of property supports both conservative and progressive conceptions of property. These tensions might be resolved in the direction of a reconception of constitutional property based on personhood in social context, which I suggest might transform the traditional triad of possession, disposition, and use. I conclude with some reflections on the significance of political power in evaluating the takings issue, in particular with respect to rearrangements of the landlord-tenant relationship in tenants' favor.

A. Tensions in the Practice of Constitutional Property

The classical liberal conception of property, with its aspects of total individual control and unfettered alienation, is the underpinning of the market society: private property plus free contract. In the classical liberal conception, property is paradigmatically fungible; everything that is property is ipso facto tradable in markets and has an objective market value. This conception of property expresses commodification: property consists paradigmatically of market commodities. There is no room in the classical liberal conception for things that are property and yet not commodified. Thus, those who hold that everything is propertizable—that all things human beings find scarce and of value can be thought of as property—embrace universal commodification. Those who hold that some things cannot be property conceive of a wall between market and nonmarket social realms, with the laissez-faire market realm being large, dominant, and the rule, and the nonmarket realm being small, subordinate, and the exception. But our constitutional property practice is not as clear about commodification and fungibility as the liberal conception is. Our practice does not find takings—nor should it—whenever commodification is curtailed.

1. The Paradox of Eminent Domain

Condemnation with compensation at "fair market value" is in our system now thought prima facie ethically and politically proper, and uncontroversially held to be "in" our Constitution. The eminent domain clause is thought to license the taking of anything for public use if the owner is paid fair market value,[78] and the term "public use" has recently been interpreted as broadly as possible.[79] In assuming that compensation is an appropriate corrective measure, that it can be "just" or make owners whole, the current idea of eminent domain assumes that *all* property is fungible—that property by nature or by definition consists of commodities fully interchangeable with money. The notion of eminent domain constitutionalizes fungibility. It constitutionalizes an ethic of exchange value. In a sense this is our strongest commitment to commodification and our strongest form of constitutionalization of the liberal conception of property.

Yet if we were really fully to constitutionalize the liberal conception of property we would return to *Lochner*.[80] We would find unfettered freedom of contract—complete market-alienability—to be inherent in the idea of property, and to be required by the Constitution, as indeed Epstein does.[81] The Court's rejection of *Lochner* despite its insistence on an unfettered governmental power of eminent domain leaves us in an ambiguous, perhaps even paradoxical, situation with regard to the constitutional status of the liberal notion of fungibility—the ethic of exchange value. The unfettered power of eminent domain affirms fungibility even while the jurisprudence of takings denies it. Perhaps the philosophical rejection of *Lochner* will ultimately require some kinds of substantive due process limitations on the eminent domain power, so as to take into account the ethical and political status of property that ought not to be treated as fungible.

2. *The Ambiguity of Individual Self-Protection*

The Court's adherence to the notion that property protects individuals—the ideology of the "small but sovereign island of one's own"—is also ambiguous. This ideological commitment can be taken as part of the liberal conception of property, but it can also point beyond it. It points beyond the liberal conception because it can be recharacterized as implicitly according more ethical importance to interests in property that are not fungible. If the "sovereign island" picture is redrawn to emphasize personal property—that which is normatively important to the freedom, identity, and contextuality of people—it would operate to create a hierarchy of property rights. Property that is bound up with individuals in a normatively appropriate sense would enjoy greater constitutional solicitude than property conforming more closely to the market commodity paradigm.

Such a revised ideological commitment would invite the Court to decide, pragmatically in the real world, in which cases property appropriately fosters individual freedom and development and in which cases it does not. The ideology of protection of the individual—if appropriately reconceived to avoid the traditional stress on negative liberty—would result in two important changes in our jurisprudence of property: it would engender different constitutional statuses for personal and fungible property, and it would undergird limits on the eminent domain power to take personal property, even if compensation is paid.

B. Reinterpretation Based on Personhood in Context

It is time to offer a few thoughts on the ultimate large question: How *should* we think about what aspects of property are protected by the Constitution? First, the Court should drop per se rules and conceptual severance. It should continue to ask the traditional pragmatic ethical question: Is it fair to ask this citizen to bear these costs for the benefit of this community? To this pragmatic ethical question the Court should add another: What conception of human flourishing—of personhood in the context of community—are we fostering by sustaining or disallowing this legislation? The latter question is explicitly a mixture of moral and political theory. It asks us to think not just about fairness to individuals, but also about our vision of democratic community, and about our understanding of the kind of community we are always in the process of creating.

1. The Significance of Personal Property in Maintaining Particular Contexts

Personal property marks out a category of things that become justifiably bound up with the person and partly constitutive of personhood. Thus, a normative view of personhood, and hence a normative view of human flourishing, is needed in order to identify which objects are appropriately personal. In my view, a normative theory of community is needed as well, because it is inseparable from a normative theory of personhood. This is so because self-constitution takes place in relation to an environment, both of things and of other people. This contextuality means that physical and social contexts are integral to the construction of personhood.

The relationship between personhood and context requires the pursuit of human flourishing to include commitments to create and maintain particular contexts of individual relationships both with things and with other people. Recognition of the need for such commitments turns away from traditional negative liberty toward a more positive view of freedom, in which the self-development of the individual is linked to proper social development. Also, proper self-development, as a requirement of personhood, can in principle limit the extent to which an individual's desires for control over things should be fulfilled, and hence limit the traditional liberal conception of property. On the other hand, when we judge some category of things to be normatively appropriate to construction of personhood, then people's control over those things is worthy of greater protection than is afforded by the mere commitment of the eminent domain clause to pay the market value.

2. Can We Find This Vision "in" the Constitution?

I will not attempt here to set forth my theory of constitutional interpretation, but I should say at least what my answer would ultimately look like to the question whether we can find a personhood vision "in" the Constitution. A constitution is only a constitution if we find "in" it our best conception of human flourishing in the context of political order; that is, it can be appropriately constitutive of us as a polity only if it embodies our commitments to notions of personhood and community. This is a view of constitutional interpretation that treats our Constitution as a "normative hermeneutic object."[82] Still, why should—or at least can—we find this vision "in" the Constitution without amending it? The answer here must be that on these particular issues our Constitution is sufficiently open-ended. The text we have commits us to protection of property, but not to the classical liberal conception of property. Property is a contested concept,[83] and so is justice—as in the "just" compensation required for legitimate exercise of eminent domain.[84] In arguing for my interpretations of these concepts as being the best now available to us, I think I am squarely within our tradition of constitutional argument.[85]

3. Possible Reflections in Practice

If we delve into our understanding of property, and the ideology of property, with our ethical commitments in mind—our ideals for ourselves of personhood and community—then liberal ideology can be usefully reinterpreted with the distinction between personal and fungible property in mind. When this is done, the liberal conception of property—hence the full panoply of liberal indicia—cannot be part of our Constitution. If commodification should be understood to be of lesser constitutional status than personal connection, then certain kinds of personal use are protected in a way that development rights or market alienability are not. How might this ideological reorientation be reflected in our constitutional practice?

Possession. Start with physical occupation—possession or the fundamental right to exclude others. From the personhood point of view, physical invasion could not be the talisman the Court thinks it is. The relevant constitutional inquiry would include asking for what reason the resource is being "occupied": Does possession in this case, or in this type of case, signify personal connection? A normative inquiry would also be required: For what types of property interests is it ethically appropriate to permit and foster interconnection with persons? Use of property as one's residence is more closely connected to personhood than use of property as a garbage dump for one's factory. The connection between people and residences is recognizable by us as normatively appropriate. Airplane overflight noise "takes" much more from a (hearing) resident[86] than from a (hearing) proprietor who already operates a noisy manufacturing business or from a (nonhearing) corporation.[87] A cable on the roof of a building the owner rents out as a fungible investment no more invades her personhood than does a utility assessment. In this visionary interpretation, we would forthrightly declare *Loretto's* reasoning (applying the moral abhorrence of invasion of one's self by others to the facts of that case) to be wrong.

Disposition. If the government curtails disposition, from the personhood point of view it makes a difference whether the regulation is aimed only at foreclosing market transactions. Market-inalienability—where it can be justified—works against wrongful commodification (wrongful treatment of something as fungible). Disallowing sale of babies should not be held to deprive parents of a property right to dispose of their children, but rather as a justifiable regulation aimed at preventing a social conception of children as fungible objects.

Partial market-inalienability (restraint on alienation in markets) can be viewed as a restriction of commodification, and sometimes respect for the interests of personhood can justify it. Here I think regulation of housing and labor are prime examples. Thus, labor regulation (such as collective bargaining, minimum wage, maximum hours, health and safety regulation and unemployment insurance) and housing regulation (such as housing codes, other habitability rights, and, under some circumstances, rent control) can be seen as an effort to foster workers' and tenants' personhood by recognizing the nonmarket personal significance of their work and homes. Such regulations need not be seen as takings.

Other kinds of dispositions (such as abandonment and destruction) should also be examined not according to their conceptual description but rather according to their connection with personhood and community. Does a corporation have a property right to blow up its plant rather than sell to a worker cooperative at fair market value?[88] (Would government action requiring such a sale be a taking?) Such legislation should not be thought of as a taking, because the corporation's property is fungible. The corporation as a profit-maximizing entity should ethically be treated as indifferent between holding assets with fair market value of x dollars and possessing x dollars in currency or securities.

Government action that required resident homeowners to sell to a corporation, on the other hand, might be considered a taking or a violation of substantive due process. The liberal "property-rule entitlement"[89] normatively demanding that market alienation be a voluntary decision on the owner's part is more readily justifiable for personal property. This suggests that courts should not always allow governments to condemn property and then transfer it to a user adjudged to benefit the community. Even if doing this satisfies the insubstantial hurdle of "public use,"[90] in the case of personal property there should be some constitutional mechanism for keeping it in the hands of its holders except in dire cases. In other words, some kind of "compelling state interest" test for compensated takings of personal, but not fungible, property seems to be appropriate. In essence, we should recognize a substantive due process limitation on the eminent domain power.

The general claim here is that from the points of view of interests of personhood and community, decisions that change the entitlement of personal property into a "liability rule" should be at least deeply suspect. For example, in *Poletown Neighborhood Council v. City of Detroit,*[91] the Michigan Supreme Court upheld Detroit's condemnation of homes in a close-knit neighborhood at the request of General Motors, which wanted the parcel for a plant. An analogous suspect case in "private" law is *Boomer v. Atlantic Cement Co.,*[92] a class action for nuisance by homeowners against a cement company whose plant spewed out dust. In *Boomer* the court granted permanent damages but not an injunction, thus allowing the company to "condemn" a portion of the homeowners' property rights. These cases are suspect because their implicit assumption that forced transfer at the market price justly compensates owners treats personal property as fungible.

Use. The "use" prong of the liberal triad requires a detailed normative breakdown. If restrictions on use are restrictions on choices internal to personal property holding—like choices about association or life-style by residents—it is not difficult to find the restrictions at least suspect. In *Moore v. City of East Cleveland,*[93] a plurality of the Supreme Court found a substantive due process right to live in an extended family despite zoning restrictions. It is not surprising that Justice Stevens would have found a property right to the same effect. Because the zoning ordinance "cut[] so deeply into a fundamental right normally associated with the ownership of residential property,"[94] Stevens thought it a taking of property without due process and without just compensation.

On the other hand, personhood interests are not obviously implicated in restricting profits on investment, or in restricting available options to change from one investment to another. Predictably (from my point of view but not Epstein's), courts have not usually found takings when the government action did not prevent the owner from making a profit.[95] Price controls are not a taking unless "confiscatory"; Penn Central (according to its own accounting) was in the black with regard to Grand Central Terminal; banning conversion of rental units to condominiums does not prevent landlords from profiting.

Restricting original development (change from vacant land to residential or commercial use) is perhaps a more complex issue. An owner of vacant land does not have a personal connection to the money she hopes to reap from development. The question of restricting original development is harder if the owner of vacant land was planning to build a residence (to live in, not for sale) and has already become bound up with those plans. Then there is a personal connection to the land, and perhaps to the architect's design of the residence, though not yet to the residence itself. It seems that someone who buys land for a personal residence and then has residential use regulated away from her has a stronger claim than the speculator. But this depends upon whether we[96] find it ethically appropriate that persons be closely connected with their residential plans for their property.

C. The Significance of Political Power
1. "Liberalism" versus "Republicanism"

Those who invest in businesses or the stock market understand that there is no right to a profit from investment, and land ownership as a fungible investment is similar when it comes to various vagaries of the market. The question is whether vagaries of governmental action are like other risks that investors face, or are different. A "liberal" understanding of politics would lead us to the conclusion that the risks associated with governmental interaction with us and our holdings are different in principle because they raise the possibility of systematic exploitation of the few by the representatives of the many. A "republican" understanding of politics perhaps does not move so quickly to the fear of systematic exploitation; instead, its central concern is preservation of self-government. Thus, a "liberal" understanding of the taking issue suggests that we evaluate takings claims by asking: Is this action a likely instance of overreaching by Leviathan? Whereas a republican understanding of the taking issue suggests that we evaluate such claims by asking: Is this action such as will undermine our commitment to self-government?[97]

I have suggested that the Court should ask the pragmatic ethical question: What conception of human flourishing do we foster by sustaining or disallowing a particular piece of legislation challenged as a taking? This question should bring explicitly into focus the fact that we have a choice in every case between "liberal" and "republican" assumptions about the situation. When we ask what conception of personhood in the context of democratic community we are fostering by sustaining or disallowing a legislative act, we must explicitly consider whether we want to think of our government as "them" (or Leviathan) and ourselves as needing protection from exploitation. Alternatively, do we want to think of our government as "us," and its disappointment of our hopes for profit from time to time as an acceptable responsibility of citizenship? If we see the government as "them" we adopt a "liberal" theory of politics, and if we see the government as "us" we adopt a "republican" theory of politics.

The reality of unequal power might lead to a conclusion that some visionary communitarians will find ironic. It may be that when the rich and powerful—like some corporate developers—complain of government action as a taking, the "republican" vision is appropriate, whereas when the poor and weak—such as welfare recipients, and indeed many homeowners—complain, we should stick to the "liberal" vision. In our nonideal world, would-be developers are in a better position to think of themselves and the government as closely connected, and hence it is more appropriate to expect them as citizens occasionally to endure disappointment of their hopes for profit. On the other hand, for most homeowners and welfare recipients, the public/private distinction better expresses their reality, and with their claims we should give more credence to the problem of systematic exploitation by Leviathan. Even admitting that the us/them picture of government should not be idealized or enshrined as a matter of principle, perhaps it is the right picture for now, at least for relatively powerless groups. Still, in order to make progress we should do two things. First, we should not assume that political relations are Hobbesian in principle, and second, we should—as Michelman recommends[98]—make empowerment and enfranchisement part of the constitutional inquiry about property.

2. Tenants and Empowerment

Tenants are both a relatively disempowered group and a group claiming both a personal and community interest in maintaining continuity of residence. Hence, the question whether the recognition of tenants' tenure rights is a taking of landlords' property rights is not difficult from my point of view, as long as the landlord's interest is fungible.[99] But the problem of political empowerment is very close to the surface in the issues of modern landlord and tenant law. As the law has developed, the issue of keeping one's home can be seen as inextricably intertwined with the issue of developing and protecting one's political voice. The retaliatory eviction defense, for example, is rooted in the understanding that if tenants are to be empowered to complain to the authorities about violations of their legal rights, and moreover if they are to be able to organize to enhance their legal status, then loss of their homes as a result of attempted political participation of this kind must be prevented. Obviously, community formation cannot proceed if the members are scattered when they try to assert themselves as group members.

In the landlord and tenant situation, the systemic problem we face is not one in which the personhood interests of individual landlords are pitted against individual tenants, but rather one in which a class of residents is unable to count on continuity of residence, hence unable to form strong political communities, because of the asserted liberal property rights of a more powerful class of investors. The systemic situation is one in which community formation and political expression, as well as individual self-development, should take normative precedence over claims of fungible holders to maintain or extend their power.

Does this situation lead us to an ethical judgment that a landlord's interest (however she subjectively feels about it) is fungible? I think the answer may well be yes, with qualifications. Some landlords live in one unit of a small building and rent out another, and on the basis of their residence we may exempt them from such an ethical judgment. But there is a broader difficulty. To what extent are subjective feelings of personal connection with one's holdings relevant to our decision that property should be recognized as personal? Clearly such subjective feelings cannot by themselves render property personal. Even if one is self-constituted by the idea of power over others through control over commodified resources, this does not translate ethically into treatment of one's investment holdings as personal, because the "compleat capitalist" embodies an inferior conception of human flourishing, and one we should reject.

But ethically more attractive subjective feelings are possible. Those who sell commodities (including commercial landlords, when they are persons and not corporations) may have a more complex subjective experience than the caricature commodity-holder (the pure self-interested profit-maximizer). They may care about the buyers and their relationships with buyers, not just about their profits.[100] Does this complex subjective experience of incomplete commodification mean we should not conceive of a landlord's interest as generally fungible? The question seems difficult, but as I see it now the answer must be no. To suggest that "good" landlords should have their property interest recognized as stronger than others as against tenants is to suggest that sellers' subjective experience of incomplete commodification should translate into greater control over their commodities, and hence greater power over buyers of them, than we would ethically accord to someone who corresponded to the caricature commodity-holder. The suggestion is morally counterintuitive. If sellers' subjective experiences of interrelationship are rewarded with more power over others, the experience of sharing that we wish to recognize as ethically appropriate would itself be undermined. The nature of the experience is essentially that power over others is *not* the essence of one's property relations; instead, one wishes to treat others as equals and as persons even while selling things they need. Therefore we do not recognize and foster human flourishing as expressed in incomplete commodification if we treat incomplete commodification as somehow giving rise to stronger property claims on sellers' part and weaker property claims on buyers' part.

III. CONCLUSION

The liberal conception of property is incompletely realized in our constitutional property practice, but a trend—as yet weak, to be sure—may be in progress toward greater realization. At the same time, long-standing tensions in our constitutional property practice pull in the opposite direction. The discourse of property has produced recurring attempts—including mine—to break down property into categories that further the ethical purposes of property and those that do not. More important, that these ethical intuitions distinguishing between personal and fungible property are played out in constitutional practice to some extent—although sporadically and ambiguously—forms a strong countercurrent to the ideological commitment to aspects of the liberal conception of property. In my view, the traditional commitments to equality of political power and respect for persons might—whether in their "liberal" or "republican" guises—extend these intuitions and their embodiment in practice, thus leading to a postliberal understanding of property.

Diagnosing the Takings Problem

"The philosopher's treatment of a question is like the treatment of an illness," said Wittgenstein, in one of my favorite remarks of his.[1] Here I would like to reflect upon the malaise that afflicts what legal scholars call the takings issue. The takings issue requires a court to determine when government action that adversely affects someone's claimed property interest should be understood to "take" that person's property. Under the Constitution, government actions that "take" property are disallowed unless compensation is paid.[2] The malaise is that no one can tell with satisfactory certainty what government actions those are.

How should we decide when "property" has been "taken"? The takings issue is central and pervasive. It is central because private property is a central commitment of a liberal legal system, a commitment that demands immunity of private holdings from defeasance. The issue is pervasive because almost all government actions make some entitlement holders worse off relative to others, yet government could not exist if it were required to undo all of its own actions by compensating everyone adversely affected by any action with distributive effects.

The takings issue is also remarkably intractable. For reasons that I hope my investigations will make clear, it is not to be solved simply by formally defining "property" and then observing that it has been "taken." Judicial efforts to develop a coherent takings doctrine have met with consistently telling criticism.[3] Often it seems that courts have not been able to do better than to tell us that when government regulation "goes too far" they will deem it a taking, whereas otherwise they will deem it within the state's normal "police power."[4] This is no more than to repeat the question, because "going too far" is a synonym for "taking." The sight of such a pervasive and central field of law in apparent disarray has enticed many able theorists, but their critical commentary has been more convincing than their efforts to reconstruct.[5]

Why is the takings problem so hard? If we cannot solve the problem, at least we can learn something by trying to understand why the solution eludes us. In the diagnosis I offer I set out three problems that are intertwined in the takings issue, which I characterize as problems of corrective justice, of the personal/fungible continuum, and of political contextuality. The upshot of my diagnosis is that two central difficulties of liberal legal and political theory are reflected especially clearly and urgently in the takings issue because of the importance of the liberal commitment to protection of private property. One difficulty is that the normative basis of liberalism resists reduction to formal rules, while rules are required by the equally important liberal commitment to the traditional ideal of the Rule of Law. The other difficulty is that the core liberal concepts of liberty, personhood, and polity are endlessly contested, while liberal political theory at the same time requires at least a basic consensus about them. If we relinquish the search for a coherent master-rule that can decide takings cases, we may find that the disarray in takings jurisprudence is somewhat alleviated. I suggest, in other words, that its disarray is partly an artifact of the commitment to formal rules and to the notion of an uncontested conception of property. Finally I take another view by considering the role of nonideal and ideal theory in trying to resolve the takings issue.

I. THREE PROBLEMS EMBEDDED IN THE TAKINGS ISSUE
A. The Problem of Corrective Justice

At first sight the takings issue appears to be a problem of compensatory justice: if private property is taken, then compensation is required. But concealed within the takings issue is a problem of corrective justice, and it forms an obverse to the compensatory justice problem. The heart of the concealed corrective justice problem is that a takings claim should, at least prima facie, be honored only if the property taken is rightfully held. If the property is wrongfully held, then corrective justice may require that the holder compensate the rightful holder or indeed return the property to her. It seems, at least prima facie, doubly wrong if instead the wrongful holder receives compensation for the taking. The theory of property that demands strong takings protection against the government also demands strong protection for individuals against theft, trespass, and nuisance, as well as any other wrongful arrogations of property rights.

The concealed corrective justice problem means that in every case where a taking is claimed we must decide whether or not the interest the government infringes is in fact justly held as a property right by the claimant. Often this threshold issue is called the baseline problem.[6] Because of the baseline problem, even what looks like a paradigm case of taking can flip-flop. Suppose the government bars Susan from land she claims to own, transfers title to itself, and then grants title to John. Susan claims that this is an unconstitutional taking. Is the answer obvious? First we need to know whether Susan is merely a trespasser against John.[7] If she is, then even though "property" has been "taken," the government should not compensate Susan for her loss.

The concealed corrective justice problem causes the most difficulty not with identifying obvious cases of claimants' thievery from, or trespass against, other individuals, although there are many nonobvious cases. The deepest difficulties instead center around identifying activities of entitlement holders that should be analogized to nuisance, deciding what to do about cases in which the government itself bears responsibility for wrongful arrogations of property rights by entitlement holders, and deciding whether, and when, settled expectations and elapsed time should turn old wrongs into new rights. I shall elaborate briefly on these three aspects of the baseline problem.

1. The Nuisance Analogy

Suppose Susan is engaging in some activity on her land that has the effect of lowering the value of neighboring land in some way.[8] Then the government regulates land use in such a way as to deny Susan the right to engage in the activity, thereby lowering the value, at least to her, of her land. Can Susan claim that she is owed compensation for a taking of her property right? First we have to know whether Susan really possessed a property right to engage in the activity in question. If not, government regulation to prevent the activity is an action of corrective justice vis-à-vis the neighbors, and not a taking from Susan.

In the constitutional takings context, the nuisance concern is often raised by asking whether the government regulation merely prevents the claimant from inflicting a harm on the community, rather than forcing the claimant to confer a benefit. If the court decides that the activity is a harm, then compensation is not decreed; if the claimant must yield up a benefit, then compensation is proper. In the analogous tort law context, it has become obvious that the nuisance issue involves a normative baseline problem that cannot yield to definitional analysis or sweeping general rules. The court must find a way to decide in each case whether the nuisance defendant's conduct was "unreasonable."[9] The decision involves a contextualized normative judgment about what level of self-restraint in light of the concerns of neighbors we think it appropriate to require of landowners.[10] It has not proved possible to formulate general rules that can either explain all past cases or predict the outcome of future ones. The only general principle is the standard of situated, case-by-case normative judgment expressed in the requirement that property owners be "reasonable."

In the takings context it has become equally clear that whether the claimant is inflicting a social harm or instead being required to confer a benefit cannot be decided by definition of "harm" and "benefit" or by general rules.[11] Situated moral judgment is required. In the famous case of *Miller v. Schoene*,[12] a government regulatory scheme ordered land-owners whose land contained cedar trees infected with rust to cut down their trees to avoid infecting other landowners' apple trees, and the Supreme Court held that compensation was not required even though the land value of the cedar owners was substantially lowered. In the celebrated case of *Hadacheck v. Sebastian*,[13] a brickyard that was originally located far from any residences was ordered to cease operations when residential uses later gradually moved next to it, and the Supreme Court held that compensation was not required even though the brickyard owner's land value was drastically diminished. More recently, in the famous case of *Just v. Marinette County*,[14] the Wisconsin Supreme Court denied that implementation of a wetlands ordinance required compensation of landowners who were prevented from building anything on their land, decreeing, or purporting to observe, that landowners have no right to change their land from its natural state.

These are all famous cases because the intuitions of many commentators run counter to the courts' decisions not to compensate. It may be easy in these "hard" cases to see that each of them requires a decision about whether the claimant landowner has a right to engage in the activity in question. *Miller* decided that there is no right to grow cedars where neighbors grow apples. *Hadacheck* decided there is no right to continue operating a brickyard when people want to live next to it. But that easy insight must be followed by the understanding that such a baseline decision is required in every case. The cases that appear "easy" (at a given time and place) merely fall more readily into widely shared and largely tacit conventional understandings about the scope of land-owners' rightful control over decision making with respect to land use. (In some more environmentally conscious future the *Just* case could come to appear easy.) So far no one has been able to reduce these conventional, intuitive, contextually contingent baseline judgments to a set of formal rules. Hence the concealed corrective justice issue tends to block any general solution to the takings problem, at least if we understand a general solution to be one that can be stated a priori in the form of a general rule.

2. Wrongful Delineation of Property Rights

Another aspect of the corrective justice problem further weakens the possibility of a general rule-like solution. How shall we treat the issue of government (and/or broadly social) responsibility for wrongful holding of property rights? Consider first the easy case in which we have all come to realize that previously recognized property rights were wrongful: slavery. It seems that it would be inappropriate to offer compensation to the dispossessed slave owners at the time of emancipation, even though their financial statements collectively showed considerably less net worth after emancipation. One reason it seems inappropriate is that abolishing property rights in human beings, and declaring that human beings simply cannot be property, seems inconsistent with paying compensation as if "property" has been taken. At least the symbolic message seems too morally mixed in such an important case.[15] We should not accept for compensation purposes the very baseline that abolition recognizes as wrongful.

Can this reasoning be generalized to other cases? Curtailing of husbands' supposed property rights in wives comes to mind. More problematic, we can consider, for example, supposed property rights of employers to maintain an unsafe workplace, of landlords to rent uninhabitable and unsafe housing, and of industrial producers to pollute air and water. Even if positive law has previously clearly recognized these supposed property rights of employers, landlords, and industries, once we decide that positive law has been wrong to do so, and that no such property rights do or should exist, it seems to contradict that recognition to turn around and grant compensation as if the property rights did exist after all.

The preceding argument will perhaps make no sense to some traditional legal positivists. Property, they will perhaps say, simply is whatever the government says it is from time to time, and the notion of mistakes about property is just incoherent. People used to be property, and now they aren't; landlords used to have the right to rent uninhabitable housing, and now they don't. From the traditional positivist point of view, the issue of whether or not to compensate when property rules change may be complicated,[16] but it cannot turn on whether the previous property regime was wrongful. For those other than traditional positivists, however, the underlying moral vision of what a property scheme should be, as it unfolds through time, must have some effect on our decision whether to grant the legitimacy to wrongful property holding that compensation bespeaks.[17] And for all of us, since the contest between affirmation and denial of the separation of law and morals in property runs deep, and perhaps we all embrace aspects of both,[18] the hope of a general rule-like solution for the takings problem recedes.

3. Settled Expectations and the Problem of Vested Rights

Perhaps the most difficult corrective justice problem has to do with when we should ignore it. The institution of private property lives in both the past and the present. It lives in the past because rightful holding depends upon an acceptable history of acquisition. It lives in the present because the mechanisms of adverse possession and prescription continually change old wrongs into new rights. The main rationale for adverse possession has always been practical: without a way to cut off old claims, not even rightful titles would be safe against lawsuits out of their distant past.[19] In the institution of property, corrective justice has its day but fades, continually overshadowed by present realities. This is a vital pragmatic compromise. Without protection against trespass and dispossession, the institution of private property could not fulfill the liberal promise of security in holdings, but neither could it do so if all holders were continually vulnerable to the successors of rival claims out of the past. Why isn't it a taking for the government to promulgate statutes of limitation that deprive holders of their rightful claims? Only because if the government omitted these statutes, the omission would "take" more.

The issue of how much we should live in the present regarding claimants' holdings causes difficulty in the takings context. Of course, if a claimant wrongfully acquired property but has achieved title by adverse possession, government deprivation can be a taking just as much as if the claimant's title were otherwise acquired. The difficulty arises in cases that are not traditional adverse possession or prescription but in which we might see a similar fading of corrective justice in light of present realities. In other words, while corrective justice concerns can cause even a case that looks like a paradigmatic taking to flip-flop, after enough time has passed it can flip-flop back again. After enough time, the entrenched status quo can come to be treated as vested rights.

Outside the bailiwick of traditional adverse possession and prescription, we have no guidance about how much time is enough, nor even whether a case is one in which the fading of corrective justice in favor of the status quo is morally appropriate. We can distinguish two kinds of cases. In the first kind the government moves to defease rights the holders thought they had (the vested rights problem). In the second kind the government must decide whether to pay off claimants for takings long past. (The second case may also pose a vested rights problem if successors to the original claimant stand to lose if the earlier claim is recognized.)

In the first kind of case, we would not want to say that settled expectations should validate ownership of slaves after we come to understand that ownership to be wrongful, even though slaveholding was a part of ordinary life for a long time. The social and legal entrenchment of slavery could not make slave ownership a vested right. On the other hand, perhaps we might think that a claimant whose long-continued activity (for example, brickmaking or pig farming)[20] eventually comes to be seen as socially "unreasonable"—nuisance-like—should nevertheless have the right to continue the activity.

In the second kind of case, we might want to honor some Indian land claims even though the takings occurred long ago.[21] On the other hand, we could not hold the government liable for all of (what we now see as) its mistakes in changing property regimes. Even if we now think the Supreme Court was wrong in 1887 to deny compensation to breweries whose business was completely destroyed by prohibition,[22] that does not mean we should seek out and compensate their successors.

What are the considerations that would go into the decision whether to allow settled expectations to override the prima facie demands of corrective justice and be treated as vested rights? No one has achieved a general theory that can answer this question, and here I only sketch a few concerns. Much more will be relevant than an observation of the length of time the claimant has mistakenly thought she enjoyed a property right. It will matter just how harmful the wrongful holding is in its present context. (Harm to how many people? To interests how central? Is their social situation favored or disfavored? Is the harm irrevocable?) It will also matter whether we think that the claimant knew or should have known that the holding was wrongful even before the government moved to defease it, and whether we can sympathize with the claimant's attachment to the holding even though we now see it as wrongful.

Similarly, what are the considerations that would go into the decision whether the government must now compensate for its old wrongs? Again, much more will be relevant than an observation of how long ago the wrong occurred. It will matter just how deep was the wrong. (Harm to how many people? etc.) The historical significance of the wrong will matter too. How important is the continuing sense of this past wrong to today's polity? If the harm has no continuing significance we can choose to live in the present. But if the harm is *too* significant, compensation may be politically impossible. Why did we compensate the victims of Manzanar but not the victims of segregation?

B. The Problem of the Personal/Fungible Continuum

The primary liberal theories of property find property to be necessary for the proper flourishing of individuals. They find—and forge—a link between private property and the differentiation, maintenance, and development of the self. Different strands of liberal thought emphasize different aspects of such a connection. Some theories emphasize a positive aspect: proper self-development and flourishing are linked to proper connection with the external world, and private property is necessary to this connection.[23] Other theories emphasize a negative aspect: proper self-maintenance and flourishing are linked to proper protection from the external world, and private property is necessary to this protection.[24] Marx declared that "bourgeois property" had abolished the connection between property and individual personhood,[25] by which he meant that private property in the context of the full-blown market society did not serve this function. But I believe that neither a complete acceptance of the liberal story about property, nor a complete acceptance of the Marxist critique, can do justice to the place of property in our form of life.

I believe, in other words, that our practice of private property, in a complex way, can validate both some aspects of the liberal conception of property and some aspects of the critique of that conception. I have attached the label "personal" to property that is connected, and is understood morally as rightly connected to the proper development and flourishing of persons, understood primarily in its positive aspect, and I have attached the label "fungible" to property that is not connected to

persons in this way but instead is understood as representing interchangeable units of exchange value. I believe that in our practice of
property we do not attach equal moral weight to all interests that we
accept as property, because we do understand, though almost always
tacitly, that property interests are morally ordered on a continuum from
personal to fungible, and that the personal interests are deserving of
greater legal protection. Homeownership carries greater moral weight
in the legal system than does ownership of vacant land held for investment. The differing strength of holders' claims greatly complicates the
takings issue. Exactly what has been taken, and from whom, matters.
Even where legal doctrines do not take account of this, the pattern of
decisions does.[26]

1. Tests for Takings and the Personal/Fungible Continuum

Market-oriented tests for whether a taking has occurred, and if so what
compensation is due, respond to the taking of fungible but not personal
property. One prevalent market-oriented test for whether a taking has
occurred is whether government action has lowered the market value of
the claimant's holding by a large enough margin, typically more than
seventy-five percent.[27] If property is personal, the claimant could experience a grievous loss even if market value decreased little, or indeed
increased.

Market value need not track—is incommensurate with—justifiable
personal connection.[28] Suppose Jack redesigns his tract house and re-
builds it into an idiosyncratic but deep architectural expression of his
personality, and in doing so he violates zoning regulations mandating
uniformity. Suppose further that uniformity increases market value. If
we recognize Jack's interest as properly personal, then we may find the
regulations to "take" property from him in a way that is unrelated to
market value.[29]

Assuming we are clear that a taking has occurred, the market-oriented
test for what compensation is due is the fair market value of the property
interest taken. This is the dominant legal standard for determining compensation, but it can seem quite wrong in cases where property interests
are apprehended as personal and incommensurate with money. In such
cases it may be difficult to decide whether compensatory justice requires
higher compensation or whether no compensation should be paid because the problem is outside the scope of compensatory justice.

A prevalent nonmarket test for whether a taking has occurred asks instead whether government action amounts to a physical invasion or occupation of the claimant's property. The physical invasion test can be understood as responsive to the central commitment in liberal theory, primarily in its negative aspect, of connection between property and personhood. It is analgous to a dignitary interpretation of the meaning of trespass: who diminishes my property diminishes me. Instead of inquiring about how much fungible wealth the claimant may have lost, this test speaks in terms of invasion and insult.

Although this test seems central to the underlying concern about persons and their connection to the external world, or persons and their cloak of protection against the external world, it cannot appropriately be treated as a systematic rule.[30] For one thing, it misses the mark when the claimant is a business entity. All property is fungible for business entities; they have nothing to lose but their wealth. So a loss that would count as trespassory, a dignitary invasion, against a person cannot be that kind of loss for a corporation.

Moreover, even when the claimant is a person, if her holding is fungible then the invasion test also misses the mark. In *Loretto v. Teleprompter Manhattan CATV Corp.,*[31] a majority of the U.S. Supreme Court held, on the basis of the physical invasion test, that it is a taking for a statute to permit a cable television operator to install a cable on a building without the owner's consent, even with provision for payment of a nominal fee to the owner. Once we accept that the strength of property claims varies depending upon whether they are personal or fungible, that is, depending upon the closeness of their fit with the core concerns of the liberal ideal of property, and once we understand, therefore, that the physical invasion test in itself responds only to government threats to personal property, the result in *Loretto* seems to push the liberal ideal way beyond its bounds. A cable on the roof of a building the owner rents out as a fungible investment no more invades her personhood than does a tax or a utility assessment.

So far I have outlined how the complexity attendant upon the personal/fungible continuum renders prevalent tests for takings partial rather than general. To this observation we should add another. Unless decisions about whether to consider property personal are susceptible to predetermination by a priori rules, that complexity also means that even when the takings tests are stated as rules, like the rule against physical invasion, those rules cannot function in the way rules are traditionally thought to. Some judgments about personal property may be rule-like, though not immutably so; for example, the judgment that in this time and place the home should be treated as personal. Other judgments about personal property may be irreducibly case-specific.

2. Further Ramifications: Limits on Eminent Domain and on Fungible Property

I also want to suggest that if we recognize the personal/fungible continuum, as I believe we do, albeit tacitly and incompletely, we might find a moral limit on the power of eminent domain. We might find, moreover, that even an otherwise clear taking of a fungible interest might not require compensation if its defeasance is required to maintain interests, even nonproperty interests, closely connected to personhood.

The broad power of eminent domain, with the requirement of monetary compensation at market value, seems, by implicitly understanding all property to be fungible, paradoxically to exclude the moral core of the liberal rationale for property.[32] To the extent that we recognize personal property, we might think that some property should not be taken at all. We might think that for some things no compensation can be "just." We might find some things to be inalienable if they are closely connected with personhood, or at least inalienable involuntarily to the government.[33] If we conceive of the body as property, can kidneys be condemned for public use?[34] While some cases may appear easy, which things ought to be inalienable on grounds of inseparability from personhood cannot be distinguished by a bright-line theoretical rule.

Recognition of the personal/fungible continuum should also lead us to conceive of conflicts between property and nonproperty personal interests, like freedom of noncommercial speech, differently depending upon whether the property is personal or fungible.[35] The concern here is connected with the corrective justice aspect of the takings problem considered earlier. In any given case we might find under the circumstances that a claimed fungible property interest is wrongly held, such that it cannot prevail against nonproperty interests that appear more closely connected with personhood. If property is fungible (for example, a large shopping center), we might find that a statute permitting political speech on the claimant's property is not a taking, even though it appears to be literally a government action permitting a physical incursion into the claimant's space and a limit on the claimant's right to exclude.[36] On the other hand, a similar statute directed against homeowners might more readily be understood as a taking.

C. The Problem of Political Contextuality

The takings issue is at first sight a problem of classifying a particular statute or a particular transaction: Does government action X take the private property of claimant Y? Yet the takings issue is deeply dependent upon political context; and how we construe the political context depends upon the political theory we accept.[37] We are deceived if we think that solving the takings problem involves scrutinizing individual statutes or transactions outside the context of political theory and political reality. The title of this subsection is itself deceptive if it suggests that the complexity of contextual judgment becomes apparent for the first time when we consider takings and politics. The largely tacit problems revealed so far, of corrective justice and the personal/fungible continuum, undermine the hope of a general solution to the takings issue just because they place each decision in a variegated moral context.

Many who tend toward traditional legal positivism, who tend to think of law as a body of rules laid down, and who tend to think of legal decision-making, at least for some majority of core cases, as uncomplicated rule-application, will also tend to think that the problems of corrective justice and the personal/fungible continuum can be solved with appropriate rules that will delineate the relevant moral distinctions.[38] I do not deny that partial, contingent rules are possible, such as the rule-like understanding that homes are personal. Where I part company from traditional positivists is in my belief that such partial, contingent rules rest only on situated experience and not on a priori master-rules. Nor do I deny that we can and should try to develop principles that can help us deal more readily with corrective justice and the personal/fungible continuum. Perhaps the difference between my views and those I characterize as belonging to a traditional positivist is one of perspective or of degree. To alleviate the perpetual disarray of the takings issue, as it appears from the traditional point of view, it is important to understand rules or principles as open-ended and inseparable from context.

Those who tend toward traditional positivism may be less able to evade contextuality when the focus is explicitly on politics. There is an affinity between traditional legal positivism and the liberal political theory now known as interest-group pluralism. Interest-group pluralism is a logrolling or dealmaking theory of politics in which interest groups try to maximize their self-interest by bringing about favorable government action, forming strategic coalitions with other groups, and making concessions to competing groups when these are strategically necessary.[39] For someone who accepts a dealmaking theory of politics, the takings issue brings contextuality to the fore in a way that cannot easily be evaded. All the typical questions we might ask about a particular transaction—How large is the loss? How much does this kind of loss interfere with personhood or dignity?—are counterbalanced, in fact engulfed, by questions about the political context. Why? Because in any particular case a claimant's loss can seem a paradigmatic taking of her property and yet be a bargained political quid pro quo.

Suppose local landlords are forced by a new ordinance to dedicate twenty-five percent of their units to free housing for the homeless, and the landlords claim this is a taking requiring compensation. Before deciding whether to pay them off, we should ask, if we accept the dealmaking theory of politics, whether the landlords bargained away these units in return for a greater gain elsewhere, for example a giant tax break. If the landlords bargained for their loss in expectation of greater gain, then no compensation should be due them.

The general point is that any loss in a particular transaction may turn out to be the price paid for gains extracted elsewhere.[40] If so, then to pay compensation is to compensate twice. Although in this political theory, at least, the self-interested claimant should be expected to try this gambit, the gambit must be defeated or politics will come to a halt. Logrolling will be foiled by a logjam.

The general point must be understood to have a temporal dimension as well. The landlords who acquiesce in the ordinance giving over some of their units to the homeless may be buying political benefits for the future rather than paying for government favors already granted. It would still be double compensation for the government both to make good on the deal and to pay them off when they scream "taking."

The dealmaking theory of politics places every takings case in a virtually unbounded dynamic context. The context is dynamic because deals, according to this theory, are always part of an ongoing process; they get unmade and remade as political give-and-take goes on. The context is unbounded because deals can be made at all levels of government. They can be made for the benefit of other groups sympathetic with one's own, or linked to one's own by a merely passing coalition. You scratch my back, I'll scratch yours. They can be made for past and future payoffs over an indefinite period. The payoffs can occur anywhere in the system and need not be observably connected with claimants' property. What if the landlords cared more for restricting abortion than for maintaining high profits in the rental business? Rent-seeking and restricting abortion make strange bedfellows. The deals can be made even when the expected payoff is uncertain, or even risky, if the interest group finds the risk to be worthwhile.

The dealmaking theory of politics does not tell us how to find out what deals have actually been made. It does not tell us how to draw the boundaries of context, nor when to stop the clock and freeze the action. It commits itself, probably in spite of itself, to contextualized pragmatic decisions. Each case requires a look at the political universe.

Suppose, though, that we reject the liberal theory of interest-group pluralism. One prevalent alternative is a version of civic republicanism.[41] Under the tenets of civil republicanism, as reinterpreted by left-liberal thinkers, a political contextuality concern still poses a deep problem for takings decisions. Republicanism rests on a commitment to the flourishing of citizens in a community by means of their self-government. Most modern republicans understand that some groups have more power than others to define and constitute the political community. In keeping with this understanding, takings decisions should be viewed through a lens of political empowerment. Groups that have power to control the legislature, or other government action, and hence actually participate, even if informally, in the lawmaking that affects their holdings, should, when they experience losses in their holdings, be more readily understood as sacrificing some of their private interests for the public interest than should less powerful groups that are largely excluded from actual participation in lawmaking. If landlords have a dominant voice on the city council, whether formally or informally, then we may judge giving over some of their units to the use of the homeless as an appropriate contribution to their community's political well-being. On the other hand, we might, as republicans, properly be more skeptical about the appropriateness of the sacrifice if low-income tenants were being asked to relinquish their units, or any important entitlements associated with tenancy. This concern means that the contextual circumstances of political power, of inclusion and exclusion from the actual governing of the community, become relevant in cases where a taking is claimed.

II. THE RULE OF LAW AND CONTESTED CONCEPTS: TWO PROBLEMS FOR LIBERAL PROPERTY THEORY AND PRACTICE

Perhaps no one would seek an a priori general rule-like solution to the takings issue if it were not for the ideal of the Rule of Law. Perhaps no one would be dismayed that all the courts are able to do is muddle through.[42] But the liberal ideal of the Rule of Law, in its traditional form, requires that people be governed by general rules that predate the action to be judged by them, and that these rules be understandable by, known to, and capable of being met by, those to whom they are addressed.[43] Muddling through does not seem to meet these criteria.

The most prevalent rationale for the requirements of the Rule of Law is that liberty depends upon them, and hence the very justifiability of government in the liberal scheme depends upon them.[44] The liberal commitment to equality—like cases must be treated alike—also seems to require a regime of general rules. The takings issue, like the death penalty, poses a crisis for the ideal of the Rule of Law, because no one has been able to bring the issue satisfactorily under a general rule or a regime of general rules.[45] If private property, a cornerstone of the complex of liberal commitments, cannot be protected in a way that lives up to the requirements of the Rule of Law, then how can governmental action affecting holdings ever be justified?

I shall not attempt here to prove a negative, to demonstrate irrefutably that it is impossible to solve the takings issue with formal rules.[46] It should be clear, at least, that each of the concerns I have delineated is at best extremely resistant to reduction to rules in the traditional sense. In that sense of rules, their preexisting meaning is supposed to dictate results of its own force. In a more modern understanding of rules, the apprehension of an action as rule-governed depends upon social consensus after the fact and not upon some a priori formal logical force. While I have not denied that partial rules, in the modern sense, are possible, the traditional sense of rules is the sense embedded in the ideal of the Rule of Law.[47] The need for shifting situational judgment in dealing with baseline problems, personal/fungible distinctions, and political contextuality highlights the inutility of the traditional conception of rules and of the traditional ideal of the Rule of Law.

One basic difficulty with the takings issue, then, is that the inherited ideal of the Rule of Law impels us to seek preexisting formal solutions where only practice-based contextual solutions are to be had. Another basic difficulty, implicitly apparent, I am sure, in the very controversiality of much of what I have said so far, is our deep pluralism regarding the values that drive these practice-based partial and temporary solutions. Property is a perennially contested concept, as are the concepts of liberty, personhood, and polity on which it is supposed to rest. We do not have consensus on the requirements of corrective justice, on the significance, if any, of the personal/fungible continuum, or on the appropriate way to theorize about politics and to construe our political practice. This pluralism does not mean that there cannot be better and worse answers, solutions, or principles associated with the takings issue. It means only that the better—the right—answers will not have the open-and-shut quality that we expect from rules and that drives the old ideal of the Rule of Law.

In my view these two intertwined difficulties, the problem of trying to achieve formal rules in the face of the stubborn relevance of circumstances, and the problem of pluralism in basic liberal values, together account for much of the disarray in takings jurisprudence. They render the takings issue resistant to general solutions. The resistance stems in part from recalcitrant theory: the continuing contestedness of moral and political theory relating to property, and our need to make decisions with broad philosophical ramifications while the philosophers are still arguing, as they always will be. The resistance arises also from recalcitrant practice: the stubborn situatedness of people and their property, and the endless variations in property relations. This protean aspect of property is part of the reason why property, like liberty, is a central value in liberal schemes, but ironically it is also the reason why property problems resist the liberal commitment to rules.

All of this is not intended to say that we cannot make takings jurisprudence better by seeking to include principles of corrective justice, personal/fungible distinctions, and dynamic contextuality in our thinking about it. We can and should seek principles and wrestle with their conjoined application. If the tacit concerns come to light and we talk about them directly, and if the traditional rhetoric of rules is relinquished, at least in its single-mindedness, then thought and decision making about takings must benefit. Once we do this, though, we must recognize that we cannot meet the requirement of the traditional Rule of Law that government act by self-evident application of preexisting general rules.

III. THE TAKINGS ISSUE AND THE TENSION BETWEEN IDEAL AND NONIDEAL THINKING ABOUT IT

As a first cut at the problem, it seems that three pervasive and intractable problems interact to make a general solution to the takings issue elude us. It also seems that their intractability is due largely to their connection with contested concepts crucial to liberal property theory and to their lack of amenability to solutions in the form of rules in the traditional sense. Now we can look at the problem another way: to understand that the takings issue presents both intractable ideal issues and intractable nonideal issues, and to examine their interaction as a problem of transition.

By ideal issues I mean issues about how we should decide the takings problem in a frictionless world of perfect good faith and perfect knowledge, including knowledge of justified theories of property and politics. In the ideal world of theory, those charged with carrying out law unfailingly do it correctly. By nonideal issues I mean issues concerning how we should decide the takings problem in our world of ignorance, including theoretical disagreement and uncertainty, mistakes, and bad faith. The problem of transition concerns how much deviance from our ideals we should mandate in practice in our present nonideal world to make the best progress toward our ideal world of theory. If our ideal, for example, is more caring interaction between landlords and tenants, should we try to implement that ideal now, in the midst of a market-oriented world, by greatly increasing landlords' duties of habitability and curtailing their profits? Or will this backfire and make the gulf between landlords and tenants even worse? Or should we stick with a largely free-market regime, hoping for happy, generous landlords and a trickle-down effect? Or will this further entrench the nonideal market order and push our ideal farther away?

The problem of transition to a better world, to the world of our theories of justice, is the problem of politics. The transition never ends; we are always in medias res. In making our decisions in practice we must recognize that those decisions not only move either toward or away from our ideals, they also continually help us to reshape those ideals, for better or for worse.

The intractability of the takings issue arises not just from the multiplicity of issues, and not just from the difficulties with contestedness and the Rule of Law, but also from our inability to specify in any general way when we should be governed by the ideal and when we should pay attention instead primarily to the nonideal. Always in the midst of the transition, we are always unsure when we should lean toward theory and our hopes for progress and when toward practical politics and our realistic appraisal of the world as it is.

The overriding ideal concern that makes the takings issue intractable is that a general solution demands a fully worked-out theory of justified property holding, which depends upon a theory of politics and the person. The contestedness of moral and political theory relating to property renders our ideals uncertain and conflicting. Perhaps we should consider its very contestedness to be nonideal. At any rate, this central ideal problem with our world of theory shades over into the nonideal, into corrective justice, our deep commitment that wrongs about property must be righted.

The need for corrective justice reflects our nonideal circumstances: wrongs happen. Corrective justice nevertheless has an aspect that relies on ideal theory. Commitment to a theory of justified property holding is necessary to identify cases of wrongful holding in which corrective justice is called for. Corrective justice also has a more immediate nonideal aspect. Corrective justice fades out in favor of the status quo. It fades out for the primary nonideal reason that otherwise the continuance of the institution of property would be under threat. When and how corrective justice should be allowed to fade will always be a serious problem of transition, a matter of controversy and pain.

Does the contestedness of ideal theory translate into ineradicable difficulties on the level of individual decisions? It seems that if theories of property are contested, because theories of politics and the person are contested, then the takings issue must remain contested. Interest-group pluralism and civic republicanism yield different patterns of justified holdings and different levels of tolerance for rearrangements. Neo-Lockeans find entrenchment where other kinds of liberals find none, and counsel corrective justice where others find no need for it. The relevance of the personal/fungible continuum remains contested, as do recognizable stopping places upon it.

To this one might try to respond that at least some paradigm cases must count as a taking under any plausible theory we can hope to devise.[48] If this response succeeds it is still only a partial solution. But I think this response must likely fail, given the range of competing political theories currently on the scene, and particularly because of the force of the dealmaking theory, interest-group pluralism. Suppose we say a paradigm case might be one in which government takes over all ownership indicia except the nominal title. In other words, say that a paradigm case looks just like an undeclared case of eminent domain. It seems that this kind of paradigm is too narrow to help much with the array of takings problems that arise. But worse, as we have seen, even what looks like a paradigm case can flip-flop, either because it runs into the non-ideal problem of corrective justice, or because it runs into the nonideal problem of political context. As we have seen, the problem of political context is especially acute for the political theory of interest-group pluralism.

The Rule of Law is another ideal problem confronting us in takings, as everywhere in a liberal regime of legality. In a sense the Rule of Law ideal is rooted in the nonideal from its source. It asks us to recognize that a regime of general rules is necessary to implement the political ideal of negative liberty, in light of the tendency of government to overreach, and in light of the shortcomings of judges and administrators.[49] The irony about the Rule of Law is that it requires general, well-understood, and self-evidently applicable rules about property, but if we were able to develop such well-behaved rules we would be more confident of decision makers' ability to make correct decisions and therefore less in need of the constraints of the Rule of Law.

Part of the complex of nonideal issues surrounding the Rule of Law is an old debate about institutional priorities. Given our theoretical uncertainties and the various possibilities of error and bad faith, should legislatures almost always have their way? Or should courts be active in attempting to correct them? The Rule of Law is often understood to include legislative deference: judges are to "apply" not "make" the law.[50] Constitutional protection of property against takings, however, is countermajoritarian. Its function is to disallow some legislative actions. Judges who are too deferential, however much deference is "too" much, will fail to "apply" the Constitution and thereby violate the Rule of Law, no less than they will violate the Rule of Law if they are not deferential enough, however much deference is "enough."

In practice it seems that those who are sure of their ideal theory, their general theory of justified property holding, especially if that theory gives little or no weight to community participation in arriving at what constitutes a system of justified holding, are likely to plump for activist judging.[51] Those who are less sure of their ideal theory, or who hold an ideal theory more dependent upon community, are more likely to favor deference to legislatures, especially at the local level.[52] Just as there are no readily apparent uncontroversial rules for justified property holding, all things considered, so there are no readily apparent uncontroversial rules for institutional priorities in deciding when a claimant has been unjustifiably deprived of property.

IV. Conclusion

The lesson of my investigations is modest. We should not seek what we cannot find: decisions that uncontestedly follow from a coherent system of rules. Some of the apparent disarray in the takings doctrine, as applied in practice, disappears if we see the courts as engaged in the pragmatic practice of situated judgment in light of both partial principles and the unique particularities of each case.[53] More still might be further eased if courts became more comfortable with their practice and less oriented toward searching for rules capable of mechanical application.

Just because the takings issue resists rationalization by a coherent master-rule does not mean we should fail to seek principles that can help organize our thinking about it. Nor does the lack of a master-rule mean that there are not better and worse valences for takings jurisprudence. In fact, I hope that takings jurisprudence can be the better for explicit cognizance of the problems I have raised in this chapter. In my investigations I have not sought to say anything novel or surprising, but only to help us see what we already know. Rather than seeking complete theories and a system of rules, we should work more consciously within the framework of the dilemmas of transition, in the tension between ideal and nonideal worlds. We should continue to work on the general principles suggested by the takings issue, but we should accept both that they always "run out" in practice and that practice always changes them. In other words, here as elsewhere in the law, we should recognize the inescapably pragmatic nature of the enterprise.

SIX

Government Interests and Takings: Cultural Commitments of Property and the Role of Political Theory

With the coalescence of a conservative Supreme Court, the level of "compellingness" of governmental interests needed to validate curtailment of private property rights has seemed to escalate in some cases. Whether or not an increased burden on the government is justified is an important question in constitutional property jurisprudence, but so are some related questions that are less often explicitly discussed. One related question is when we should consider the government's interest to be *maintaining and enforcing* a prior property regime, and when we should consider the government's interest to be *changing* the prior regime. As soon as that question is asked, we must also ask another: How do we decide whether a government action is one that "enforces" or one that "changes" a property regime? (Indeed, how do we decide the government is "acting"?) These questions about how we determine the government's interest, and how we characterize government actions in light of it, implicate both our prevailing cultural commitments of property and a political theory of government action. They are questions that are in a sense prior to our determination of how "compelling" the interest is, and prior to our determination of whether that level of "compellingness" is enough to justify action.

The government's interest can also be characterized as its purpose or its reason for acting, at least when interest, purpose and reason are characterized at a high level of generality. If the government's interest is maintaining the existing scheme of property rights, for example, then when it acts to prevent trespass, its ultimate purpose or reason for doing so is to maintain the scheme of property rights. In this essay I focus on the takings issue. I investigate the ways in which perceived government reasons figure in deciding whether government has acted to change a property regime in a way that should be regarded as unconstitutional.

When a takings claim raises the question whether the government's interest is in maintaining and enforcing or in changing the prior property regime, there are four subtopics of inquiry. One is how an owner's "bundle of sticks" fluctuates, and another is when we should consider these fluctuations the government's doing. Another is how we go about attributing reasons for an action to the government or to a governmental entity, and another is how we go about judging those attributed reasons for action as good or bad, legitimate or illegitimate. As my procedure will show, I don't think these subtopics can remain ultimately discrete in useful thought and discussion of them. I can say in advance that when we think the government has bad reasons for doing something in specific circumstances, we are also going to think that its interest is weak or nonexistent in those circumstances, and we are most likely to call its action a "taking." Conversely, when we think the government has good reasons for doing something in specific circumstances, we are also going to think that its interest is strong or even "compelling" in those circumstances, and we are less likely to call its action a "taking."

I hope to flesh out these observations by showing how cultural commitments of property structure our perception of government interests, as well as our evaluation of those interests. I want to show that evaluation of government interests—the legitimacy of attributed purposes or reasons for action—also depends upon our political theory of government decision making. Moreover, I want to show that the process of evaluation is intertwined with the issue of when we perceive "change" and when we perceive it as due to government "action"; and that these perceptions in turn are also structured by cultural commitments of property.

In these inquiries I shall take as examples two areas of change in property regimes: the movement of beach property away from a strict private property regime and in the direction of commons, and the rearrangement of entitlements in the landlord-tenant relationship. Recent Supreme Court cases serve to focus some of the discussion. In *Lucas v. South Carolina Coastal Council,*[1] the Court declared that land use regulations that deprive an owner of all economic benefit of property are per se a taking (regardless of the government's purpose in enacting them) unless previous legal understandings of the scope of property rights show that the owner's "bundle of sticks" did not include the rights claimed. Justice Scalia wrote the opinion in *Lucas,* as he did in the 1987 case of *Nollan v. California Coastal Commission.*[2] In *Nollan,* a divided Court found that the Coastal Commission acted illegitimately (working a taking) when it conditioned its grant of a beachfront development permit on the Nollans' dedicating a lateral public access easement through a portion of their property beyond their seawall. Justice Scalia's opinion conceded that the Commission could legitimately have denied the permit outright.

Conservatives fared less well when it came to landlords' entitlements. In *Yee v. City of Escondido*,[3] the Court declined to equate trailer park rent control with physical invasion of the landlord's property, thus foreclosing one conservative strategy for bringing back laissez-faire markets. In the 1987 case of *Pennell v. City of San Jose*,[4] the Court was unanimous in assuming that local jurisdictions legitimately have broad discretion to impose rent control on residential housing, and only Justice Scalia (joined by Justice O'Connor) found the specific ordinance before the Court to be constitutionally objectionable in any respect.

I. Changing Property Regimes and Government Action
A. Justice and the Existence of Property Rights: the Cultural Commitments of Property

It may seem at first that the relationship between government action and how entitlements change is obvious: an owner has more or fewer entitlements after the government acts to change the rules so as to add to or take away from her entitlements. I think, however, that upon reflection the relationship must seem more complicated, at least for anyone who is not a straightforward positivist. Consider the abolition of slavery. Do we simply say that before the Emancipation Proclamation people could be property, and after it they couldn't? Or do we want to say that in some sense people never were "really" objects of property, even though the government allowed them to be officially conceived of and legally treated as such? Again, do we simply say that before the Emancipation Proclamation slave owners had property rights in these objects, and afterwards they didn't? Or do we want to say that in some sense the wrongfulness of slavery attenuated the rights associated with ownership even before the government recognized that wrongfulness?

Perhaps we want to say both, but neither categorically. The point of these rhetorical questions is that the existence of property regimes, their phenomenological detail, is connected with culture and not just with government action narrowly conceived. The point, more specifically, is that our very recognition of the existence of property rights is intertwined with our perceptions of their justice. There is no sharp demarcation between empirical and normative questions, and cultural commitments are reflected in the way we view either kind of question.

Moreover, to the extent our cultural commitments are not monolithic but rather reflect conflict and pluralism, the question of the existence of property rights, as well as the question of their justice, may remain contested.

We sometimes use the notion of natural rights to ground insights about how the wrongfulness of a regime, and the need for corrective justice, can undermine the sense of property itself. To steer clear of philosophical red herrings, for purposes of this discussion I am considering the content of natural right as a cultural possession, without arguing about whether natural rights can only exist as commitments of a particular culture or can be said to exist independent of any culture.

In saying that property regimes, in their phenomenological detail, are connected with culture and not just government action narrowly conceived, I add the qualifier to suggest that more broadly conceived, government and culture are not separate. Legal regimes both express and help to shape culture, and in that function they have symbolic force; and I think their symbolic force contributes to what we perceive as government action. In other words, what we see as action, how we attribute it to the government as actor, depends to some extent on the surrounding cultural circumstances.

Let me try to relate what I have said to the changing property regimes for beaches and the landlord-tenant relationship. In these evolving regimes, can we see surrounding cultural circumstances as being implicated both in how an owner's "bundle of sticks" fluctuates, and in when we consider these fluctuations to be the government's doing?

B. The Beach: From Private Property to Commons?

The prevalent common law property regime for coastal lands reserved in the sovereign a nonextinguishable public servitude for fishing and navigation over the tidelands (the area between the mean low tide and mean high tide lines),[5] but allowed the sovereign to pass the tidelands into private ownership otherwise.[6] The regime allowed for ordinary private property ownership with full exclusion rights for beach land inland of the mean high tide line (including the dry sand area between the vegetation line and the mean high tide line). Thus the coastal property regime was a limited commons in the tidelands, and otherwise private property.

In some areas the traditional coastal property regime has changed in the direction of a commons, in various ways. In Oregon the Supreme

Court declared that owners could not exclude the public from the dry sand area of the beach, because from time immemorial everybody used the beach as a matter of customary right.[7] In California the content of the tidelands public servitude was found to be expandable to suit changing times, and thus now to include public recreation rights as well as fishing and navigation.[8] Also, California's voters enacted, by direct initiative, a Coastal Zone Conservation Act that curtailed the free rein of private decision-making about the use of coastal private property.[9]

These California developments figure in the *Nollan* case, and in *Lucas* Justice Scalia made explicit the dependence of property rights upon cultural commitments. But before I go into that, pause to consider how we might characterize the evolution of the coastal property regime, as I have cursorily sketched it. Some coastal owners of course felt that any change in the direction of commons "took" their private property. But the Oregon court said it wasn't changing anything about the scheme of rights.[10] It only wanted to change what owners were actually doing so as to accord with the official legal regime. Coastal owners were mistaken to think they had those particular property rights that would enable them to exclude people who want to use the beach. The beach was always, or always should have been, as a matter of natural right, partially a commons. This reasoning implied that owners' habit of exercising their supposed property rights to exclude people was wrongful against the public and that owners had no legitimate expectation of continuing to exercise them. The court saw itself as acting not to change the property regime but to enforce property rights under the existing regime.

Unlike the Oregon court, the California court thought itself to be implementing change.[11] But it said that the possibility of change was always understood—I would say as part of the cultural commitments of property. It said, in other words, that the scope of the public rights was always meant to change with the times.[12] Thus the court understood itself to be reaffirming, rather than changing, the underlying expectations of property ownership. Owners belong to the culture of property. They can be understood to participate in it and therefore to understand the areas of flexibility, the areas where evolution is to be expected. Although disappointed, owners of land subject to the public trust servitude lost nothing they could reasonably have expected to keep forever in a rigid way.

These court decisions were not separate from the culture that produced them. They were not, or not merely, "new" rules laid down by (judicial) legislation as a sort of deus ex machina. The culture of private property, at least in some states, seemed to be evolving toward an understanding that beaches are a special resource not treated the same as ordinary objects of property. The legal system influenced this cultural evolution, but the cultural evolution also influenced the legal system. The understanding seemed to be that both free public access to enjoyment of the resource, and conservation of the resource for future public enjoyment, were important enough to operate to attenuate, as a matter of natural right, the possibilities for full private ownership of beach property. The cultural understanding seemed to be that the stereotyped private property regime, with its broad discretion of owners to control use and exclusion was, with respect to this particular resource, wrong. In California the public seemed both to express and further this cultural shift when the Coastal Zone Conservation Act was enacted by a direct initiative ballot measure. In South Carolina the legislature declared erosion and despoliation of the coastline to be a public harm.[13]

Do we (should we) consider these judicial and legislative activities as government action that changes the property regime? Or are they mere implementation of the regime that we are already committed to? About these legal developments it does seem to me we might want to say both things at once. We might say (let us call it the positivist response) that legal rights were changed to bring them into accord with a newer, non-legal ideal view. At the same time, we might say (let us call it the non-positivist response) that because nonlegal and legal rights are inseparably intertwined, legal rights already coincided with the newer ideal view. Then legal entities acted not to change the rights but to see that they were not ignored in practice. Which response we want to affirm more strongly will make the difference in whether we see something relatively unambiguously as government action changing the scheme or relatively unambiguously as mere implementation of the scheme.

Justice Scalia saw the activities of the South Carolina legislature and the California Coastal Commission unambiguously in the positivist sense, as government action changing property rights. But in both cases the situation was at least considerably more ambiguous. The South Carolina legislature may be understood not as taking away coastal owners' rights to act in ways that lead to erosion and despoliation, but rather as recognizing a background culture of property in which these acts are not within the scope of owners' rights. Analogously, the easement that the Nollans were asked to dedicate might very well have already belonged to the public, under the California law I have sketched. If so, when the Nollans bought the property they did not acquire what they alleged the Commission deprived them of. The Commission's activity in asking for the recorded document affirming the easement could readily be seen, in context, as merely an attempt to coalesce and clarify the existing legal regime. The Commission had done the same thing for most of the other tracts along that stretch of beach. In context, the Commission could readily be seen more as enforcing than as changing the property scheme.

Among other things, Scalia's positivist view is insensitive to the idea that in South Carolina and in California the state legal regime, insofar as it is interdependent with the cultural commitments of property, may have begun to deviate, for coastal land, from the liberal ideal of full private property. Scalia's view tends to impose a general regime (i.e., a federal interpretation) of property and foreclose state deviance from it. This view appears in tension with the Court's view in an analogous earlier decision, *PruneYard v. Robins,*[14] that refused to recognize any federal regime of property rights, and in particular refused to federalize any absolute right of an owner to exclude others. In *Nollan,* Scalia was not able to take seriously the idea that California's property regime may have renounced (or at least attenuated the strength of) certain exclusion rights on the part of beach owners, and thus that the right of passage may already have belonged to the public (or may have more likely belonged to the public than not). In *Lucas,* Scalia did not even entertain the idea that cultural background principles may already have foreclosed private ownership of the rights Lucas claimed.[15] Of course, if Scalia was wrong, then his decisions, and not the actions of the Commission or the legislature, are government actions that change the state's property regime.[16]

C. Residential Tenancy Before and After

It is widely said that the law of residential tenancy has undergone a revolution. The ordinary common law property scheme of landlord and tenant was caveat tenant, and the scheme largely prevailed as little as thirty years ago. Then came the revolution.[17] Before: Tenants were entitled only to bare possession, with no warranties of habitability; tenants assumed the risk of injury caused by dangerous conditions in and around the rented premises, and landlords were not liable to them in tort; tenants had no ongoing tenure rights, and landlords could terminate tenancies for any reason or no reason, as long as they notified the tenant at the proper time; tenants had no right to prevent landlords from setting any price they wished; tenants' waivers of what legal rights they did have against landlords were fully valid; landlords had the advantage of summary eviction process and the doctrine of independent covenants, which thwarted the possibility of defending against eviction with counterclaims against the landlord; and landlords were of course free to get rid of their tenants and demolish their units or convert them to condos or business use. After: Tenants are entitled to habitable premises, and landlords are under a legal obligation to maintain habitability; landlords are fully liable to tenants in tort for injuries due to dangerous conditions both patent and latent within the dwelling, as well as for failure to protect properly against outside intruders and for intentional infliction of emotional distress; tenants have tenure rights against the landlord's attempting to terminate the tenancy for a bad reason, including various forms of prohibited discrimination as well as retaliation against the tenant for exercising legal rights; in many urban jurisdictions tenants have the benefit of rent control and landlords no longer have the right to set whatever price they wish; tenants' entitlements are largely not waivable (i.e., the revolution is more than a change in the default rules); the doctrine of independent covenants has been abolished, meaning that tenants can defend against eviction for nonpayment of rent by raising the landlord's breaches as setoffs; and in many jurisdictions there are limits on the landlord's exit.

It is obvious that the landlords have lost a lot of the "sticks" in their "bundle" and the tenants have gained a lot in theirs. Many landlords of course felt that this change, in the aggregate, or indeed specified aspects of it, amounted to a "taking" of their property. Yet landlords' "taking" claims have resoundingly failed, as we can see in *Yee* and *Pennell* and their background. But before I get to that, pause to consider how we might characterize the evolution of the landlord-tenant scheme, as I have cursorily sketched it.

Housing codes established standards of habitable housing and made it a misdemeanor to rent substandard housing. Eventually, courts found that this recognition of a standard, enforceable (if only nominally) through the criminal law, had an effect on tort and contract doctrines as well.[18] It did not make sense for a landlord to be criminally liable if the ceiling was falling down, but not liable in tort for the injuries to whoever was under it when it fell. It did not make sense to declare the landlord open to criminal prosecution for renting an uninhabitable dwelling, yet force the tenant to pay for it as if nothing were wrong with it. It did not make sense to recognize legal rights to habitable housing, yet leave all periodic tenants vulnerable to losing their homes the minute they tried to get these rights enforced. Many of these judicial developments were then written into legislation; and the next round of judicial developments relied upon coherence with that legislation.[19] The landlord-tenant revolution was not a sudden coup d'état; it gradually manifested itself through a long series of interactions between courts and legislative bodies.

Clearly there has been a marked change in the property regime for residential tenancy. But whose "action" accomplished it? Who or what did it? Do we want to think of the spread of housing codes as the government action that worked this profound change in the property regime? Even if we are inclined toward this positivist response, I don't think it can be unambiguous. It is too simplistic to think that enactment of housing codes is clearly the "action" from which all else follows. We might also think that housing codes followed and did not lead; we might think that they primarily responded to and did not create (although they symbolically helped to reinforce) a change in the culture of property toward recognition of a tenant's entitlement to minimally decent housing as a matter of natural right. Moreover, the state of our cultural commitments is complex and perhaps contradictory here. I think we should recognize that there has been a change in the culture of property toward a right to decent housing. At the same time, we have to think that the change toward such a recognition is seriously ambivalent, since there seems to be little political will to implement the kind of wealth redistribution that would make these tenants' entitlements mean much to poor tenants.[20]

Perhaps we don't want to say that the advent of housing codes was the government "action" that "caused" the revolution. Perhaps we don't want to take wholly at face value judicial decisions that say they are merely recognizing the ramifications of the existing regime, and seeking to enforce it properly in practice, rather than changing the regime. But then there is no particular decision, either judicial or legislative, that can count as "the" action that effected the revolution. For there to be a taking, first there has to be a government action, an action that takes away property rights that are rightly held. If we don't see the series of incremental shifts in the official landlord-tenant regime as a series of rules laid down, but rather as the reflection of a shift in the underlying culture of property, then it is hard to see the change as due to government action.

No one denies that the allocation of property rights between landlord and tenant has changed markedly in the tenant's favor and at the landlord's expense. So, perhaps the most interesting thing about the revolution, jurisprudentially speaking, is that, with the exception of rent control, almost none of it has even entered the arena of high constitutional argument. The Supreme Court declared in the 1970s that there is no fundamental right to housing, or to any particular quality of housing,[21] but (analogous to *PruneYard*, and not *Lucas* or *Nollan*) it found no federal right that prevented states from finding otherwise. No high court due process or takings cases review housing codes or the implied warranty of habitability or the New Jersey tenant tenure statute. A challenge to rent control failed in *Block v. Hirsch*[22] in 1921, and failed again in *Pennell v. City of San Jose*[23] in 1988.[24]

In *Pennell* the landlords apparently didn't even argue that price control per se is unconstitutional; at any rate, no one on the present Court would have taken the argument seriously. This surprises my students, and, I am sure, many landlords. An owner's freedom to set prices is an important "stick" in the bundle of property rights as liberal ideology has constituted them, and old-fashioned liberal ideologues do still argue that price control is a taking.[25] But their arguments have the ring of the *Lochner* era.[26] Without reviving *Lochner* it appears that the Justices—however some of them may sympathize with the old-fashioned ideologues—cannot regard the freedom to set prices as other than a merely economic right subject to broad regulation constrained only by the required due process inference of rationality. The ghost of *Lochner* is hence probably the main explanation why *Pennell* was only concerned with the hardship tenant provision in the San Jose rent control ordinance, staying well clear of the issue of price control in general. The hardship tenant provision permitted an administrative body the discretion to deny a landlord a rent increase it determined to be otherwise reasonable, for a specific unit, if the rent increase would cause too much hardship to a low-income tenant of that unit. Although Justice Scalia dissented, the majority of the justices held that even this part of the ordinance could not be declared unconstitutional on its face.

The classic liberal ideology that makes freedom of alienation in a laissez-faire market an absolute property right still has its cultural resonance. Yet I think it's fairly clear that, in spite of the outrage of some landlords, and for deeper reasons than fear of *Lochner,* the cultural commitments of property now disfavor freedom of price setting in many contexts, whether the object is housing or something else. Especially freedom of price setting is disfavored where that freedom would price some people out of a necessity of life.

As any economist can quickly explain, price and quality are interrelated. A landlord can exercise her freedom of profit taking, if there is such a freedom, equally by lowering quality and maintenance, or by raising the price. If it is readily accepted that there exists a right against lowering quality beyond the point of human decency, at least when the expense to landlords is only a lesser profit, it seems that we are similarly committed to a right against raising the price to a point that disrupts communities and causes homelessness, at least when the expense to landlords is only a lesser profit.

Did San Jose "act" to change property rights? Whether it acted to enact the ordinance seems unproblematic. In this case almost everyone would side with the commonsensical positivist in thinking that San Jose "acted." But what was the nature of the "action"? Did it "change" property rights? I have suggested that the issue is at least ambiguous. All I'm trying to do here is muddy the waters, because my purpose is to show how decisions about government action are connected with cultural commitments about property. Whether it acted to change property rights depends upon what property rights existed before the ordinance was enacted, and in turn to some extent upon our evaluation of the justice of the property regime, and in particular upon whether or not we think the action is one of corrective justice.

When government acts to divest someone of property rights she claims, and the rights are wrongly held at the expense of a rightful holder, the government action restoring or confirming the rights in the rightful holder does not "change," but rather "enforces," the property regime. If San Jose merely acted to bring the official property regime into line with already existing cultural commitments about the property regime of landlord and tenant, then it is harder to characterize the action as one that "changes" property rights.

I am qualifying this suggestion because a thoroughgoing positivist would claim that the official ("legal") regime exists in a robust sense, regardless of its rightness or wrongness; so acts changing wrong "property rights" into right ones are no less changes than any other kind of changes. The official ("legal") regime, for such a positivist, is completely autonomous from any culturally embedded evaluations of it. I tend to think that at bottom few of us are really such straightforward, thorough-going positivists about the autonomy of law. That is the substance of my claim about the muddiness of the waters in these cases. Evaluative commitments that judge the official ("legal") regime as unjust also tend to weaken the force of our commitment to its existence in that particular form.

To sum up what I have been saying so far, in order to evaluate government action changing property regimes, first we must see something as government action, and as action that "changes" the existing regime. These are judgments that are made largely tacitly, and seemingly as a matter of common sense; but these judgments depend upon our understanding of the existent regime. That understanding depends to some extent, in turn, both upon substantive evaluative commitments and also upon how deeply we are committed to try to ignore those commitments if we are also committed to positivism as our implicit jurisprudential theory. So judgments about government action depend in part upon an implicit jurisprudential theory. They also depend, in a way I now want to explore, on an implicit theory of politics.

II. ATTRIBUTING REASONS TO GOVERNMENTAL ACTORS
A. Attributing Actions and Reasons to Persons

I want to argue that what will be considered a taking is related not only to the "rightness" or "wrongness" of the property claims, but also the "goodness" or "badness" of government reasons, and I want to argue that the way we attribute actions and reasons to governmental entities is interdependent with our commitment (often implicit) to a political theory. I suggest that in approaching this question it will be helpful to start with how we attribute reasons for acting to individuals (persons). Famous philosophical puzzles attend the questions of exactly what is going on when we attribute reasons, motives, purposes, or intentions to actors, and indeed attend the question of what is an act (attributable to an actor). I cannot recapitulate these debates here. Rather, I will just sketch in a general way my own position, which I consider to be pragmatic and Wittgensteinian.

"What is she doing?" "Why is she doing it?" When we have occasion to ask these questions (and we are not doing philosophy), we are located within practices that characterize our form of life. Many activities associated with persons evoke standardized or stereotypical responses in us. In context, we know what it means to wink, beckon, point something out, etc. The stereotypes are what mark us as being socialized in this particular form of life. They are practically useful, indeed necessary to us, and we are justified in using them unless something about the circumstances tells us otherwise.

For example, suppose Mary is standing in her front yard with a hose in her hand, and water from the hose is spraying on the grass growing there. We see this as watering the lawn; we apprehend her intent or purpose as getting the grass to grow. Almost always this conventional response will correspond with the actor's inner state about what she is doing; that is what makes the response conventional, and makes it useful. After we see this scene, we are entitled to say, "I saw Mary watering the lawn" and "Mary intended to make her grass grow," and others will understand us and will know what kind of scene we saw.

Notwithstanding this, it is possible that the conventional or social perception of Mary's activity and her intent do not correspond to her self-perception or inner experience. It is possible that if we have the opportunity to ask Mary what she was doing and why, she will tell us something different. Some responses ("I am rinsing out the hose") we might find plausible, especially if she tells us some special circumstances that do not fit our stereotype ("Somebody poured maple syrup in it"). If so we can use them to correct our stereotypical default assessment.

On the other hand, some responses ("I am feeding the baby," "I am trying to cut the grass") might make us cast doubt upon Mary's sanity or her status as one of us. That is because we have a view of what a person is: a person uses means to act toward practically rational ends, and the person uses appropriate instrumental means to achieve those sorts of ends. These views about what a person is are implicit in the way we understand what we see persons as doing, and what we see them as intending by what they do. In other words, our perceptions about a person's actions and the reasons for that action are connected with a theory about what a (sane, well-socialized, ordinary, typical) person is. Two aspects of that general theory of the person interest me here: a theory that judges what is reasonable for persons to want to accomplish, and a theory of instrumental rationality that judges what means are suited to bring about whatever it is the person wants.

B. Attributing Actions and Reasons to Entities That Are Not Persons But Are Composed of Persons

I want to suggest that we attribute actions and reasons to certain kinds of nonpersons in an analogous stereotypical way. We have an implicit theory of what the nonperson is, or what its function is. We use that theory to impute reasonable goals to the nonperson, and then couple that with an imputation of instrumental rationality in trying to achieve those goals. (I think the nonpersonal entities we attribute actions and reasons to in this way have to be limited to those composed of persons in some way, because I don't think my suggestion holds for attributing actions to rocks. But I'll exclude from consideration here the issue of what sorts of entities we attribute actions and reasons to, as well as the issue of why our theories of such entities are more various and contested than our theory of the person.)

To see how we attribute actions and reasons to an entity, consider business entities. If a business entity cuts its prices, what is it trying to do? A prevalent implicit theory about business entities is that they are profit-maximizing black boxes. If that is the theory we accept, then we will normally impute only one "intent" to a business entity, the goal of maximizing profits, and we will see the entity as engaging in activities that we regard as suitable instrumental means for maximizing profits. An entity that cuts its prices will be seen as engaging in predatory pricing, or it will be seen as engaging in keeping itself in business by adjusting its prices to the realities of demand. It will not be seen as attempting to liquidate itself. It will not be seen as trying to help the poor community, unless, perhaps, we are told that there are special circumstances such that if the poor community ceases to be viable, then the entity will have to go out of business.

C. Legislative Intent

Legislative intent has been as famous a morass in jurisprudence as personal intent has been in philosophy of mind and action. Theories that posit a group mind have been well debunked, and so have theories that suggest we hunt for some aggregation of the subjective intentions as experienced by the individual legislators.[27] I think the pragmatic view of actions and motives that I have sketched can suggest a more attractive alternative, a commonsense view of legislative intent that is the one that most lawyers and judges implicitly accept.

When we are characterizing the actions and intents of a legislative entity, I think that we treat it as we do the business entity, not as a group but as an abstract nonpersonal unit. In order to see how and why this nonpersonal unit acts, we need to understand what goals it would be appropriate or reasonable for such a unit to have, and see whether its activities are instrumentally rational in light of those goals. For example, in a case familiar to thousands of law students,[28] a court observed that Congress over a period of twenty years had always rejected amendments to the Interstate Commerce Act that would increase regulation of farmers and had always accepted amendments that would increase farmers' exemption from regulation; and the court further observed that these exemptions saved farmers money. Using an implicit theory of the person in which it is considered beneficial to save money, and using an implicit theory of Congress that treated it as an abstract unit (ignoring, for example, that the membership had changed over the years in question), the court inferred that the intention of Congress was to benefit farmers.

How do we decide what goals it is appropriate or reasonable for a legislative unit to have? Just as an implicit theory of personhood enables us to see what persons do as actions with particular purposes, so an implicit theory of what a legislature is enables us to see what legislatures do as actions with particular purposes. In other words, we see legislative activity in light of our implicit political theory, in our case a theory of democracy.

It further seems that our use of an implicit theory of democracy usually has a salient normative aspect. That is, mostly we interpret legislatures by and large as doing what (by our lights) they should do, and mostly for the motives that (by our lights) they should have. Just as we don't assume in the ordinary course of events (absent special circumstances) that a person is trying to kill herself, hurt herself, or decrease her own welfare, we don't, under any political theory, easily impute suicidal or egregiously immoral motives to a democratic legislature. We don't impute the motives of subverting national security, wasting the taxpayers' money, or fomenting war or domestic discontent. Most of the time we don't impute the motive of subverting the separation of powers, for example by enacting an unconstitutional statute.

Moreover, we don't impute the motive that the legislators mean to line their own (or their supporters') pockets.[29] It could well be in any given instance that the reason a bill passed, in the sense of but-for causation, is that various legislators owed political favors to its sponsor. It could be, if asked what they intended to accomplish in passing the bill, and assuming that they had taken a truth serum, that these legislators would answer, "I intended to pay off my political debt." Nevertheless, when we are looking for "legislative intent" we will not seek such evidence, and if we do find out about it we will likely view it as irrelevant.

We will impute intent instead by asking what a more nearly ideal legislature (whatever our ideal may be) would reasonably have been trying to do by passing that particular bill. We will do this by combining our judgments about instrumental rationality with our judgments about reasonable goals, just as we do when we perceive that Mary is watering her lawn, and intends to make her grass grow. In Mary's case, we know something about the needs of plants and what kind of plant grass is, so that it is instrumentally rational to try to make it grow by giving it water, and we know something about how in our culture people with lawns like to keep their grass, so that it makes sense to assume that Mary wants it to grow. In the case of the bill, we (under whatever political theory we hold) "know" something about the needs of the polity, and we also know that legislatures "intend" to serve the needs of the polity, so we look for the most obvious of those needs that can be seen as the end for which the bill can be seen as a rational means. We know that legislatures "intend" to serve the needs of the polity because that is what our theory of democracy tells us they are *for*. Moreover, this attribution of appropriate intent is reinforced (if we are judges) by the aspect of our traditional theory of democracy—the separation of powers—that tells us not to question the activities of legislative entities unless something about the situation forces us to.

D. What Triggers Displacement of Default Assumptions?

Usually we displace our stereotypes or default assumptions when the facts turn out to be other than typical. It could turn out, when we see Mary's life in its narrative context, that she needs to rinse out her hose; or, less likely, it *could* turn out that grass is not the sort of plant we thought it was or not a plant at all. We also displace our default assumptions by deciding that the person is other than typical. It could turn out that we can't link what Mary says she's doing with the activity as we see it, or that the activity as we see it doesn't further any goals that are reasonable for the person as we have constructed personhood; in which case, we'll decide that Mary has a screw loose.

I suggest there might be analogous conventional ways for displacing our default assumptions about the activities of a governmental entity. It might be the case that when taken in the narrative context of the particular polity the entity's action should not be seen in the stereotypical way. Or it might be the case that the governmental entity has a screw loose. It could have a screw loose, in our view, either if it is not acting with instrumental rationality, or if it is not acting in the way that our theory of democracy posits for that sort of entity. It will be easy, I hope, for the reader to link up what I have said so far with the conventional doctrinal metaphors of scrutiny. The deferential rhetoric of "rational basis" tests corresponds to use of our default assumptions, and the rhetoric of "heightened scrutiny" corresponds to the displacement of those assumptions for some reason. What kind of reasons jolt us out of our default assumptions?

Three main kinds of circumstances tend to displace our conventional acceptance of the ordinary day-to-day activities of governmental entities. First, we tend to think the entity has a screw loose if the activity looks instrumentally goofy with respect to ordinary goals we think proper for it. Without a special story the activity may be judged "irrational," or we may decide that its stated goals are merely a cover for its "real" goals, which we find are illicit. Second, we also tend to think the entity has a screw loose if the activity seems obviously to go against our theory of democracy (for example, by failing to respect fundamental rights or equal treatment of persons). In this case we need a special story ("compelling" or overriding interest under "heightened scrutiny") in order to save our assumptions about the nature of the entity (i.e., that it is an appropriate democratic governing body). For similar reasons, we also look for a special story to explain/justify the action if the immediate or long-range narrative context shows that we should not take the activity at face value (for example, when facially neutral regulations in context can be seen to be aimed at specific disfavored groups). These are the types of circumstances in which we require a special story in order to understand the action attributed to the government as appropriate. In the next section I want to go back to my property regime examples and see what can be said about when we see a governmental entity as having a screw loose.

III. Evaluating Governmental Actions with Respect to Property Regimes
A. Relationship to Trends in Political Theory

One traditional view of democracy is that government acts in the public interest—for the benefit of the polity as a whole. In such a political theory, the default position is that a legislature or other governmental entity is behaving properly. That is, we assume that the government is acting for the polity, as democratic theory says it should, unless a special story (for example, bribery or corruption) jolts us out of this assumption. But there is considerable pressure placed upon such a default position if the prevalent political theory changes to a vaguely Hobbesian public choice variety.[30] In such a Hobbesian theory, governmental entities (as well as individuals) are pictured as selfish profit-maximizers, or as aggregates of logrolling maximizers of interest-group satisfaction. The way governmental entities "ought" (i.e., are expected) to behave is that they will "naturally" try to overreach or cheat.

If a judge holds this type of Hobbesian theory, she expects government entities routinely to try to "take" property to see if they can get away with it. Just as in the analogous theory of the person, not paying is to be preferred to paying, and whatever means seem efficacious will be used to avoid paying. Such a judge may conceive her role as requiring her to be ever on the lookout for this kind of manipulation. She may likewise view her role as requiring her to deal harshly with it when it is discovered, in order to deter as much of it as possible (though her theory tells her it can never really be repressed). Such a judge will find a tension between her view of what governmental entities do and the doctrines that tell her to keep her judicial hands off except in cases that stand out as egregious. If enough judges hold these Hobbesian views, we can predict that these doctrines will begin to give way.[31] Deference will become judicial activism if the general pressure to view governmental activities with suspicion becomes strong enough to overcome the traditional positivist rhetoric that casts the judge as a passive implementation tool.

I believe something like the scenario I have been sketching underlies the posture of at least Justice Scalia, and on occasion Justice Rehnquist, in constitutional property cases.[32] It explains the short shrift given to the need for local government flexibility in *First Evangelical Lutheran Church*,[33] for example. (That case found mere invalidation of a regulation of property to be a constitutionally inadequate remedy and required governmental entities to pay damages dating from the time of their action in the event the courts later decide that the entity's action amounted to a taking.) To the protest that the majority's result will chill and deter local governments from acting with respect to property regulation, Justice Rehnquist would no doubt reply that that's the point.

One might also speculate that the result in *Agins v. City of Tiburon*[34] would have been different if the Hobbesian trend had taken hold at the time it was decided. In that case, Tiburon had originally brought condemnation proceedings against the property in question, but dropped them and accomplished preservation of open space by means of stringent zoning regulation instead. A Hobbesian judge would readily see this activity as meaning that Tiburon "knew" that the property rights in question could only rightfully be acquired by paying for them, but "intended" to try first to get them for free. (Of course, for one less Hobbesian in outlook, it could just as well be that Tiburon "realized" that it would not be "going too far" to regulate the Aginses' expected use in this way, and therefore "intended" by regulating without paying for the rights to avoid a windfall gain to the Aginses at the community's expense.)

B. Looking for a Nexus

It seems to me that the aberrational nexus test introduced into takings law by Justice Scalia's opinion in *Nollan* can be understood in terms of this tension between traditional doctrine and the public choice style of interpretation of the activities of governmental entities. Justice Scalia was very mistrustful of the Coastal Commission. It was possible, as I suggested earlier, to see the legal entitlements as at least ambiguous. It was possible to see the Commission as mediating in good faith between the desires of individuals to own beachfront private homes and the already present cultural commitments about preservation of the resource and public access. No one denied that the Commission could constitutionally have denied the building permit outright in order to prevent any increase in density of coastal construction. Instead it granted the permit on condition that the Nollans confirm the existence of the lateral public access easement. It had done the same thing for most of the houses on that beach.

Instead of seeing the Commission as acting presumptively properly under an old-fashioned public interest theory, Justice Scalia was looking for the overreaching and extortion we expect under the public choice theory. Unless you show him a special story, in the form of an "essential nexus" between the imposition of the easement and the purposes that would have been served by denying the permit outright, he is predisposed to see the Commission's action as "an out-and-out plan of extortion."[35] As he makes clear in a footnote, if we don't deter governmental entities from conditional regulatory activities that are more lenient than permissible outright prohibitions, we can expect to see a public choice nightmare: "leveraging of the police power" by creating a regime of "stringent land-use regulation which the State then waives to accomplish other purposes."[36]

Justice Scalia's reasoning in *Nollan* shows how the "nexus" test is related to inference of legislative intent. The argument takes the form of a standard syllogism:

> *Major premise:* If granting the permit on condition that the easement be dedicated fails to implement the legitimate purpose that would have been served by denying the permit outright, then the government's motive becomes one of illegitimate extortion.
>
> *Minor premise:* Granting the permit on condition that the easement be dedicated fails to implement the legitimate purpose that would have been served by denying the permit outright.
>
> *Conclusion:* Therefore, the government's motive is illegitimate extortion.

The major premise of this syllogism reflects the pragmatic theory I have sketched about how lawyers and judges infer governmental purpose. Scalia is willing to presume that denying the permit outright, if that is what the Commission chose to do, would have been for the legitimate purpose of preserving the public's view of the beach. But if granting the permit on condition that a lateral easement be dedicated looks instrumentally goofy with respect to this purpose, Scalia now changes his view of what the Commission's motive is; that is why he says the motive "becomes" one of illegitimate extortion. (What should change in light of perceived means/ends failure, says Scalia, is our inference about what the government's motive is.)[37]

There are special circumstances, of course, in which even a vaguely public interest traditionalist would indeed see such extortion. For example, if a governmental entity conditioned its grant of a low-cost housing development permit upon the developer's voluntary commitment to pay for redecorating the governor's mansion, the traditionalist would probably see the entity as behaving improperly (having a screw loose in terms of our implicit democratic theory). It appears in some sense that the decision to impose the costs of redecorating the governor's mansion on someone who seeks a development permit is not appropriately democratically arrived at; perhaps because it's akin to a bill of attainder, perhaps because it's not properly debated on its own merits, or not evaluated independently for its costs.[38] But seeing conditions as extortion is not the traditional default position.

Justice Scalia's greater willingness to see extortion where those who hold a more traditional implicit theory see ordinary give-and-take is shown by the way he apprehended the purpose (or public interest) that would have been served by the admittedly constitutional outright ban on further beachfront development. The Commission suggested that some of the reasons it could have denied the permit included protecting the public's ability to see the beach, breaking down the "psychological barrier" imposed by dense beachfront development, and preventing congestion on the public beaches.[39] In spite of the Commission's views of its own purposes, Scalia seized on "protect[ing] the public's view of the beach"[40] as the sole purpose he was willing to attribute to the Commission. He then decided that the lateral access easement had nothing to do with the view, so must fit into the extortion category.

In *Lucas* Justice Scalia maintains his mistrustful stance. He goes so far as to hold that what a state legislature says it is doing—in this case, preventing harm to the public—may not be taken at face value.[41] For Scalia, when one sees government regulation as leaving the owner "without economically beneficial or productive options"—which "typically" occurs when the government requires land to be "left substantially in its natural state"—we should mistrust the government's motive. For Scalia this kind of regulation signifies "heightened risk that private property is being pressed into some form of public service under the guise of mitigating serious public harm."[42] Thus, legislatures are foreclosed from declaring the state of the background principles delineating property rights; only the courts may do that, it seems, primarily through their decisions in nuisance cases.[43]

I have suggested that imputation of intent or purpose to governmental entities is analogous to imputation of intent or purpose to persons. Consider *Nollan*. If we knew that a person had the duty of regulating shorefront development to preserve public access, both visual and physical, and to prevent degradation of the resource by overdevelopment, what would we think the person intended to accomplish by repeatedly demanding of those who wished to build that lateral access be confirmed if development was to become more dense? We would probably think, under our ordinary implicit view of persons, that the person intended to make up for the detrimental effect of the private houses by facilitating travel along the public shoreline—by owners like the Nollans as well as everyone else—in spite of the density of private houses.[44]

Justice Brennan's dissenting opinion characterized the Commission's purpose as we would such a person's.[45] His perception has the ring of common sense, I think, for most of us who have not become public choice theorists. Once the purpose is seen that way, it has no trouble passing the nexus test, which is just another way of saying that nothing about the entity's action sticks out like a sore thumb and makes us infer or suspect that the entity has (in terms of democratic theory) a screw loose.

C. Reevaluating Rationality

Suppose we hold a straightforward economic theory of politics. What the government is supposed to do is act to maximize general welfare; that is what legitimates its restraint of us. (Some would equate this with a mandate to act to forestall us from being frustrated—by market failure, transaction costs, rent seeking, or whatever—in our own attempts to maximize welfare.)[46] If we hold this theory, how will we view instrumental rationality? A governmental entity that enacts something whose consequences we believe cannot possibly be welfare-maximizing will be seen to have a screw loose, in the sense that the action will be seen as instrumentally irrational: enacting *this* is simply not consistent with the theoretically posited normative end of maximizing welfare.

Many who hold this economic theory of politics, either implicitly or explicitly, are also Hobbesians. Hence we can put the economic normative view (what the government is supposed to do is act to maximize general welfare) together with what I have just been saying about the Hobbesian view of governmental action (governmental entities should be expected routinely to betray general welfare for the gain of special interests). Then, when enacting *this* is seen as economically irrational, enacting *this* therefore must be (just as we expected) an instance of cheating, overreaching, or rent seeking.

Rent control now becomes an interesting question. One would expect that there is internal pressure on judges with these kinds of views to find that rent control fails the rational basis test. It seems to be (to my mind rather simplistic) gospel among economists that rent control is always and necessarily counterproductive when it comes to welfare-maximizing. For the economically minded judge, nothing more is needed to see rent control as irrational with respect to the achievement of the government's legitimate goal. Thus, I am not surprised that Judge Kozinski, writing for the Ninth Circuit, cast doubt on "[t]he rationality of rent control *vel non.*"[47]

What is surprising, perhaps, is that Justice Scalia has so far been so measured about it. In *Pennell* Justice Scalia boldly suggested that any regulation diminishing an owner's "bundle of sticks" is a taking unless there is "a cause-and-effect relationship between the property use restricted by the regulation and the social evil that the regulation seeks to remedy."[48] But he went on to treat rent control very gingerly:

> The same cause-and-effect relationship is popularly thought to justify emergency price regulation: When commodities have been priced at a level that produces exorbitant returns, the owners of those commodities can be viewed as responsible for the economic hardship that occurs. Whether or not that is an accurate perception of the way a free-market economy operates, it is at least true that the owners reap unique benefits from the situation that produces the economic hardship, and in that respect singling them out to relieve it may not be regarded as 'unfair.' That justification might apply to the rent regulation in the present case, apart from the single feature under attack here.[49]

Perhaps this delicate treatment is mostly explained, as I suggested above, by the ghost of *Lochner*. The need for the delicate treatment—the delicacy of the position in which Justice Scalia finds himself—is created by his implicit public choice view of the activity of governmental entities.

The "cause-and-effect" test Scalia tries to introduce here is very similar to the "nexus" test he introduced in *Nollan,* and he deploys it for the same reason. We should expect that governmental entities will always be trying to achieve wealth transfers for favored groups without going through the democratically mandated long cut of openly debating and weighing them in the taxing and spending process. Our suspicions about this can be allayed in cases where we see a special story: those who bear the burden of the regulation are the "cause" of some social evil, and the regulation will operate to ameliorate the social evil. "Once such a connection is no longer required, however, there is no end to the social transformations that can be accomplished by so-called 'regulation,' at great expense to the democratic process."[50]

Justice Scalia wants such a special story to be required in *all* regulatory takings cases; otherwise we should presume that the legislative body has a screw loose (is acting contrary to democracy). Justice Scalia's inclination toward "heightened scrutiny" in takings cases has, I would therefore hypothesize, nothing to do with the imposition of conditions that happened to be the focus in *Nollan*, and everything to do with his general theory of what a governmental entity is and how it can be expected to behave when it is behaving "naturally."[51]

Justice Scalia went on to decide in *Pennell* that San Jose's hardship tenant provision violated this cause-and-effect test: the neediness of the particular hardship tenants could not possibly have been caused by the particular landlords in whose buildings they happened to reside. But in order to validate rent control in general under his test, Scalia had to say that landlords "can plausibly be regarded as the source or the beneficiary of the high-rent problem," and he had to say as well, or at least imply, that rent control can plausibly have the consequence of alleviating the problem.[52] In light of what he has allowed us to know of his views, I don't think he did this with a straight face. How long can the evanescent fog of *Lochner*'s ghost keep the mind in tension and hold back economic "rationality"?

Now I can offer a speculation; take it for what it's worth. As I said earlier, in the economic view price control is substantively no different from quality control or other nonprice restraints on the decisions of owners who market their commodities. But *Lochner*'s ghost, because of its contractual aura, holds more sway over price control than over nonprice restraints. So if I am right about the tension between traditional doctrines of judicial review and the Hobbesian view of governmental action, we should expect to see constitutional challenges to nonprice restraints on property owners becoming more viable.

In particular, the economic view holds that the consequences of the nonwaivable implied warranty of habitability, as well as the other nonwaivable tenant entitlements such as those involving tenure, are as counterproductive and "irrational" as rent control. By now the implied warranty of habitability is a well-entrenched part of the legal landscape, and landlords when they purchase their property will be expected (by positivistic economists) to have taken it into account and thus probably to have no "property" expectation that it be overturned. But governmental entities that attempt to implement tenants' entitlements not previously unambiguously inscribed in the official "legal" regime (for example, the right to tenure during good behavior) may well face a constitutional challenge that will be taken seriously. A strong coalition may develop between old-style conservatives who unabashedly find freedom of alienation in a laissez-faire market to be a fundamental natural right and new-style Hobbesians who find that the judge's role is to be ever-vigilant against the natural rent-seeking behavior of governmental entities.

IV. CONCLUSION

As we can see most readily in cases like *Lucas* and *Nollan,* whether a governmental entity will be seen to have "taken" someone's property depends very much both on whether the person is seen to hold the property right at all, or to hold it rightfully, and whether the governmental entity can be seen to have behaved instrumentally rationally with respect to the ends our theory of democracy holds that it should appropriately have. Our traditional theories of what governmental entities are doing have been vaguely of the public interest variety; and this implicit theoretical commitment correlates with the traditional view of the judicial role. But economics and public choice theory may change that. For someone whose theory of democracy holds both that government ought to maximize welfare *and* that it ought to be expected routinely to subvert its own supposed ends, judicial activism—regarding almost all governmental actions with skepticism—seems to be required. Of course, such judges have yet to face the full implications of the idea that their own activities, as individuals and as governmental actors, should also be interpreted as rent-seeking.

SEVEN

The Rhetoric of Alienation

I want to muse on some wordplay in property theory, wordplay that I think is also very serious. This wordplay has not often been noticed in the ordinary discourse of legal academics, who do not often (at least professionally) puzzle over interesting twists of rhetoric. Yet the rhetoric of property—the shared discourse of property—is deeply implicated in how we construct ourselves and our world. I shall begin by drawing out some implications of two puns or double entendres in the rhetoric of property. One is a double meaning of the word "property" itself; the other is a double meaning of the word "alienation." They can both be encapsulated in this question: If property is a property of persons, does alienation reflect alienation? After that I shall consider the double meaning of my title—the rhetoric of alienation.

I. DOUBLE MEANINGS
A. Object-Property and Attribute-Property

In the legal and moral discourse of private property—that is, when we are speaking of property law or of the justification of property—the word property is always identified with something owned, an object of ownership. Property refers to an owned object ("this book is my property") or to rights and duties of persons with respect to control of owned objects ("to exclude you from my land is one of my property rights"). This meaning of property I shall call the "owned object" aspect, or the "object" aspect for short, and sometimes refer to it as "object-property." This meaning of property is entrenched in ordinary language. In fact, I once encountered a first-year law student who said that property is inherent in the object, by which I understood him to mean that the fact that an object is private property is independent of the minds, relationships, or institutions of human beings. (Surely an extreme "objective" view!)

The second meaning of the word "property" is not found in the legal and moral discourse of private property, but rather in other philosophical discourses such as metaphysics and the philosophies of mind, language, and personhood. Here property means an attribute: of a thing, concept, argument, person, etc. Whatever are the appropriate attributes that characterize or constitute X are the properties of X. ("In one view of semantics, the meaning of a word is described as a conjunction of properties." "Self-consciousness and autonomy are properties of personhood.") This meaning of property I shall call the "attribute" aspect, and sometimes refer to it as "attribute-property."

The thrust of my musings will be that in the ideology of private property and free contract the two meanings coexist in deep tension because they correlate with opposing views of personhood. Object-property correlates with an object-fungibility thesis underlying commodification and market freedom. Attribute-property correlates with a personal-continuity thesis underlying stable expectations needed for self-constitution.

B. Contract-Alienation and Estrangement-Alienation

In traditional legal and moral discourse about property, the word "alienation" means "transfer." Alienability of property rights, or freedom of alienation with respect to property, is one of the most important indicia of liberal (capitalist) private property. The infrastructure of the free market is a system of private entitlement linked to a system of private transferability: private property plus free contract. Freedom of alienation of property rights expresses the "free contract" part of this nexus. The market theorist argues both that in order for private property to be complete or well developed it must be freely alienable and that in order for free contract to flourish there must be a well-developed system of private entitlements. Everything must be both ownable and salable. In the free-market system, at least, alienation is constitutive of the system and a good to be pursued. This meaning of alienation I shall call the "free-contract" aspect, and sometimes refer to it as "contract-alienation."

The other meaning of alienation refers to a pathology to be avoided. It is more familiar to users of ordinary language. Alienation in this sense means estrangement, painful or hostile isolation of the self, a feeling of being cut off or ostracized from one's appropriate social environment, a psychological malaise caused by lack of commitment or loss of meaning in life. The concept of alienated labor developed by the early Marx is related to this pathological meaning of the word alienation.[1] Under capitalism, workers sell their labor to create fungible market objects with which the workers have no further connection. The workers are alienated from their material environment, from the objects of their creation, and from themselves viewed as laboring commodities. This meaning of alienation I shall call the "estrangement" aspect, and sometimes refer to it as "estrangement-alienation."

C. Linkage

Contract-alienation is linked to object-property. Alienation is accomplished when an owned object is transferred from one holder to another. Estrangement-alienation is linked to attribute-property. Alienation comes about when attributes of personhood are sundered. Contract-alienation and estrangement-alienation are linked by the general notion of separation. In the free-contract aspect of alienation, a separation of an entitlement, and hence a property object, from its holder takes place when it is transferred to another holder. The separation is viewed as constitutive or expressive of the market system. By market adherents it is viewed as an exercise of liberty. In the estrangement aspect of alienation, the separation of the person from her proper physical or social environment, or from her creations, is pathological and harmful to the person, and signifies unfreedom rather than freedom.

In English, at least, the two meanings of alienation can be linked in an ironic pun about capitalist private property.[2] The workers alienate their labor—in both senses—to create alienable objects for the market. The objects are alienated—in both senses—by and from the various market actors who deal with them. This is one way to understand the fetishism of commodities described by Marx in a famous passage in *Capital*:

> A commodity is therefore a mysterious thing, simply because in it the social character of men's labour appears to them as an objective character stamped upon the product of that labour; because the relation of the producers to the sum total of their own labour is presented to them as a social relation, existing not between themselves, but between the products of their labour.
>
> . . . Since the producers do not come into social contact with each other until they exchange their products . . . the labour of the individual asserts itself as a part of the labour of society, only by means of the relations which the act of exchange establishes directly between the products, and indirectly, through them, between the producers.[3]

In the traditional liberal ideology of property, the two meanings of the word property are also sometimes linked. If private property is necessary for autonomy or liberty, and autonomy or liberty is a necessary attribute of persons, then property (object-aspect) is a property (attribute-aspect) of persons. The link is shown, for example, in Locke's use of "the general name, *Property*," to refer to people's "Lives, Liberties and Estates."[4] For us, life and liberty are attribute-properties of persons and estates are object-properties, but for Locke (given that estates originally referred to status, not mere landholding) there was probably not this clear distinction. Now if we hold fast to the traditional theory that property is a property of persons, and at the same time accept the modern distinction between object-property and attribute-property, the lurking pun can also cause dissonance and paradox. When property is a property of persons, my liberty is my property. Does this mean I abdicate personhood if my liberty is voluntarily relinquished? Apparently yes, if property means attribute-property. But if at the same time property also means object-property, then voluntarily relinquishing my liberty is also an instance of contract-alienation, and in traditional liberal ideology this is an instance of self-expression and fulfillment of personhood rather than its negation. Abdication of liberty is both destructive of personhood and expressive of it. The pun is the surface manifestation of a deep fissure in liberal ideology.[5]

II. RHETORICAL TROUBLE AND THE SUBJECT-OBJECT DICHOTOMY

It is particularly the German "will" or "personality" theory of property that runs into difficulty on this kind of question, because of its ambivalent position on the subject/object dichotomy. The difficulty comes from stressing a link between object-property and attribute-property (persons need object-property in order to exist as persons; property is a property of persons), while at the same time trying to uphold the ideology of alienation or free contract. Hence, this difficulty is where the ambiguities of "property" and "alienation" meet. It is appropriate to characterize the difficulty as involving the subject/object dichotomy, as we shall see, because the "object" meaning of property and the "free-contract" meaning of alienation assume that there is a bright line between subjects (persons) and objects (property), while the "attribute" meaning of property and the "estrangement" meaning of alienation undermine the notion of such a natural divide between persons and objects.[6]

In order to explicate this, let me briefly recall Hegel's property theory as an example of this rhetorical difficulty. Hegel held that private property is necessary to realize or actualize the will of a person, which is necessary for freedom and concrete personhood.[7] Thus property in objects is necessary for well-developed personhood, and property-holding becomes an attribute of persons. Hegel thought alienability of property to follow easily from the premise that it is the presence of a person's will that makes an object her property; take away the will and property ceases.

> The reason I can alienate my property is that it is mine only insofar as I put my will into it. Hence I may abandon . . . anything that I have or yield it to the will of another . . . , provided always that the thing in question is a thing external by nature.[8]

The presence of the will makes an object into (object-)property, but first the object must truly be an object. That is the import of the proviso that the thing in question must be "a thing external by nature." It follows that whatever is mine but is not "a thing external by nature" is an inalienable attribute of personhood. These inalienable attributes include, for Hegel, the "goods, or rather substantive characteristics" that constitute personality itself and the essence of self-consciousness.[9] Hegel considered forbidden alienation of the personality itself to include slavery, serfdom, disqualification from holding property, encumbrances on property, "and so forth."[10] Transferring to someone else full power to direct one's actions or to prescribe duties of conscience or religious truth, "etc.," would be forbidden alienation of intelligence, rationality, morality, religion.[11] All of these are presumably substantive characteristics of personhood (hence attribute-properties) and not things external by nature.

Thus in order to tell the difference between attribute-properties (permanently inside the person) and alienable property (external by nature) we need to be able to draw clearly the distinction between things external by nature and substantive constitutive elements of personality. This external/substantive distinction is just the subject/object dichotomy. For Kant and Hegel the distinction between persons and things, or subjects and objects, seemed natural and obvious. Yet Hegel himself undermined it in his property theory.

To see why, consider the dynamic nature of Hegel's theory. Objects go from things in themselves to bearers of a person's will, and the person's will goes from abstract to actual through embodiment in the object. According to Hegel the essence of private property ("the true and right factor in possession")[12] is just that it is necessary to embody the will and actualize personality. Hence objects may start out external but they do not remain so; they become constitutive of well-developed personality. The distinction between objects and persons becomes blurred. So too must the distinction between attribute-properties and object-properties.

Now it seems as though if personality is inalienable, so may be property once personality is constituted through it. But Hegel's argument is instead that any inalienability of property would itself be a violation of inalienable personality. Why? One reading is that when it comes to contract-alienation he is reverting to a pure subject/object view. Yet if we accept the blurring between subject and object—between attribute-property and object-property—that lies buried in Hegel's property theory, this view of contract-alienation contains the core of estrangement-alienation. If we take seriously the view that property can bridge the gap (or blur the distinction) between the person and the environment of objects, that personhood can be bound up with objects in the environment in a constitutive sense, then to affirm at the same time the free-market view of alienation that assumes all objects are fungible through exchange value is indeed to countenance painful separation and harm to personality.

The tension arises because Hegel seems to be more of a market theorist in his view of alienation than in his view of property. In fact, in his contract theory he says that "the concept" (that is, the Idea or Spirit or universal reason) *compels* alienation of external objects qua property.[13] At the same time, Hegel's property theory is compatible with a nonmarket view of object-relations, since it is based upon embodiment of the will in objects and not upon trade. It is unclear why reason or the concept would compel trade, just as it is unclear why any inalienability of property rights would violate personality. Rather one would expect that any object-property that had bridged the gap and become significantly like the core attribute-properties would thereby become inalienable, because no longer wholly "external," or at least cease to be presumptively alienable.

III. DISAGGREGATION

Now let me bring this discussion back to the present. The double meanings of property and alienation have uncovered a tension or contradiction at the heart of liberal property theory as it is still practiced. The ideology of property as it has come down to us affirms what I would call a personal-continuity thesis: that property is necessary to give people "roots," stable surroundings, a context of control over the environment, a context of stable expectations that fosters autonomy and personality. Property is a property of persons; and this understanding of property is held to be necessary for human freedom. Yet at the same time, the ideology of contract (free trade) affirms what I would call an object-fungibility thesis: that the value to persons of all property objects is measured only by their exchange potential with other objects, that all objects must be free to be traded about, and that the context of persons should constantly be rearranging itself in response to market forces. This understanding of free-contract-alienation is held to be necessary for autonomy and freedom. But if property is a property of persons, then alienation of property breeds alienation of persons. If the person-object bond is broken, the stable context destroyed or prevented from forming, the basis of plans and memories ignored or smashed, then the autonomy of freedom of contract can be merely a sign of the estrangement of persons.

One way to try to resolve this tension or mediate the paradox at the heart of liberal property ideology is to disaggregate property.[14] That is, perhaps we could recognize that some categories of property rights do justifiably become bound up with persons and then ought not be prima facie subject to rearrangement by market forces, while at the same time recognizing that other categories of property rights do not, or do not justifiably, become bound up with persons and are appropriately left to market forces. In other words, we could delineate categories in which the distinction between object-properties and attribute-properties justifiably becomes blurred. This is a strategy that I and others have pursued.[15] I have called the first kind "personal" property, and the second kind "fungible."

This strategy has a number of important results. For one thing, it has the result that persons have stronger claims to retain some objects than do corporations. Condemnation with compensation at fair market value can place a corporation in as good a wealth position as it was before, whereas to a person the money might be meaningless as a replacement for the valued object, or even an insult. Forced sale is not an injury to corporationhood where the corporation's wealth position is held constant, because a corporation is defined as a wealth-maximizing entity.

Forced sale is sometimes (but not always) an injury to personhood. It is not an injury to personhood where the person is appropriately thought of as a wealth-maximizing entity holding fungible property, but it is an injury to personhood where personal property, taking on the attribute-aspect, is involved.

Another result, then, is that objects held by persons for purposes of wealth gain through market trading are to be thought of differently from objects held as integral to personal continuity. For example, it would be prima facie fair for the government to confiscate a fungible object worth ten dollars on the market if it would be fair for the government to tax the holder ten dollars; but it would not be prima facie fair to take a personal object whose exchange value was also ten dollars, even if the holder were paid the ten dollars. Wedding rings are not the same kind of property as widgets.

A third important result of the disaggregation strategy, at least as I have pursued it, is that there is a normative element in recognizing some property to be personal in the sense of partaking of the attribute as well as object senses of the word. The claim of the holder is not just that her personal continuity is bound up with the object, but that it is justifiably so. Thus a theory of the good or well-developed person, or a concept of human flourishing, is required to tell when objects are appropriately treated as personal. I have not yet tried to lay out the ramifications of a concept of human flourishing for all manner of person-object relations. But it is nevertheless possible to argue piecemeal for a few positions that seem clear. "The compleat capitalist," someone who claims to be personally bound up with a vast empire of property that she uses to dominate other people, is not justifiably bound up with her property, because she has embraced what we can recognize as an inferior concept of human flourishing. On the other hand, it seems that attachments to one's home, whether as an owner or as a tenant, are justifiable.

A fourth important result of the disaggregation strategy is that the grammar of contract-alienation must be modified for personal property. We should not presume that such items are replaceable by fair market value. We should also not presume that a holder's attempt to market such an item expresses autonomy and not coercion.[16] Some items of personal property (or, some personal properties) perhaps ought not to be salable by anyone, because this would degrade the social world for everyone. The strongest argument for noncommodification of sexuality may be that we do not wish to unleash market forces onto the shaping of our discourse regarding sexuality and hence our very conception of sexuality and our sexual feelings. On the other hand, with some kinds of personal objects, perhaps most of them, it seems easy to countenance both selling and sharing, as the holder may choose. Yet there is at least a change in how we view such sales, amounting to a shift of presuppositions or presumptions about them. Trade of items that are usually personal (and may justifiably be personal) requires stricter scrutiny for coercion. If we see someone trade something personal as if it were fungible, and have no other information, we may assume, as ordinary moral observers, that the trade is coerced.

IV. ALIENATION AND MARKET RHETORIC

Now I would like to return to the double meaning of the title of this essay and ask: Is the rhetoric of contract-alienation also the rhetoric of estrangement-alienation? Here I want to consider rhetoric specifically, apart from actual markets. Could it be alienating to conceive of events, desires, interactions, and feelings in market rhetoric even if no resources are actually bought and sold?

The extreme enthusiasts of law and economics treat the human world as one giant market. (For that reason I call them universal commodifiers.) Every object that people need or desire, either individually or in groups, is potentially a good or commodity. This includes, for example, leisure time, family life, safe working conditions, a healthful environment, and the coordination and management functions of government. Whatever some people are willing to buy and others are willing to sell (i.e., where demand and supply exist for a scarce "good") should be subject to free market exchange. The only exceptions are for market failure; that is, where free-market results for some reason cannot be achieved through free-market means. These are exceptions that prove the market rule.

Moreover, where people are not willing to buy and sell something, nor even to characterize it as a scarce good—babies, for example—the universal commodifier offers an explanation in market rhetoric to explain why not. (For example, the marginal benefit of these "moralisms" exceeds their marginal cost; people are trading off some "utils" of pleasure or leisure time for these utils of rhetorical preference in how they talk about allocation of babies.)

Market rhetoric is the rhetoric of cost-benefit analysis, which includes the notion that human satisfactions are composed of fungible "utils"; it conceives of all things that can be desired as goods that can be possessed and assigned a monetary equivalent. All this is of course the heritage of Hobbes and Bentham. For universal commodifiers the rhetoric of contract-alienation is the only rhetoric of human affairs. Among Marxists there are, on the other hand, universal anticommodifiers. For them, all markets and market rhetoric are related to estrangement-alienation both as symptoms and cause. That is to say, the market perpetuates estrangement-alienation and at the same time the existence of markets and market rhetoric reflects the underlying alienation.[17]

Is there a defensible middle way? Most of us are neither universal commodifiers nor universal anticommodifiers. We think, without really thinking deeply about it, that there is some appropriate realm for market trading and market rhetoric. The paradigm of corporation A selling widgets to corporation B, and the conception of widgets as fungible objects, does not invoke images of dislocation and distress. The corporate world is a world of fungibility, of profit-maximizing entities. Persons who hold shares of stock or certificates of deposit are presumed, with respect to these investment holdings, to be similar wealth-maximizers. But most of us think that that appropriate realm for market trading and market rhetoric only occupies a subset of the whole fabric of human interaction and discourse; and that that realm is transgressed when we speak of baby markets, or political power markets.

If these transgressions reflect or cause estrangement-alienation, then they would answer the question I am asking: When is the rhetoric of contract-alienation also a rhetoric of estrangement-alienation? Where the proper boundaries of the market are transgressed. But this leads to two further questions: First, does the transgression of market boundaries—the commodification of what ought not to be commodified—in fact reflect or cause alienation? Second, can we say anything in general about the market boundaries; or, how do we determine that something ought not to be commodified because to do so would transgress the appropriate realm of the market?

I shall bypass here the second question, the normative boundaries of the market, except to say that I am inclined to see it as allied to the problem of nonfungible property. That is, the pure free market, with its assumed fungibility of goods, is unwelcome in areas where the "goods" in question are particularly important for personhood. This includes human beings' homes, work, food, education, health, bodily integrity, sexuality and procreation. At the same time, I think the problem of the normative boundaries of the market is also allied to the problem of community. Certain "goods" are rights and duties (or better, attributes) of citizenship, and it is degrading and harmful to community or political life to conceive of them as market commodities. My thesis is that "goods" that are important to personhood and community should be, and mostly are, noncommodified or incompletely commodified.[18]

Let me spend a little more time on the first question: Is there really a connection between estrangement-alienation and wrongful commodification? One could certainly say that wrongful commodification of slaves and child labor caused extreme alienation, among other things. The point that I would like to focus on here, however, is the purely rhetorical one. Does the use of market rhetoric (even if the items are not actually, or legally, bought and sold) sometimes reflect or cause alienation? As a concrete example, consider whether women are alienated by the discussion of rape in terms of cost-benefit analysis, and whether the cost-benefit analysis of rape reflects the fact that women are alienated.

In a famous article, Guido Calabresi and A. Douglas Melamed argued that there should be a "property rule" protecting bodily integrity. They argued that an "indefinable kicker" in terms of extra cost to the rapist should be added to give the right incentive structure to achieve the optimal amount of rape, given our assumptions that, in general, victims value their bodily integrity more than attackers value invading it.[19] What is wrong with this? For all but the economics enthusiast, cost-benefit analysis seems out of place here. For some it may seem merely silly, while for others (perhaps primarily women) it seems to trivialize and insult the value being talked about.

What is it about the rhetoric of cost-benefit analysis that seems to trivialize and degrade women's interest in bodily integrity even as it purports to protect it? The problem with thinking of rape in terms of economic analysis is that the market rhetoric implicitly treats as fungible what we (women, at least) know is personal. Hence the feeling of discomfort, insult, and trivialization; and alienation. Systematically treating what is personal as fungible is threatening to personhood, and alienates the person who is treated not as a whole person but as the holder of a fungible commodity. The rhetoric assumes, in other words, a separation or separability between myself and my commodity, when I know there is no such separation; so the rhetoric both reflects and creates alienation between the speaker and me. The speaker supposes that an attribute-property is an object-property. That the speaker has no difficulty in so supposing reflects his alienation from women's self-consciousness. If my bodily integrity is made fungible, hence hypothetically valued in money, that feels like valuing *me* in money, for the same reason: I know that there is no divide between myself and my commodity, but the speaker supposes there is. This reinforces alienation.

Moreover, the use of market rhetoric in this or analogous situations may in fact make it easier to value people in money, as repositories of exchange value. To think in terms of costs to the rape victim and her sympathizers weighed against benefits to the rapist is to assume that raping "benefits" rapists; that somehow raping is a personal gain or self-enhancement to rapists. What conception of personhood or of human flourishing can this bespeak? Moreover, the cost-benefit analysis also implicitly assumes that there might be some situations where those "benefits" would outweigh the costs. In these situations rape would not only not be morally wrong but would instead be morally commended.

Perhaps it does not go too far to say that this market rhetoric, if adopted by everyone (at least by everyone in whatever dominant group can shape moral discourse) would transform our world of persons into a world of alienable objects. To be more precise, it would transform our world of concrete persons whose uniqueness and individuality is expressed in specific personal attributes into a world of disembodied, fungible, attributeless entities possessing a wealth of alienable, severable objects. That is at least an alien conception of personhood. Though it has been embraced or implied in theories of property from Kant onwards, it is now foreign to the main conception of personhood we embrace in our lives and institutions; at least, for now. But it is only partly alien; it is an alien in our midst. If this alien conception of personhood at the heart of market rhetoric tends to degrade the conception of personhood that is properly ours, and to make impossible our development into the persons we can be, and to divide us both internally and from each other, then it is "alienating" as well as (partly) alien. Then contract and fungibility is a rhetoric of estrangement and dissonance; the rhetoric of alienation is indeed a rhetoric of alienation.

Notes

Introduction

1. Peevyhouse v. Garland Coal & Mining Co., 382 P.2d 109 (Okla. 1963). A farm family was promised by a strip mining company that their land would be returned to its original state, but when that turned out to be expensive for the company, the court allowed the company to pay $300 in damages instead. (My students and I discussed this case in property class, although it is taught in contracts.)

2. Ch. 1, sec. IVC.

3. Hilary Putnam, *Afterword,* 63 S. CAL. L. REV. 1911, 1914–15 (1990).

4. *Id.*

5. Ch. 1, sec. IIC.

6. *Id.*

7. Ch. 2, sec. II (n. 17).

8. "Private property has made us so stupid and one-sided that an object is only *ours* when we have it—when it exists for us as capital, or when it is directly possessed, eaten, drunk, worn, inhabited, etc.,—in short, when it is *used* by us. Although private property itself again conceives all these direct realizations of possession as *means of life,* and the life which they serve as means is the *life of private property*—labour and conversion into capital." Karl Marx, *Economic and Philosophical Manuscripts of 1844, in* THE MARX-ENGELS READER 73 (R. Tucker ed. 1st ed. 1972).

9. One thing I did say now seems to me wrong or at least misleading. *See* ch. 1, sec. IIB. Kant argued that property is required to give full scope to freedom of the will, and therefore should not be read to say that there is no necessary connection between persons and property.

10. Ch. 1, sec. IIIB.

11. Ch. 2, sec. II.

12. *See, e.g.,* RICHARD RORTY, PHILOSOPHY AND THE MIRROR OF NATURE 61–69, 343–56 (1979).

13. *Cf.* Joseph William Singer, *The Reliance Interest in Property,* 40 STAN. L. REV. 614 (1988).

14. In Lyng v. Northwest Indian Cemetery Protective Ass'n, 485 U.S. 439 (1988), the Supreme Court ruled that timber harvesting in and constructing a road through federal land that had traditionally been used for tribal religious purposes did not violate the guarantee of free exercise of religion. *See, e.g.,* David C. Williams & Susan H. Williams, *Volitionalism and Religious Liberty,* 76 CORNELL L. REV. 769 (1991).

15. Charles Reich, *The New Property,* 73 YALE L.J. 733 (1964).

16. Bruce Ackerman, *Liberating Abstraction,* 59 U. CHI. L. REV. 317, 342–46

(1992). In Bowers v. Hardwick, 478 U.S. 186 (1986), the U.S. Supreme Court ruled that no constitutional due process or liberty rights prohibit states from criminalizing "sodomy" as practiced by homosexual lovers.

17. *See* Guido Calabresi & A. Douglas Melamed, *Property Rules, Liability Rules, and Inalienability: One View of the Cathedral,* 85 HARV. L. REV. 1089 (1972). This locution is discussed in chapter 1, section IVC.

18. *See* Richard A. Posner, *An Economic Theory of Criminal Law,* 85 COLUM. L. REV. 1193 (1985).

19. That debate is largely absent from these essays, perhaps because I was seeking primarily to identify aspects of our property practices that could be widely accepted as a basis for further evaluation, rather than seeking primarily to explore deep conflicts. Nevertheless the debate comes to the fore in "The Rhetoric of Alienation" (chapter 7). My consideration of it continues in another book, tentatively titled *Commodification: Justice and the Market Domain.*

20. I have not attempted to update my surveys, so readers should be wary in some areas—particularly the law governing what searches and seizures are permissible under the Fourth Amendment; there have been substantial changes during the past decade. In a footnote I invited others to consider waste, specific performance, artists' personality rights, exemptions in bankruptcy, special protection for homeowner-mortgagors, and servitudes.

21. An economist replying to my article suggested that the fact that tenants do not typically bargain for long-term leases shows that they do not have desires for stability similar to homeowners. My guess is that it shows wealth constraints instead. *See* Timothy J. Brennan, *Rights, Market Failure, and Rent Control: A Comment on Radin,* 17 PHIL. & PUB. AFF. 66 (1988), and Margaret Jane Radin, *Rent Control and Incomplete Commodification: A Rejoinder,* 17 PHIL. & PUB. AFF. 80 (1988).

22. Ch. 4, sec. IIC.

23. Ch. 4, sec. IIC.

24. Lochner v. New York, 198 U.S. 45 (1905). The *Lochner* Court found that state regulation of working hours for health and safety reasons was unconstitutional because it violated a substantive due process right to freedom of contract. *Lochner* and the constitutionalization of laissez-faire market principles were thoroughly repudiated during the New Deal era.

25. For an excellent critical review, see Thomas C. Grey, *The Malthusian Constitution,* 41 U. MIAMI L. REV. 21 (1986).

26. Robert C. Ellickson, *Rent Control: A Comment on Olsen,* 67 CHI.-KENT L. REV. 947, 953 (1992).

27. Indeed, the argument may seem similar to the radical vision of Roberto Unger, who endorses context-smashing as constitutive of human flourishing. ROBERTO MANGABEIRA UNGER, FALSE NECESSITY 491–506 (1987).

28. For reviews see, for example, Thomas Nagel, *Libertarianism without Foundations, in* READING NOZICK: ESSAYS ON ANARCHY STATE AND UTOPIA 191–205 (Jeffrey Paul ed. 1981) [hereafter READING NOZICK]; Cheyney C. Ryan, *Yours, Mine and Ours: Property Rights and Individual Liberty, in* READING NOZICK, *supra* at 323–43; Thomas Scanlon, *Nozick on Rights, Equality, and the Minimal State, in* READING NOZICK, *supra* at 107–29; Robert Paul Wolff, *Robert Nozick's Derivation of the Minimal State, in* READING NOZICK, *supra* at 77–104.

29. *See* ROBERT NOZICK, ANARCHY, STATE AND UTOPIA 228 (1974). Perhaps

the real complaint is not that Rawls treats natural endowments as alienable, but that he treats them *as already alienated* (to the community), whereas the libertarians want to treat them as alienable but only by the self voluntarily. (Another way to say this is that Rawls puts the voluntariness that does the alienating into the decision in the original position, whereas the libertarians want to preserve it for real life.) If this is the real complaint, then the libertarian is adopting a thin theory of the self.

30. *Id.* at 331.

31. *See* Stephen J. Schnably, *Property and Pragmatism: A Critique of Radin's Theory of Property and Personhood,* 44 STAN. L. REV. 347, 352 (1993).

32. BERNARD YACK, THE LONGING FOR TOTAL REVOLUTION (1986). These two critical rhetorics seem not to be readily reconcilable. An inclination to deconstruct whatever stable understanding presents itself is at odds with an inclination to commit oneself to an overarching theory of transformation. In Roberto Unger's work there is an attempted reconciliation that is attractive to some on the left. The reconciliation is that context-disruption ("plasticity") is a good in itself. *See* Unger, *supra* note 27. I do not find this reconciliation plausible. *Sometimes* context-disruption is a good; but *sometimes* context-stability is a good. Which is which depends upon the context! It is true that much of my writing about property has focused on the need for context-stability, where appropriate. Some critics on the left, looking for overarching theory, may have misunderstood me to say that the need for stability is the whole picture. But as a pragmatist I meant my investigations to be understood as partial.

33. *See supra,* sec. IV.

34. Otto Neurath, *Protocol Sentences, in* LOGICAL POSITIVISM 199, 201 (Alfred J. Ayer ed. & George Schick trans. 1959). "We are like sailors who must rebuild their ships on the open sea, never able to dismantle it [sic] in dry-dock and to reconstruct it there out of the best materials."

35. O'Brien v. O'Brien, 489 N.E.2d 712 (N.Y. 1985).

Chapter One

1. The personality theory, the labor theory, and the utilitarian theory are respectively associated with Hegel, Locke, and Bentham. *See* G.W.F. HEGEL, PHILOSOPHY OF RIGHT (T. Knox trans. 1942) (1821); J. LOCKE, SECOND TREATISE OF GOVERNMENT (P. Laslett ed. 1960) (1690); J. BENTHAM, THEORY OF LEGISLATION (R. Hildreth trans. 2d ed. 1871) (1802). The sociobiological/psychological "territorial imperative" theory may be a fourth type stemming roughly from Darwin and Freud. *See* S. Freud, *Civilization and its Discontents, in* 21 THE STANDARD EDITION OF THE COMPLETE PSYCHOLOGICAL WORKS OF SIGMUND FREUD 111–14 (J. Strachey ed. 1964).

Locke's theory has long been defended or characterized by modern writers as a labor-*desert* theory. One must somehow *deserve* to own items mixed with one's labor, rather than simply dissipate one's labor. *See, e.g.,* R. NOZICK, ANARCHY, STATE AND UTOPIA 175 (1974) (Nozick's example: If I empty a can of tomato juice into the ocean, do I own the ocean?). Bentham's theory has been reincarnated in the economic analysis of law. *See, e.g.,* R. POSNER, ECONOMIC ANALYSIS OF LAW (2d ed. 1977); Demsetz, *Toward A Theory of Property Rights,* 57 AM. ECON. REV. 347 (1967).

2. Economic language, though awkward in this realm, would say that the holder

of such an object has a large amount of consumer surplus that would be very difficult to ascertain accurately. The holder typically would not think about the object in monetary terms at all. Applying economic reasoning to things of high sentimental value presents difficulties because such things are likely to represent a large proportion of a person's total "wealth." *See* Kennedy, *Cost-Benefit Analysis of Entitlement Problems: A Critique,* 33 STAN. L. REV. 387 (1981). *See also* Baker, *The Ideology of The Economic Analysis of Law,* 5 PHIL. & PUB. AFF. 1 (1975).

3. The distinction is not simply between consumer property and commercial property. While it is likely that most commercial property is not property for personhood but rather held instrumentally, a great deal of consumers' property is also not property for personhood in the special direct sense I am trying to bring out. Many items—e.g., pots and pans, lawn mowers, light bulbs—can also be characterized as valued instrumentally, not in the same sense as something one holds only for exchange, but in the related sense that they are held in order to perform a service and it is the service that is substantively valued.

4. The distinction is between conceptions of negative freedom ("freedom from"), characteristic of English liberalism, and positive freedom ("freedom to"), typical of Hegel's and other continental theorists' views. *See* I. BERLIN, TWO CONCEPTS OF LIBERTY (1958); Berki, *Political Freedom and Hegelian Metaphysics,* 16 POL. STUD. 365, 365 (1968). The principal difference between the theories of Locke and Hegel is that for Locke the source of entitlement is labor, whereas for Hegel it is will. The Lockean individual has a natural right to property and broad negative freedom regarding that right. Hegel's notion of rights—autonomy or freedom in the positive sense—is logically bound up with entitlement to external objects. The historical importance of this distinction between negative and positive freedom is that Hegel's intellectual descendants tend to consider property rights as socially based, while Locke's followers tend to remain individualistic.

5. *See generally* THE IDENTITIES OF PERSONS (A. Rorty ed. 1976) (collection of conflicting views about criteria for personal identity).

6. I. KANT, FUNDAMENTAL PRINCIPLES OF THE METAPHYSICS OF MORALS (T. Abbott trans. 1949).

7. This seems to describe the persons in John Rawls's original position, who are called upon to develop a social contract to which all would consent purely on the basis of rationality, in ignorance of their individual particularities. *See* J. RAWLS, A THEORY OF JUSTICE (1971). Recently Rawls has distinguished three conceptions of the person: (1) an artificial agent of construction in the original position, possessing only rational autonomy; (2) an ideal of the person affirmed by the citizens of a well-ordered society, possessing full autonomy; and (3) an actual citizen in her personal affairs, possessing particular attachments and loves, and particular religious and philosophical commitments. Rawls, *Kantian Constructivism in Moral Theory,* 77 J. PHIL. 515, 533–35 (1980). The conception of person I refer to in the text as Kantian is, according to Rawls, for both Kant and himself merely a philosophical construct for abstracting principles of justice, and not the same as the notion of person in society or everyday life.

8. J. LOCKE, AN ESSAY CONCERNING HUMAN UNDERSTANDING bk. II, ch. XXVII, § 9 (A. Fraser ed. 1894) (1st. ed. London 1690).

9. David Wiggins builds on Locke, arguing that in seeking to create a personal identity condition we are seeking to describe "a persisting material entity essentially

endowed with the biological potentiality for the exercise of *all* the faculties and capacities conceptually constitutive of personhood—sentience, desire, belief, motion, memory, and so forth." Wiggins, *Locke, Butler and the Stream of Consciousness: And Men as a Natural Kind,* in THE IDENTITIES OF PERSONS 139, 149 (A. Rorty ed. 1976).

10. The ontology of the person is not a settled matter in philosophical discourse. *See e.g.,* B. BRODY, IDENTITY & ESSENCE (1980); S. SHOEMAKER, *Are Selves Substances?,* in SELF-KNOWLEDGE & SELF-IDENTITY 41 (1963); Shoemaker, *Embodiment and Behavior,* in THE IDENTITIES OF PERSONS 109 (A. Rorty ed. 1976).

11. This view seems overinclusive: Is a dead body or a body that is alive but exhibits no brain function a person?

12. P. F. Strawson argues that person is a primitive concept to which two classes of predicates both apply: "M-predicates" which are applicable to mere material bodies, and "P-predicates" which imply possession of consciousness and are not applicable to mere material bodies. P. STRAWSON, INDIVIDUALS: AN ESSAY IN DESCRIPTIVE METAPHYSICS 87–116 (1959); *see also* B. WILLIAMS, *Are Persons Bodies?* in PROBLEMS OF THE SELF 64 (1973); B. WILLIAMS, *Bodily Continuity and Personal Identity,* in PROBLEMS OF THE SELF 19 (1973); B. WILLIAMS, *Personal Identity and Individuation,* in PROBLEMS OF THE SELF 1 (1973).

13. L. WITTGENSTEIN, PHILOSOPHICAL INVESTIGATIONS 178 (G.E.M. Anscombe trans. 3d ed. 1958). Part of what Wittgenstein meant by this must have been that "when we are asked to distinguish a man's personality from his body, we do not really know what to distinguish from what." B. WILLIAMS, *Personal Identity and Individuation,* in PROBLEMS OF THE SELF 12 (1973).

14. *See, e.g.,* Williams, *Persons, Character and Morality,* in THE IDENTITIES OF PERSONS 197 (A. Rorty ed. 1976). The Kantian view does not do justice to "the importance of individual character and personal relations in moral experience," *id.* at 201; "such things as deep attachments to other persons will express themselves in the world in ways which cannot at the same time embody the impartial view." *Id.* at 215. With regard to the Lockean emphasis on memory, see Wiggins, *supra* note 9, at 149–50.

15. *See, e.g.,* Dennett, *Conditions of Personhood,* in THE IDENTITIES OF PERSONS 175, 177–78 (A. Rorty ed. 1976). Dennett distinguishes six themes, each familiarly claiming to be a necessary condition of personhood. They are: (1) that persons are rational beings; (2) that persons are beings to which states of consciousness are attributed; (3) that whether something counts as a person depends on the stance others take in relating to it—i.e., that it is treated as a person; (4) that the object of the personal stance must be capable of reciprocating its treatment as a person; (5) that persons must be capable of language and verbal communication; and (6) that persons have a special consciousness or self-consciousness distinguishing them from other species.

16. D. HUME, *Of Personal Identity,* in A TREATISE OF HUMAN NATURE bk. I, pt. IV, § VI (1888).

17. The familiar "economic man" is simply that entity which applies pure instrumental rationality to satisfy its arbitrary tastes and desires. How would such an entity be conventionally recognized? Perhaps by an equilibrium that becomes stable enough to persist over time, i.e., the status quo. *See generally* J. BUCHANAN, THE LIMITS OF LIBERTY (1975).

18. S. Freud, *The Ego and the Id,* in 19 THE STANDARD EDITION OF THE COM-
PLETE PSYCHOLOGICAL WORKS OF SIGMUND FREUD 18 (J. Strachey ed. 1961).

19. *See, e.g.,* J. Habermas, *Historical Materialism and the Development of Normative Structures,* in COMMUNICATION AND THE EVOLUTION OF SOCIETY 95,
100 (T. McCarthy trans. 1979) (linguistic development contributes to ego
development).

20. J. LOCKE, *supra* note 1, ch. V, § 27.

21. As Macpherson and others have pointed out, to say "must" at this point
requires a capitalist mentality. *See* C. MACPHERSON, THE POLITICAL THEORY OF
POSSESSIVE INDIVIDUALISM: HOBBES TO LOCKE 13 (1962).

22. J. LOCKE, *supra* note 1, ch. V, § 25.

23. Hence a touching of one's clothes or cane, etc., can be a battery. W. PROSSER,
LAW OF TORTS § 9 (4th ed. 1971).

24. Whether society should permit bodily parts to become commodities is controversial. *See A Brazilian Tragedy—Desperation: Selling Your Eye, Kidney,* L.A.
TIMES, Sept. 10, 1981, § I, at 1, col. 1; *Man Desperate for Funds: Eye for Sale
at $35,000,* L.A. TIMES, Feb. 1, 1975, § II, at 1, col. 3. *See generally* G. CALA-
BRESI & P. BOBBIT, TRAGIC CHOICES (1978) (reasons society might disallow such
transactions).

25. The first inquiry raises the point that the parameters of personal identity may
be scalar rather than binary; but that we may leave to the philosophers of personal
identity. *See, e.g.,* Parfit, *Later Selves and Moral Principles,* in PHILOSOPHY & PER-
SONAL RELATIONS 137 (A. Montefiore ed. 1973).

26. *See* J. RAWLS, *supra* note 7, at 17–22.

27. Since objects do not become bound up with the person considered as abstract
rationality, one might expect a tendency of Kantian rational persons to treat all
property as fungible.

28. The process by which a person develops object relations and an appropriate
differentiation from the environment of other people and things is the subject of
large portions of psychological and psychoanalytic theory. *See, e.g.,* H. KOHUT, THE
ANALYSIS OF THE SELF (1971); D. WINNICOTT, *Transitional Objects and Transitional Phenomena,* in COLLECTED PAPERS 229 (1958); Steele & Jacobsen, *From
Present to Past: The Development of the Freudian Theory,* 5 INT'L REV. PSYCHOANALY-
SIS 393 (1977).

29. The connection between certain kinds of property rights and the person
viewed as continuing character structure was recognized by Bernard Bosanquet in
1895. *See* B. BOSANQUET, *The Principle of Private Property,* in ASPECTS OF THE
SOCIAL PROBLEM 308, 311, 314 (1895).

30. J. BENTHAM, *supra* note 1, at 112.

31. *See* Moore, *Legal Conceptions of Mental Illness,* in MENTAL ILLNESS: LAW &
PUBLIC POLICY 25 (B. Brody & H. Engelhardt eds. 1980); Morse, *Crazy Behavior,
Morals, and Science: An Analysis of Mental Health Law,* 51 S. CAL. L. REV. 527
(1978).

32. *See* J. Murphy, *Incompetence and Paternalism,* in RETRIBUTION, JUSTICE AND
THERAPY 165 (1979); P. STRAWSON, *Freedom and Resentment,* in FREEDOM AND
RESENTMENT 1 (1974).

33. Whether any kind of consensus can ever be a source of objective moral judgments is the subject of philosophical dispute. I have argued elsewhere that our pres-

ent state of philosophical enlightenment on the subject of moral objectivity seems to be consonant with the argument that "deep" moral consensus—not mere social consensus, or subjective preference counting—should be treated as objective for political purposes. Radin, *Cruel Punishment and Respect for Persons: Super Due Process for Death,* 53 S. CAL. L. REV. 1143, 1176 n.109 (1980); Radin, *The Jurisprudence of Death: Evolving Standards for the Cruel and Unusual Punishments Clause,* 126 U. PA. L. REV. 989, 1030–42 (1978). *See* Rawls, *Kantian Constructivism in Moral Theory, supra* note 7, at 570–71.

34. There has not been much philosophical analysis of perversion; but see Nagel, *Sexual Perversion,* in MORTAL QUESTIONS 39 (1979). There are varying philosophical approaches to the necessary criteria or indicia for recognizing someone as one of us. For Moore, *supra* note 31, the criterion is rationality, the ability to carry out intelligible rational syllogisms. Drawing out these notions of intelligibility, Morse, *supra* note 31, at 581–90, distinguishes "crazy urges" and "crazy reasons." Strawson, *supra* note 32, speaks of responses to entities in terms of personal or objective attitudes. Dennett, *supra* note 15, speaks of the indicia of "intentional systems."

35. K. MARX, CAPITAL ch. I (S. Moore & E. Aveling trans. 1889).

36. If we deny the caricature capitalist the claim that her empire is personal, that still leaves her with an empire of fungible property; and Marx would probably be quick to point out that its fungible character in the hands of the capitalist makes it no less oppressive to the propertyless. Thus, the hypothetical caricature capitalist brings up a further aspect of the fetishism problem: the effect of one person's claimed property rights on the personhood of others. The extent to which a liberal government may permit private individuals to engage in practices which impinge on the personhood of others is a difficult question of political theory. It is the inverse of the problem of welfare rights—that is, to what extent certain interests in personhood (regardless of whether embodied in property or not) ought to be guaranteed by the government even against the claimed property interests of the rich. This is a problem not directly addressed in the present essay, though it is further noticed in sections IVD and VC.

37. The standard English translation of GRUNDLINIEN DER PHILOSOPHIE DES RECHTS is HEGEL'S PHILOSOPHY OF RIGHT (T. Knox trans. 1942) [hereinafter cited as PR]. Citations in this essay are to the Knox translation; in a few quotations I have made minor emendations for the sake of clarity. The text of the work consists of numbered sections, "remarks" added to the text by Hegel [hereinafter cited with "R" following the section number], and "additions" obtained by early editors from collating student lecture notes [hereinafter cited with "A" following the section number]. The English title of the work is slightly misleading, because right does not capture the full sense of "*Recht,*" by which Hegel means "not merely what is generally understood by the word, namely civil law, but also morality, community morality [*Sittlichkeit*], and world-history . . . . " PR § 33A. *Cf.* PR § 29 ("[*Recht*] therefore is by definition freedom as Idea"). Thomas Hill Green, a nineteenth-century British Hegelian, understood *Recht* as meaning the system of positive law, but wished it to connote instead both "moral duty in regard to actual [i.e., positive, legal] obligations, as well as . . . the system of rights and obligations as it should become." T. GREEN, LECTURES ON THE PRINCIPLES OF POLITICAL OBLIGATION § 10 (1927) *reprinted from* II GREEN'S PHILOSOPHICAL WORKS (L. Nettleship ed. 1886); *see also id.* §§ 9–11; *cf.* § 11 n.1.

Although the *Philosophy of Right* is a philosophy of law, Anglo-American legal
scholars have not systematically examined it. The best discussion I have found of
Hegel's property theory in English is Stillman, *Property, Freedom, and Individuality
in Hegel's and Marx's Political Thought,* in NOMOS XXII, PROPERTY 130 (J. Pennock & J. Chapman eds. 1980). *See also* S. AVINERI, HEGEL'S THEORY OF THE
MODERN STATE (1972); Stillman, *Person, Property and Civil Society in the* Philosophy of Right, in HEGEL'S SOCIAL AND POLITICAL THOUGHT 103 (D. Verene ed.
1980); Stillman, *Hegel's Critique of Liberal Theories of Rights* 68 AM. POL. SCI. REV.
1086 (1974).

38. Hegel puts this as follows:

"35. The universality of this consciously free will is abstract universality, the self-
conscious but otherwise contentless and simple relation of itself to itself in its individuality, and from this point of view the subject is a person . . . .

"35R. Personality begins not with the subject's mere general consciousness of
himself as an ego concretely determined in some way or other, but rather with his
consciousness of himself as a completely abstract ego in which every concrete restriction and value is negated and without validity . . . .

"36. (1) Personality essentially involves the capacity for rights and constitutes the
concept and the basis (itself abstract) of the system of abstract and formal right.
Hence the imperative of right is: 'Be a person and respect others as persons.' PR
§§ 35, 35R, 36. *Cf.* T. GREEN, *supra* note 37, § 27 ("[The proposition that all
rights are personal] means that rights are derived from the possession of personality—a rational will.").

39. PR § 41; *cf.* PR § 39 ("Personality is that which struggles . . . to give itself
reality, or in other words to claim that external world as its own [*jenes Dasein als das
ihrige zu setzen*]."). Since Hegel, like Plato, was an idealist, something must exist as
Idea in order to be actualized or real.

40. PR § 41.

41. "But I as free will am an object to myself in what I possess and thereby also
for the first time am an actual will, and this is the aspect which constitutes the
category of *property,* the true and right factor in possession." PR § 45.

42. PR § 44. It is unclear why Hegel referred in this passage to the thing becoming "mine" [*die Meinige*] rather than "the person's." Perhaps by this lack of parallel-
ism he meant to suggest the change from abstract personhood to concrete
individuality brought about by embodiment of the will.

43. PR § 45R. To understand why Hegel says property is only the first embodiment of freedom, one must understand both the structure of the *Philosophy of Right*
and the Hegelian meaning of freedom. Hegel's *Philosophy of Right* is divided into an
introduction and three parts, entitled, "Abstract Right," "Morality," and "Community Morality" [*Sittlichkeit*]. (On Hegel's special use of *Sittlichkeit, see* note 54, *infra.*)
The first part considers relationships among individuals viewed as persons or as
abstract autonomous entities possessing arbitrary free will in the contexts of property, contract, and crime. The second part considers individuals as subjective entities
having a consciousness and conscience which direct the individual will towards its
own conception of the good. The third part considers individuals as grounded in an
objective ethical order consisting of the customs, history, and spirit of a nation. This
discussion covers the family, civil society, and the state. Hegel argues that freedom
is finally realized when the individual will unites with and expresses itself as part of

the objective ethical order—an absolute mind or spirit (*Geist*) embodied by the state. *See* Solomon, *Hegel's Concept of "Geist,"* in HEGEL: A COLLECTION OF CRITICAL ESSAYS 125, 125 (A. MacIntyre ed. 1972) ("What clearly emerges from Hegel's writings is that 'Geist' refers to some sort of *general consciousness, a single 'mind' common to all men.*"); *cf.* C. TAYLOR, HEGEL AND MODERN SOCIETY 111 (1979) (*Geist* is "cosmic spirit. . . . [It is] spiritual reality underlying the universe as a whole.").

For Hegel, real freedom (rather than just its initial stage) depends upon the individual's assumption of an appropriate role in the properly developed state, a concept quite different from the notion of (negative) liberty, or freedom from external constraints.

44. "Since property is the *embodiment* of personality [*Dasein der Personlichkeit*], my inward idea and will that something is mine is not enough to make it my property; to secure this end occupancy [*die Besitzergreifung*] is requisite." PR § 51.

45. PR § 64R. Hegel thus makes it clear that prescription or adverse possession is *not* based on an "external" theory that a statute of limitations is needed to cut off the "disputes and confusions which old claims would introduce into the security of property." *Id.* Rather, things become unowned when they are "deprived of the actuality of the will and possession." PR § 64.

46. Alienability also follows; things which have become property are alienable simply by withdrawing one's will. PR § 65. Those things which constitute the will or personhood must, however, be inalienable. PR § 66. The concept of mind [*Geist*] could not be actualized if persons could dispose of their personhood. PR § 66R.

47. Hegel believes that his argument yields not only a property relationship, but *private* property. "46. Since my will, as the will of a person, and so as a single will, becomes objective to me in property, property acquires the character of private property; and common property of such a nature that it may be owned by separate persons acquires the character of an inherently dissoluble partnership in which the retention of my share is explicitly a matter of my arbitrary preference." PR § 46. Hegel believes that "[o]wnership therefore is in essence free and complete." PR § 62. The notion of divided ownership poses "an absolute contradiction." What is mine is "penetrated through and through by my will," but that cannot be if the "impenetrable" will of another is supposedly present in the same thing. *Id.*

Although Hegel thought his argument necessitated private property, he did not think it had anything to do with who gets what. He took care to point out that in this sphere of abstract right, where he considers only units of personal autonomy and no forms of social interaction or social entities, there are no issues of justice in distribution. Hegel discusses here only the "rational aspect"—that individuals possess property as expressions of their wills; he does not consider here the "particular aspect"—that how much one possesses depends on "subjective aims, needs, arbitrariness, abilities, external circumstances, and so forth." PR § 49.

Hegel adds: "At this point, equality could only be the equality of abstract persons as such, and therefore the whole field of possession, this terrain of inequality falls outside it.

"We may not speak of the injustice of nature in the unequal distribution of possessions and resources, since nature is not free and therefore is neither just nor unjust . . . . On the other hand, subsistence is not the same as possession and belongs to another sphere, i.e., to civil society." PR § 49R. Hegel means by "civil society" (*die bürgerliche Gesellschaft*) roughly what most liberals mean by the state; that is, the sphere of political economy in which individuals pursue their own selfish ends. *See* PR §§ 182–256.

48. PR § 40R.

49. In fact, he remarks that the civil law's traditional classification of rights, derived from Justinian, was confused because of its "disorderly intermixture of rights which presuppose substantial ties, e.g., those of family and political life," with those stemming from personhood simpliciter. PR § 40R. This distinction presents a basic question for interpreters of Hegel's property theory: To what extent are his considerations of property rights from the first part of *Philosophy of Right* ("Abstract Right") superseded in turn by the considerations in part two ("Morality") and part three ("Community Morality" [*Sittlichkeit*])? Hegel thought of these dialectic stages as both historical and conceptual, occurring successively in history as well as in logic. The Idea, the concept of absolute mind as the perfection of both the universal and all particulars, was the ultimate goal of both his conceptual system and the process of history. Hegel's initial sphere of abstract right might be considered comparable to a Hobbesian state of nature from a Kantian perspective. Conceptualizing a person merely as a separate autonomous unit possessing arbitrary will leaves out the "later" spheres of moral sentiments and participation in family and community. Do Hegel's remarks on property apply to a society in which these later stages are to some degree already actualized?

If one interprets the structure of the *Philosophy of Right* according to the most usual understanding of the Hegelian dialectic, then earlier stages are "*aufgehoben*" (transcended) by the later. They are at once destroyed, transcended, and incorporated into a new synthesis. *See, e.g.,* C. TAYLOR, HEGEL AND MODERN SOCIETY 49, 53–66 (1979); Findlay, *The Contemporary Relevance of Hegel,* in HEGEL: A COLLECTION OF CRITICAL ESSAYS, *supra* note 43 at 1; Findlay, *Some Merits of Hegelianism,* 56 PROC. ARISTOTELIAN SOC'Y 1 (1955). T. M. Knox, the translator of the *Philosophy of Right,* thought that abstract right and morality are both "absorbed into ethical life [*Sittlichkeit*] as its constituents." Knox, *Translator's Foreword* to HEGEL'S PHILOSOPHY OF RIGHT, *supra* note 37, at x. If this is correct, then the type of community entity that realizes the Idea would contain property relationships of the sort he set out in the sphere of abstract right. That is, the Hegelian ideal state would still contain the property relationships characteristic of liberalism.

50. PR § 167. Marriage is one of the "absolute principles" on which community morality depends, PR § 167R, and in a family one has "self-consciousness of one's individuality within this unity" as a "member," not as an "independent person." PR § 158.

51. PR § 169.

52. PR § 171. Hegel also argued that children are not property since they are "potential freedom." PR § 175. He conservatively favored inheritance but disfavored freedom of testation. PR §§ 178–80. He also endorsed the traditional roles of husbands and wives. PR § 166.

53. PR § 257. The state is "absolutely rational," PR § 258, and the "actuality of concrete freedom," PR § 260, and in the state "personal individuality and its particular interests . . . pass over of their own accord into the interest of the universal," which they "know and will" and "recognize . . . as their own substantive mind." *Id.* In contrast, Hegel conceives of civil society as "an association of members as

self-subsistent individuals." PR § 157. By voluntarily contracting with each other, the autonomous units in civil society fulfill each other's needs. In the sphere of political economy, Hegel draws conclusions very similar to those theorists who derive a "minimal" state from strictly individualist premises. Civil society, as an aggregate of autonomous units of arbitrary will, is an aggregate of private property-owning individuals. "As the private particularity of knowing and willing, the principle of this system of needs contains absolute universality, the universality of freedom, only abstractly and therefore as the right of property." PR § 208.

54. Hegel's special use of the word *Sittlichkeit,* the subject of the third part of his work, causes a translation problem. Knox translated this word as "ethical life" to distinguish it from *Moralität,* the subject of the second part of the work, even though both words ordinarily mean "morality." Hegel differentiated the two because he wanted *Moralität* to connote the morality of the individual conscience and *Sittlichkeit* to connote the collective morality of a society including the totality of its history and customs. PR §§ 33, 141; *cf.* Knox, *Translator's Notes* to HEGEL'S PHI-LOSOPHY OF RIGHT 319 n.75 (*Moralität* is abstract morality; *Sittlichkeit* is concrete morality.). A more suggestive translation of *Sittlichkeit* might be "community morality," which I use in this essay, although most Hegel scholars either leave the word untranslated or use Knox's "ethical life." [Today I would leave the word untranslated, because "community morality" raises problems of its own.]

55. *See* PR § 260; note 53, *supra.* Hegel objects to classical liberal theories of the state: "If the state is confused with civil society, and if its specific end is laid down as the security and protection of property and personal freedom, then the interest of the individuals as such becomes the ultimate end of their association, and it follows that membership of the state is something optional. But the state's relation to the individual is quite different from this. Since the state is objective mind [*Geist*], it is only as one of its members that the individual himself has objectivity, genuine individuality [*Wahrheit*], and community morality [*Sittlichkeit*] . . . . [The individual's] particular satisfaction, activity, and mode of conduct have this substantive and universally valid life as their starting point and their result." PR § 258R.

56. PR § 305. *See also* K. MARX, CRITIQUE OF HEGEL'S "PHILOSOPHY OF RIGHT" (1843).

57. The insight that there are two kinds of property appears in quite disparate contexts. In addition to the critiques discussed in the text of this section, see B. ACKERMAN, PRIVATE PROPERTY AND THE CONSTITUTION 116–18, 156 (1977) (social property and legal property); Berle, *Property, Production and Revolution,* 65 COLUM. L. REV. 1, 2–3 (1965) (property for production and property for consumption); Cohen, *Property and Sovereignty,* 13 CORNELL L.Q. 8 (1927) (property for use and property for power); Donahue, *The Future of the Concept of Property Predicted from Its Past,* in NOMOS XXII, PROPERTY 28, 56, 67 n.104 (J. Pennock & J. Chapman eds. 1980) (suggesting a distinction between offensive and defensive use of property).

58. For Locke, the paradigm case was mixing one's labor with the environment in a state of nature. J. LOCKE, *supra* note 1, ch. V, ¶ 27.

59. *Id.* ¶¶ 36–50.

60. Critiques of Locke that reflect this view are T. GREEN, *The Right of the State in Regard to Property,* in LECTURES ON THE PRINCIPLES OF POLITICAL OBLIGA-TION, *supra* note 37, §§ 211–32; C. MACPHERSON, *supra* note 21, at 197–221. A

critique of Hegel in a similar vein is Piper, *Property and the Limits of the Self,* 8 POL. THEORY 39 (1980).

61. Marx said that private property resting on the labor of others is the "direct antithesis" of private property resting on the producer's own labor. K. MARX, CAPITAL ch. XXXIII, at 790 (S. Moore & E. Aveling trans. 1889). Marx's two kinds of property could not coexist; rather, they are viewed as distinct historical stages. Capitalist or bourgeois property, resting on wage labor, was the historical successor of forms of property resting on the fruits of one's own labor. *Id.* ch. XXXII.

62. K. MARX & F. ENGELS, THE COMMUNIST MANIFESTO 96 (Penguin Books ed. 1979) (S. Moore trans. 1st ed. 1888).

63. Hobhouse, *The Historical Evolution of Property, in Fact and in Idea,* in PROPERTY: ITS DUTIES AND RIGHTS 3, 9–11 (2d ed. 1922). This distinction was later noted by Morris Cohen, *supra* note 57; and most recently by C. B. MacPherson, *The Meaning of Property,* in PROPERTY: MAINSTREAM AND CRITICAL POSITIONS 1, 12 (1978).

64. Hobhouse, *supra* note 63, at 9–11.

65. *Id.* at 23. This, of course, sounds similar to Marx's insistence that property resting on the employment of others' labor must inevitably be the historical successor of property resting on the employment of the producer's own labor. *See* note 61 *supra.* Yet English reformers such as Hobhouse—and T. H. Green before him—did not assert that capitalism must necessarily result in propertyless (and therefore dehumanized) proletarian masses. They merely argued that, insofar as capitalist laws and institutions do result in such a propertyless proletariat, they are unjustified and should be reformed. *See* GREEN, *supra* note 37, §§ 227–31.

66. On Marx and property, see Stillman, *Property, Freedom, and Individuality in Hegel's and Marx's Political Thought, supra* note 37; Brenkert, *Freedom and Private Property in Marx,* 8 PHIL. & PUB. AFF. 122 (1979). Suggestive passages are found in Marx & Engels, *The German Ideology,* in THE MARX-ENGELS READER 110 (R. Tucker ed. 1st ed. 1972), and in Marx's discourse on estranged or alienated labor in Marx, *Economic and Philosophic Manuscripts of 1844,* in THE MARX-ENGELS READER 52 (R. Tucker ed. 1st ed. 1972). Marx's point was not that object-relations are unimportant, but that wage-labor perverts them. Wage-labor makes man's "life-activity, his *essential* being, a mere means to his *existence.*" *Id.* at 62. "Private property has made us so stupid and one-sided that an object is only *ours* when we have it—when it exists for us as capital, or when it is directly possessed, eaten, drunk, worn, inhabited, etc.,—in short, when it is *used* by us. Although private property itself again conceives all these direct realizations of possession as *means of life,* and the life which they serve as means is the *life of private property*—labour and conversion into capital." *Id.* at 73.

67. *See* note 61, *supra.*

68. "Species being" stems from Marx's term *Gattungswesen.* In the section of the *Economic and Philosophic Manuscripts* on estranged labor, Marx stated: "In creating an *Objective world* by his practical activity, in *working-up* inorganic nature, man proves himself a conscious species being . . . . This production is his active species life." Marx, *Economic and Philosophic Manuscripts of 1844, supra* note 66, at 62.

69. This distinction assumes the existence of a market society. Marx did not hold that merely producing commodities for exchange with other commodities was alien-

ating; rather, he held that alienation was produced by the "fetishism of commodities," that is, producing commodities for market exchange. K. MARX, CAPITAL, *supra* note 35, ch. I, § 4. In a society based on barter between producers who know each other, this fetishism of commodities would not develop.

70. *See* K. MARX, CAPITAL, *supra* note 35 ch. I, § 1. "Exchange value" is basically what economists call market value. "Use value" is the utility to the consumer: "Use-values become a reality only by use or consumption: they also constitute the substance of all wealth, whatever may be the social form of that wealth." *Id.* at 2–3. Marx used the term "value" simply to refer to the amount of labor socially necessary to produce a commodity. *Id.* ch. I. For more discussion of these concepts, see Cohen, *Labor, Leisure, and a Distinctive Contradiction of Advanced Capitalism,* in MARKETS AND MORALS 107 (G. Dworkin, G. Bermant & P. Brown eds. 1977).

71. It also exhibits the logical problem that all property gives power over others in the sense that it confers enforceable claims on the holder and hence power to have them enforced.

72. *E.g.,* Cohen, *supra* note 57.

73. This is a cultural-historical interpretation of Posner's "universality" criterion for an efficient system of property rights. R. POSNER, *supra* note 1.

74. Calabresi & Melamed, *Property Rules, Liability Rules, and Inalienability: One View of the Cathedral,* 85 HARV. L. REV. 1089 (1972). Their hierarchy is not really a dichotomy, since they also designate a category of "inalienable" entitlements. No one may choose to submit to murder or to sell herself into slavery. In general, it seems that the inalienable entitlements they point to are not of the sort traditionally thought of as property rights.

75. The Calabresi-Melamed use of the term "property rule" seems to bend the language. In the incarnation of utilitarianism known as economic analysis of law, there is no role for a distinction between personal rights and property rights. An entitlement to bodily integrity or free speech is not different in kind from an entitlement to exclusive use of some object or resource in the external world. All are simply goods; all have prices.

76. Or by inalienability rules. *See* note 74, *supra.* But inalienability would often be disfavored by market theorists on efficiency grounds. *See, e.g.,* R. POSNER, *supra* note 1, at 111–16 (sale of babies should be legalized).

77. *E.g.,* Polinsky, *Controlling Externalities and Protecting Entitlements: Property Right, Liability Rule, and Tax-Subsidy Approaches,* 8 J. LEGAL STUD. 1 (1979); Polinsky, *On the Choice Between Property Rules and Liability Rules,* 18 ECON. INQUIRY 233 (1980).

78. Of course, such an exercise is trivial to thoroughgoing ethical subjectivists; in the Calabresi-Melamed terminology these reasons are mere "moralisms," just another word for strong subjective preferences. Calabresi & Melamed, *supra* note 74, at 1111–13.

79. [I returned to develop the topic of inalienability, with its connotations of anticommodification, in Margaret Jane Radin, *Market-Inalienability,* 100 HARV. L. REV. 1849 (1987).]

80. While residences are not specially protected against eminent domain, such legal protections as homesteading and special mortgage redemption rights show a degree of special concern.

81. The claim that fungible property should not override personhood interests of others is not considered radical when the personhood interest at stake is so close to personhood that we hold it to be inalienable.

82. All entitlements are treated alike in the economic model. Economists typically rely on efficiency criteria and not on the perspective of autonomy or personhood in seeking to determine whether certain entitlements should be accorded greater protection than others. In a neo-Lockean natural rights scheme, property rights might swallow up other concerns. Such a scheme might hold that personal rights or civil liberties are derived from property rights, which exist a priori in persons. Once the government has mechanisms for ensuring that people's a priori rights are not violated, whatever pattern of entitlements that results from the voluntary interaction of the rights-holders must not be disturbed. Under such a scheme, a political system must protect property, thereby doing all it can to protect autonomy or personhood.

83. *See, e.g.,* Grey, *Property and Need: The Welfare State and Theories of Distributive Justice,* 28 STAN. L. REV. 877 (1976); Michelman, *Welfare Rights in a Constitutional Democracy,* 1979 WASH. U. L.Q. 659.

84. Another approach that also has the effect of doing away with any intrinsic difference between property and nonproperty rights is simply to identify all claims or interests that the government ought to protect, and then call them "property." This is the tendency of Reich's "functional" approach; he calls for "new property" rights in government largess to the extent necessary to maintain people's independence from government. Reich, *The New Property,* 73 YALE L.J. 733 (1964).

85. Grey argues that the distinction between property rights and nonproperty rights loses its significance when a "bundle-of-rights" conception of property is substituted for a "thing-ownership" conception of property. Grey, *The Disintegration of Property,* in NOMOS XXII, PROPERTY 69 (J. Pennock & J. Chapman eds. 1980). Such a transformation aids in curtailing property rights for the sake of the goals of the welfare state, and is one response to perceived injustices of a Lockean natural rights scheme. I would argue, however, that recognizing the distinction between fungible and personal property might be a preferable approach leading to a similar result. It would allow curtailing fungible property rights without relinquishing the notion of thing-ownership in personal property, where thing-ownership seems embedded in the ideas of self-constitution through object relations.

86. For example, paying attention to the notion of personal property would lead not merely to a right to shelter in general, but a right to a particular house or apartment.

87. This might follow from Reich's argument that largess should become "property" so it could fulfill the function—making people independent of the government—which he saw the prevailing pattern of property rights as failing to fulfill, *see* Reich, *supra* note 84, if one assumes that independence from government is necessary for self-constitution and that government must make self-constitution possible.

88. For example, it would tell the government to curtail landlords' rights against tenants, rather than simply distribute money to tenants (or provide housing itself).

89. 394 U.S. 557 (1969).

90. "Georgia contends . . . that there are certain types of materials that the individual may not read or even possess . . . . Whatever may be the justifications for other statutes regulating obscenity, we do not think they reach into the privacy of

one's own home. If the First Amendment means anything, it means that a State has no business telling a man, sitting alone in his own house, what books he may read or what films he may watch." 394 U.S. at 565.

91. *See, e.g.,* L. TRIBE, AMERICAN CONSTITUTIONAL LAW 906–07, 984–85 (1978).

92. *See* Javins v. First Nat'l Realty Corp. 428 F.2d 1071, 1078–79 (D.C. Cir. 1970), *cert. denied,* 400 U.S. 925 (1970):

> Today's urban tenants, the vast majority of whom live in multiple dwelling houses, are interested, not in the land but solely in "a house suitable for occupation."
>
> . . . In a lease contract, a tenant seeks to purchase from his landlord shelter for a specified period of time. The landlord sells housing as a commercial businessman and has much greater opportunity, incentive and capacity to inspect and maintain the condition of his building.
>
> . . . .
>
> . . . The inequality in bargaining power between landlord and tenant has been well documented . . . . Various impediments to competition in the rental housing market, such as racial and class discrimination and standardized form leases, mean that landlords place tenants in a take it or leave it situation.

See also Birkenfeld v. City of Berkeley, 17 Cal. 3d 129, 158–59, 550 P.2d 1001, 1022–23, 130 Cal. Rptr. 465, 486–87 (1976); Green v. Superior Court, 10 Cal. 3d 616, 517 P.2d 1168, 111 Cal. Rptr. 704 (1974).

93. A number of states have enacted the UNIFORM RESIDENTIAL LANDLORD AND TENANT ACT (1974) [hereinafter cited as URLTA], with its liberal positions on tenants rights and remedies, and the implied warranty of habitability has become the majority rule on the duty to maintain the premises. *See* RESTATEMENT (SECOND) OF PROPERTY §§ 5.1–5.6 (1977); Abbott, *Housing Policy, Housing Codes and Tenant Remedies: An Integration,* 56 B.U. L. REV. 1 (1976).

94. A similarity exists between the development of tenure rights in residential tenancies and tenure rights in jobs. *See* M. GLENDON, THE NEW FAMILY AND THE NEW PROPERTY 143–205 (1981). One might explain both of these developments on the basis of general norms for wealth distribution or on the basis of moral reasoning about what rights are necessary to protect personhood. The connection with personhood is the need for food and shelter. Yet I would argue that something is "left over" with regard to residential tenancies, and that is the sanctity of the home, the attachment of self to a particular place with its particular context of objects.

95. Courts imposing warranties of habitability often say they are simply applying contract rules to leases, arguing that the parties bargain on the assumption that habitable premises will be supplied. *See, e.g.,* Javins v. First Nat'l Realty Corp., 428 F.2d 1071 (D.C. Cir. 1970), *cert. denied,* 400 U.S. 925 (1970). The difficulties with this are (1) reasonable parties would not assume habitable premises will be supplied if the common law rule were still in effect; and (2) making the habitability rights inalienable (nonwaivable) moves them out of the realm of contract and into the realm of property.

96. *See, e.g.,* N.J. STAT. ANN. § 2A:18–61.1 (West Supp. 1981): "No lessee or tenant . . . may be removed by the county district court or the Superior Court

from any house, building [etc.] leased for residential purposes, other than owner-occupied premises with not more than two rental units . . . except upon establishment of one of the following grounds as good cause. . . . "

Although this kind of statute seems to be a direct manifestation of the personhood perspective when it is enacted alone, where it is proposed in conjunction with rent control it may simply be a safeguard designed to assure the success of the redistributive scheme. Restricting the grounds for eviction is necessary to implement the statute, especially where rent control statutes allow uncontrolled price increases when the units are vacated.

97. The autonomy and individuality of the landlord is more clearly implicated when the landlord is not simply a commercial investor. If the prevailing pattern of leaseholds in a given time and place is that both landlord and tenant occupy the land at the same time, then the need for sanctity of the home would not favor the tenant. *Cf.* N.J. STAT. ANN. § 2A:18–61.1 (West Supp. 1981) (exemption to tenant's tenure for landlords who reside on premises and maintain only one or two rental units).

98. The doctrine began with the notion that the landlord would not be able to end a month-to-month tenancy if her motivation for eviction was to retaliate against the tenant for complaining of housing code violations on the premises; the rationale was that to permit such evictions would render the housing codes, which depended on private enforcement, ineffectual. *See* Edwards v. Habib, 397 F.2d 687 (D.C. Cir. 1968), *cert. denied,* 393 U.S. 1016 (1969). Some jurisdictions have enacted legislation that defines certain landlord conduct, such as eviction, increasing the rent, or cutting off the heat, as impermissibly retaliatory if motivated by tenant activities. *See, e.g.,* URLTA § 5.101; CAL. CIV. CODE § 1942.5 (West Supp. 1982).

99. Ackerman, *Regulating Slum Housing Markets on Behalf of the Poor: Of Housing Codes, Housing Subsidies and Income Redistribution Policy,* 80 YALE L.J. 1093, 1171 (1971). Ackerman does not show that the costs of habitability standards are in fact borne by landlords. Rather, he constructs a model to show that landlords would bear the expense of bringing apartments up to code standards under strict code enforcement (and therefore also under the imposition of warranties of habitability) if his model's assumptions held true. Some of the important assumptions of his model are: landlords are perfectly competitive, not collusive or oligopolistic; landlords make sufficient profit to absorb all costs of maintaining apartments up to code standards and still stay in the landlord business (or, to the extent they cannot, the government will enter the market to make up the deficit in supply); all interchangeable local low-income housing is brought up to standard at once so that people fleeing from an unreconstructed ghetto will not bid up the prices in a neighboring reconstructed ghetto; the marginal ghetto dweller is completely indifferent to better housing and will not pay a penny more for it (i.e., the demand curve won't shift so as to enable a rent increase); and that ironclad race or class prejudice will keep outsiders from moving into the ghetto even if ghetto housing substantially improves in quality (i.e., the demand will not increase relative to supply so as to enable a rent increase).

It is difficult to suppose that all of these assumptions would hold true for any given community. The last one is the most ironic: in order for a code enforcement scheme to benefit those who suffer from racial or class oppression, the prejudices supporting their oppression must continue unabated. Those who observe "gentrification" in areas subject to code enforcement (like Washington D.C.) argue that this is not the case; when the housing improves the middle class moves in.

100. *Id.* at 1173.

101. Ackerman's tentative argument that the law should enforce landlords' moral obligation to respect tenants' dignity is consonant with his later elaboration of the morality required of the citizens and lawmakers in the liberal state. *See* B. ACKERMAN, SOCIAL JUSTICE IN THE LIBERAL STATE (1980).

102. Payton v. New York, 445 U.S. 573, 589–90 (1980); *see also* United States v. Watson, 423 U.S. 411 (1976).

103. The challenged New York statute permitting the practice had been in effect for nearly 100 years and was in fact thought to be the common law rule. *See* Payton v. New York, 445 U.S. 573, 582, 591–98, 604–05 (1980) (White, J., dissenting).

104. *Id.* at 582 n.17. "[T]he 'physical entry of the home is the chief evil against which the wording of the Fourth Amendment is directed.'" *Id.* at 585 (quoting United States v. United States Dist. Court, 407 U.S. 297, 313 (1972)). The Court endorsed the statement of the dissenters below that "the purpose of the Fourth Amendment is to guard against arbitrary governmental invasions of the home." 445 U.S. at 582. The *Payton* majority also adopted the passage from Coolidge v. New Hampshire, 403 U.S. 474 (1971), recognizing "a distinction between searches and seizures that take place on a man's property—his home or office—and those carried out elsewhere." 445 U.S. at 586 n.25. And it quoted the classic passage from Boyd v. U.S., 116 U.S. 616, 630 (1886): "[T]he principles reflected in the Amendment . . . 'apply to all invasions on the part of the government and its employees of the sanctity of a man's home and the privacies of life.'" 445 U.S. at 585.

105. In United States v. Chadwick, 433 U.S. 1, 7 (1977), the Court quoted this phrase from Katz v. United States, 389 U.S. 347, 351 (1967). In *Chadwick* the court held that a locked footlocker, seized on the probable cause grounds that it contained contraband when its owners were arrested, could not be opened and searched in official custody without a warrant. The majority opinion said that the government was wrong in arguing that "only homes, offices, and private communications implicate interests which lie at the core of the Fourth Amendment." 433 U.S. at 7. Both the concurring and dissenting opinions agreed with this view. *Id.* at 16 (Brennan, J., concurring); *id.* at 17 (Blackmun, J., dissenting). Similarly, the three dissenters in *Payton* argued that "the Fourth Amendment is concerned with protecting people, not places, and no talismanic significance is given to the fact that an arrest occurs in the home rather than elsewhere." 445 U.S. at 615 (White, J., dissenting).

106. 116 U.S. 616 (1886).

107. *Id.* at 626.

108. *Id.* at 627–28, (quoting Entick v. Carrington, 95 Eng. Rep. 807, 810 (1765)).

109. *See* Warden v. Hayden, 387 U.S. 294 (1967). In *Warden,* the Court noted that in Gouled v. United States, 255 U.S. 298, 309, 311 (1921), it had "derived from *Boyd v. United States, supra,* the proposition that warrants 'may be resorted to only when a primary right to such search and seizure may be found in the interest which the public or the complainant may have in the property to be seized, . . . or when a valid exercise of the police power renders possession of the property by the

accused unlawful and provides that it may be taken'"; to seize the accused's property otherwise "'would be, in effect, as ruled in the *Boyd* case, to compel the defendant to become a witness against himself.'" 387 U.S. at 302. On the Fifth Amendment aspect of *Boyd,* see Gerstein, *The Demise of* Boyd: *Self-Incrimination and Private Papers in the Burger Court,* 27 UCLA L. REV. 343 (1979).

110. *See, e.g.,* Silverman v. United States, 365 U.S. 505 (1961).

111. 387 U.S. 294 (1967).

112. 389 U.S. 347 (1967).

113. *See* note 104 *supra.*

114. 387 U.S. at 301.

115. *Id.* at 304.

116. Katz v. United States, 389 U.S. at 351.

117. *Id.* at 361.

118. *See* Smith v. Maryland, 442 U.S. 735, 740 n.5 (1979).

119. *See, e.g.,* Coolidge v. New Hampshire, 403 U.S. 433 (1971); Carroll v. United States, 267 U.S. 132 (1925).

120. Chambers v. Maroney, 399 U.S. 42 (1970).

121. South Dakota v. Opperman, 428 U.S. 364 (1976); Cady v. Dombrowski, 413 U.S. 443 (1973).

122. In Cardwell v. Lewis, 417 U.S. 538 (1974), the Court stated: "One has a lesser expectation of privacy in a motor vehicle because its function is transportation and it seldom serves as one's residence or as the repository of personal effects." *Id.* at 590. In spite of the Court's statement, most people undoubtedly use their private automobiles as repositories of personal effects. The Court has also found a diminished expectation of privacy in cars because they are licensed and subject to many regulations, and because inventory searches of impounded vehicles had been made standard operating procedure by certain police departments. *See, e.g.,* Cady v. Dombrowski, 413 U.S. 439 (1973). But some inchoate feeling that cars are indeed personal may have influenced the outcome in Wooley v. Maynard, 430 U.S. 705 (1977) (state may not constitutionally force one to display license plate motto as condition upon using one's car).

123. Hindering the Court's development of a normative inquiry for the Fourth Amendment has been distaste for the exclusionary rule, which sometimes allows criminals to go free because of technical violations. Because of their discomfort with the rule, some justices seize upon whatever rationale is handy to validate searches. In Rakas v. Illinois, 439 U.S. 128 (1978), a plurality held that people riding in a car do not have standing under the Fourth Amendment to challenge a search unless they own the car or the item whose seizure is challenged. This provoked the dissenters to invoke the irony of *Katz:* "The court today holds that the Fourth Amendment protects property, not people . . . . " 439 U.S. at 156. The result in *Rakas* is not inconsistent with the personhood perspective, but seems too narrow. The important issue for the personhood perspective is not the state of the legal title, but the state of the person's relationship with the object, if that relationship is deemed legitimate by society.

An issue similar to the status of "mere passengers" in a car is the Fourth Amendment "standing" of household visitors. As to items found in the apartment, the court has granted standing to (recognized a protected interest in) those who essentially treat the place as home, i.e., have some continuing relationship with it. *See* 439 U.S.

at 141. This is not inconsistent with the property-for-personhood perspective. (Even casual visitors have a protected interest in their "persons"—physical body— because the Fourth Amendment protects "persons," as well as "houses, papers and effects.") *See* Ybarra v. Illinois, 444 U.S. 85 (1979).

124. *See* Michelman, *Property, Utility and Fairness: Comments on the Ethical Foundations of "Just Compensation" Law,* 80 HARV. L. REV. 1165 (1967). Michelman proposes a sophisticated utilitarian calculus designed to explain many of the anomalies of the case law. He rationalizes four incomplete strands of case law in terms of judicial intuitions relating primarily to this inherent utilitarian structure. The "physical invasion" test relates to high demoralization costs and low settlement costs. *Id.* at 1227. The "diminution of value" test boils down to an approximation of the "physical invasion" test. *Id.* at 1233. The "balancing" of the claimant's losses with society's gains relates to demoralization costs, *id.* at 1235, and the "harm and benefit" test is aimed at identifying "antinuisance" measures which merely rectify a preexisting unilateral redistribution and hence do not properly raise a compensation issue. *Id.* at 1239.

125. In Penn Cent. Transp. Co. v. City of New York, 438 U.S. 104 (1978), Justice Brennan, for the majority, wrote: "The question of what constitutes a 'taking' for purposes of the Fifth Amendment has proved to be a problem of considerable difficulty . . . . [T]his court, quite simply, has been unable to develop any 'set formula' for determining when 'justice and fairness' require that economic injuries caused by public action be compensated by the government, rather than remaining disproportionately concentrated on a few persons." *Id.* at 123–24.

126. B. ACKERMAN, PRIVATE PROPERTY AND THE CONSTITUTION 113–67 (1977).

127. Such a way of thinking is postulated in Michelman, *supra* note 124, at 1234.

128. *See* note 124 *supra.*

129. A government should not take such an object from me unless my hypothetical relationship with the object were viewed as fetishism or slavery to material things rather than constructive of personhood. *See* sec. IIC.

130. Such an implied limitation might well be couched in terms of substantive due process. *See* Moore v. City of East Cleveland, 431 U.S. 494 (1977), where a plurality found a substantive due process right to live in one's home with one's extended family, hence a substantive due process limitation on the power of local government to zone for occupancy by nuclear families only.

131. *See* Sager, *Property Rights and the Constitution,* in NOMOS XXII, PROPERTY 376, 378 (J. Pennock & J. Chapman eds. 1980): "While exercises of the power of eminent domain nominally depend for their legitimacy upon the existence of a 'public purpose,' that requirement has passed beyond the pale of serious judicial enforcement. In practice, eminent domain may be employed for any scheme a governing body that has not utterly taken leave of its corporate senses might choose to undertake."

132. Pillar of Fire v. Denver Urban Renewal Authority, 181 Colo. 411, 509 P.2d 1250 (1973).

133. *See* Joint Tribal Council of the Passamaquoddy Tribe v. Morton, 388 F. Supp. 649 (D. Me. 1975), *aff'd,* 528 F.2d 370 (1st Cir. 1975). The legislative settlement of the Indians' claim that the state had unfairly obtained some of their ancestral territory provided for extraordinary protection against state eminent do-

main once certain lands were reacquired for the Indians. In contrast, it is well established that the federal government may "take" Indian land without even monetary compensation, unless a federal treaty promises that it will not, in which case just compensation will be due. *See* United States v. Sioux Nation of Indians, 448 U.S. 371 (1980); Tee-Hit-Ton Indians v. United States, 348 U.S. 272 (1955).

134. B. ACKERMAN, *supra* note 126, at 142; Michelman, *supra* note 124, at 1233 (1967).

135. "Inverse condemnation" refers to an action brought by a property owner claiming that a government action not officially in eminent domain has in fact "taken" her property. Whether compensation and transfer of title to the condemnor would be the appropriate remedy in this type of action is currently in controversy. *See* Agins v. City of Tiburon, 447 U.S. 255 (1980); San Diego Gas & Elec. Co. v. City of San Diego, 450 U.S. 621 (1981).

136. 56 Wis.2d 7, 201 N.W.2d 761 (1972).

137. This inference helps explain the "mere" in some courts' reference to "mere diminution of market value," considered not compensable even though it may amount to huge losses of expected return on investment. *See, e.g.,* Agins v. Tiburon, 24 Cal. 3d 266, 598 P.2d 25 (1979), *aff'd,* 447 U.S. 255 (1980).

138. *See* Michelman, *supra* note 124, at 1238. Unfortunately, it would be difficult to prove that courts' deference to land use regulations stems from perception of the affected property as fungible. Actions are not likely to be brought by those who have put down roots into a prior permitted use, because, when new regulations are imposed, local bodies usually exempt preexisting nonconforming uses. *See, e.g.,* R. ELLICKSON & A. TARLOCK, LAND USE CONTROLS: CASES AND MATERIALS 190, 194—98 (1981). Local bodies sometimes provide that nonconforming uses must be "amortized" over a number of years, although, as Ellickson and Tarlock make clear, this would not be applied to a home or other personal property.

139. Marsh v. Alabama, 326 U.S. 501 (1946); Amalgamated Food Employees Union Local 590 v. Logan Valley Plaza, Inc., 391 U.S. 308 (1968); Lloyd Corp. v. Tanner, 407 U.S. 551 (1972); Hudgens v. NLRB, 424 U.S. 507 (1976).

140. Hudgens v. NLRB, 424 U.S. 507 (1976), declared that Lloyd Corp. v. Tanner, 407 U.S. 551 (1972), had effectively overruled Amalgamated Food Employees Union Local 590 v. Logan Valley Plaza, Inc., 391 U.S. 308 (1968).

141. 447 U.S. 74 (1980).

142. This intuition is nascent in Justice Marshall's opinions in the cases cited in note 139 *supra*, although he relies primarily on the quasi-public property argument. For example, in *Logan Valley,* Marshall implies that the speakers should prevail over commercial property owners but not homeowners, because homeowners have a privacy claim and commercial owners do not. 391 U.S. at 324. It appears that to Marshall "privacy" invokes the same complex of protected values I associate with "personhood." Dissenting in *Lloyd Corp. v. Tanner,* Marshall explicitly balanced "the freedom to speak, a freedom that is given a preferred place in our hierarchy of values, [with] the freedom of a private property owner to control his property." 407 U.S. at 551, 580.

143. Tribe argues that there is a problem with the "public function" analysis in that it makes First Amendment rights depend on speech content. L. TRIBE, *supra* note 91, at 1167. From the personhood perspective, both the moral status of the shopping center property (roughly fungible) and the moral status of the claimed

speech interests (related to personhood?) are relevant. If the speech interest were wholly commercial, it would not be characterized as closely tied to personhood. Consequently there would be no compelling reason to prefer the would-be speaker over the shopping center owner. Thus, a content distinction becomes relevant, similar to the distinction evinced in theories of freedom of speech that rest on personal dignity or autonomy. *See, e.g.,* Baker, *Commercial Speech: A Problem in the Theory of Freedom,* 62 Iowa L. Rev. 1 (1976). A parallel theory of freedom of association would hold that the interest in forming a corporation is less important than the interest in forming a political party or religious group.

144. *See, e.g.,* State v. Shack, 58 N.J. 297, 277 A.2d 369, 372 (1971) (state trespass law cannot be enforced by farmer against OEO worker seeking entry to aid migrant workers): "Title to real property cannot include dominion over the destiny of persons the owner permits to come upon the premises." *See also* Agricultural Labor Relations Bd. v. Superior Court, 16 Cal. 3d 392, 546 P.2d 687, 128 Cal. Rptr. 183 (1976); Donahue, *The Future of the Concept of Property Predicted from its Past,* in NOMOS XXII, Property 28, 67–68 n.104 (J. Pennock & J. Chapman eds. 1980).

145. 378 U.S. 226 (1964).

146. The Court remanded *Bell* so that the state court could consider whether Maryland's subsequently-enacted Public Accommodation Law would apply to void the trespass convictions. 378 U.S. at 228. The issue became moot because the Civil Rights Act of 1964, 28 U.S.C. § 1447, 42 U.S.C. §§ 1971, 1975a–d, 2000a–h (1976), prohibits discrimination in places of public accommodation.

147. 378 U.S. at 246.

148. The corporation owning the restaurant refused service not because of dislike for blacks but because "'it' thought 'it' could make more money by running a segregated restaurant." *Id.* at 245 (Douglas, J., concurring). The dilemma here is that restaurants as businesses would presumably prefer to serve everyone because that will maximize their profit. But if most white customers would prefer to dine without blacks, then no restaurant can afford to serve blacks unless it can make more profits serving blacks only than serving whites only. The dilemma disappears when all businesses agree to serve blacks, or if a court or legislature imposes this "agreement" on them.

The possibility that relying solely on the personhood perspective may permit "discrimination" on the part of small proprietors may be more important in the landlord-tenant context. Is it fair to ask someone who rents out the basement of her home to live in close proximity with a person who represents something personally repugnant to her? (Imagine a Jew whose parents died in the holocaust being asked to rent part of her home to a member of the American Nazi Party.) Perhaps some such feeling of the limiting case justifies the exemption in Title VIII of the 1968 Civil Rights Act for single-family homes sold or rented by the owner and for small multiple-unit dwellings in which the owner resides. 42 U.S.C. § 3603(b)(1), (2) (1976). But clearly this limitation would apply only to a narrow class of cases, which might be narrowed still further by other moral arguments not based solely on individual personhood.

149. [It is important to remember that the mere fact someone is genuinely self-invested in property rights needed to implement prejudice cannot make that self-investment justifiable and hence cannot make the property rights personal.]

150. 416 U.S. 1 (1974).

151. The village restricted land use to single-family dwellings. "Family" was defined to mean "[o]ne or more persons related by blood, adoption, or marriage, living and cooking together as a single housekeeping unit, exclusive of household servants. A number of persons but not exceeding two (2) living and cooking together as a single housekeeping unit though not related by blood, adoption, or marriage shall be deemed to constitute a family." 416 U.S. at 2. The six students, who attended nearby SUNY, Stony Brook, leased the house for 18 months. The owner-landlord and three tenants brought the action to invalidate the ordinance after the village threatened to enforce it against them.

For insightful thoughts of commentators who keep recurring to the puzzle posed by the case, *see* L. TRIBE, *supra* note 91, at 975–80, 985, 989–90; Michelman, *Political Markets and Community Self-Determination: Competing Judicial Models of Local Government Legitimacy,* 53 IND. L.J. 145, 187–99 (1977–1978). Part of the difficulty comes in trying to fathom why the court went the other way in Moore v. City of East Cleveland, 431 U.S. 494 (1977), where a plurality found a substantive due process right to live in one's home with one's extended family, hence a substantive due process limitation on the power of local government to zone for occupancy by nuclear families only. One justice found this right to be a property right. The personhood insight helps to explain the overlap of property rhetoric with substantive due process rhetoric; the right to live with her extended family was important to Mrs. Moore as constitutive of herself as an individual and member of a group. Thus a government that must respect persons should not prevent her from choosing to live this way, unless it can show a morally compelling reason to override her choice.

From the personhood perspective, Mrs. Moore had a better case than the students in Belle Terre, since it would be much more difficult for her to leave the community in which she made her home to express her life-style elsewhere, and since her choice is more clearly self-constitutive. At the same time, East Cleveland, a town of 40,000, had a much less plausible claim than did the 700 people of Belle Terre that a crucial claim of personhood for its people depended on upholding the ordinance. The village's claim would have been more plausible had the residents' group values not represented the American cultural mainstream.

152. Warren & Brandeis, *The Right to Privacy,* 4 HARV. L. REV. 193 (1890).

153. The survey of its manifestations in section V *supra* was meant to be suggestive and by no means exhaustive. Some other legal fields in which property for personhood seems relevant are:

(1) The doctrine of ameliorative waste probably now rests implicitly on the assumption that the reversioner or remainderman has personhood interests at stake that are irrelevant to the valuations of the marketplace. In the well-known case of Melms v. Pabst Brewing Co., 104 Wis. 7, 79 N.W. 738 (1899), Pabst, the holder of a life estate *pur autre vie* in the Melms residence, demolished it to add the land to its brewery next door. The Melms remaindermen sued for waste, but it was not readily believable that the homestead was personal, since it now stood in an industrial wasteland. The court denied relief but based its decision on a utilitarian rationale.

(2) The doctrine of specific performance gives enforcement of contracts for "unique" goods, but it simply assumes land is "unique" and it does not give ade-

quate scope to the uniqueness of other goods to some holders. Neither does it take into account the fact that the item may be personal to the seller and fungible to the buyer seeking enforcement, which would be a ground for denying specific performance in some cases (i.e., land transfers) where it is now routinely granted. *See* Schwartz, *The Case for Specific Performance,* 89 YALE L.J. 271, 296–98 (1979).

(3) An interesting recent development that seems to stem directly from the civil law tradition of which Hegel was a part is the granting to artists of rights over their work after it has passed out of their hands. This kind of claim is called *droit moral* (moral right) or *Urheberpersonlichkeitsrecht* (author's personality right). It goes beyond copyright, which protects only against economic exploitation of one's work by others, to give the artist the right to prevent owners of her work from altering or destroying it. The California Art Preservation Act, CAL. CIV. CODE § 987 (West Supp. 1982), declares "that the physical alteration or destruction of fine art, which is an expression of the artist's personality, is detrimental to the artist's reputation, and artists therefore have an interest in protecting their works of fine art against such alteration or destruction; and that there is also a public interest in preserving the integrity of cultural and artistic creations."

California also went beyond copyright in enacting the *droit de suite* in the California Resale Royalties Act, CAL. CIV. CODE § 986 (West Supp. 1982), granting artists additional property rights in the form of a five percent royalty most times a work changes hands. *See* Note, *The California Resale Royalties Act As a Test Case for Preemption Under the 1976 Copyright Law,* 81 COLUM. L. REV. 1315 (1981).

(4) The law has long allowed bankrupted persons to preserve some property claims against their creditors. The creditors' claims are clearly fungible and the exempt items may be personal. For example, the federal Bankruptcy Code exempts the debtor's interest (not to exceed $200 per item) in "household furnishings, . . . books, animals, crops, or musical instruments that are held primarily for . . . personal, family, or household use," 11 U.S.C. § 522(d)(4) (Supp. III 1979), and $500 worth of "jewelry held primarily for . . . personal, family, or household use." *Id.* § 522(d)(4). *See* 3 COLLIER ON BANKRUPTCY ¶¶ 522.01–.26 (15th ed. 1981).

(5) Special protections for homeowners who borrow on purchase-money mortgages are common. *See, e.g.,* CAL. BUS. & PROF. CODE § 10242.6 (West Supp. 1982) (limiting prepayment charges for loans on owner-occupied single-family residences); CAL. CIV. CODE § 2949 (West 1974) (prohibiting declaring default or acceleration upon further encumbrance of owner-occupied single-family residence). The UNIFORM LAND TRANSACTIONS ACT (1978) grants enhanced rights to a "protected party"—defined essentially as a homeowner mortgagor—in many circumstances (e.g., longer notice before instituting foreclosure and a ban on deficiency judgments). *See* § 1–203 and Commissioners' Comment to § 1–203.

(6) The common law requirement that parties' attempts to create servitudes upon land will be honored only if they "touch and concern" the land could be related to preservation of autonomy and human dignity. *See* Reichman, *Judicial Supervision of Servitudes,* 7 J. LEGAL STUD. 139, 143–50 (1978).

Chapter Two

1. *See, e.g.,* Werner Z. Hirsch, *From "Food for Thought" to "Empirical Evidence" About Consequences of Landlord-Tenant Laws,* 69 CORNELL L. REV. 604, 610 (1984).

2. In this situation rent control would not worsen allocative efficiency over

laissez-faire, and we might deem the wealth transfer from (relatively richer) monopolizing landlords to (relatively poorer) tenants to be normatively appropriate. Efficiency would not actually be improved by rent control, however, unless setting rents at the competitive price somehow gave rise to an increase in supply of rental housing from the restricted monopoly level. By assuming that landlords have been able to maintain a monopoly, we have assumed that entry by new landlords has been difficult, perhaps because the landlord monopoly controlled the issue of building permits to potentially competitive landlords, or for other reasons. Unless imposition of rent control could simultaneously ease barriers to entry, it would not give rise to the increase in supply which would improve allocative efficiency.

3. Economic rents are "payments to inputs that are above the minimum required to make these inputs available to the industry or to the economy." Edwin Mansfield, Microeconomics: Theory and Applications 370 (2d ed. 1975). Some people might tend to think of economic rents as excess profits, since they are profits above the rate of return required to keep the productive resources allocated to their current use.

4. The term is meant to be a contrast to the term "ideal theory" used by John Rawls in A Theory of Justice 9 (1972).

5. The same normative issue arises in the context of legal habitability rights, insofar as they attempt to raise quality (hence landlord's costs) while not raising the price to the tenant. *Cf.* Bruce A. Ackerman, *Regulating Slum Housing Markets on Behalf of the Poor: Of Housing Codes, Housing Subsidies and Income Redistribution Policy,* 80 Yale L.J. 1093 (1971).

6. I refer to an uncritical reader of Richard A. Posner, Economic Analysis of Law (2d ed. 1977); *see, e.g., id.* at 367. The "mere" redistribution would be acceptable to the Posnerian, of course, only if it were accomplished without transaction costs, including "demoralization costs." Posner himself would postulate unacceptable costs to almost any proposed redistribution. *See id.* ch. 16.

7. I refer, of course, to an uncritical reader of Robert Nozick, Anarchy, State, and Utopia (1974).

8. This seems to be the dominant view of the classical theorists on property and contract, the necessary institutions of the free market. *See* John Stuart Mill, Principles of Political Economy II ch. II, § 1 (1848) ("The right of property includes . . . the freedom of acquiring by contract"). Hume's view was more instrumental: free transferability by consent is the remedy for the "grand inconvenience" that property rights might not originally be held by those most suitable. David Hume, *Of the Transference of Property by Consent,* in A Treatise of Human Nature pt. II, § IV, 514 (Lewis Selby-Bigge ed., with text rev. and variant readings by P.H. Nidditch, 2d ed. 1978).

9. I should say here that I think such a "pure" Nozickian would be inconsistent with (some of) Nozick's own views. Nozick did recognize, although he did not dwell on the issue, that in the real world the existing entitlement structure can be unjust. Transfers of entitlements occur by rip-offs and fraud as well as free contract. In order to uphold the absolute nature of the rights of private property plus free contract, a prophylactic corrective justice theory is necessary. Therefore, a Nozickian less oriented solely to an ideal form of entitlement theory might admit that under some circumstances rent control is permitted or required by what Nozick called a theory of rectification. Under nonideal circumstances Nozickian libertarianism does

not forbid all forms of redistribution. If the landlords' chain of title to their wealth contains any taint of coercion or conquest, it does not follow that they are entitled to keep it. Nozick did not develop a theory of rectification. For those who consider the bitter details of historical oppression to be the paramount "nonideal" factor for ethics and politics, the requirements of a developed theory of rectification would no doubt engulf most of Nozick's ideal libertarian conclusions.

10. Probably where rent control is enacted, it is predicted that more tenants would be forced out by rising uncontrolled rents than by side effects of controls. The prevalence of concomitant safeguards such as restrictions on condominium conversions shows that this factor is worrisome. *See infra* sec. IV.

11. There might be alternatives other than rent control to respond to these considerations. For example, some government entity could subsidize all tenants to offset the market increases. In this article I do not consider such alternatives because my aim is to contribute to evaluating the primary solution our political order has generated. I would be inclined to suppose, however, that enactment of rent control by grassroots political organizing is preferable to subsidies granted at higher levels of government. For various reasons, accomplishing regulation in one's favor is not the same thing as receiving a dole.

12. Someone might interpose here, What if the tenant chooses not to press the claim? There could be tenants who don't much care whether or not they stay very long in one residence. Why grant a price break against landlords who care very much about their profit levels? If such a subclass of tenants can be singled out, it can be exempted from rent control (for example, an exemption for transient accommodations). Insofar as such a subclass cannot be singled out, one would have to be convinced that the risk of error against the personal interests of other tenants who do very much care justifies the errors of a blanket rule that includes this subclass of indifferent tenants. The strength of our conviction about this will vary, but it is my guess that there are many circumstances in which this conviction would prevail.

There could also be tenants who would value the money they might get by "selling" back to the landlord their rent-control rights more than they value a right to keep their apartments. This could come about if we made rent control waivable by the tenant, and if circumstances were such that the landlord would charge a lower price "up front" for a non-rent-controlled apartment, knowing she could raise the rent at will, than she would charge for a rent-controlled apartment, knowing she would be stuck with the original price for as long as the tenant stayed. Then some tenants might choose to waive rent control in exchange for lower initial rent.

Since no rent-control ordinance permits such transactions to take place, the tenant's rent-control right is inalienable, much as the tenant's habitability right is inalienable where the legal implied warranty of habitability is nonwaivable. The restraint on alienation on the seller's side (the landlord's limited freedom to set prices and terms of transfer) is matched by an inalienability on the buyer's side (the tenant's inability to waive or sell back rights for a subjectively perceived benefit). The normative analysis of this kind of inalienability, which is typical of incomplete commodification, is partly beyond the scope of the present essay. [*See* Radin, *Market-Inalienability,* 100 HARV. L. REV. 1849 (1987).]

13. I do not wish to imply that the would-be tenants have no claim to rent control or housing regulation in general; they may well, under any number of approaches to moral claims involving necessities of life, including shelter. In arguing

that incomplete commodification of housing is proper, I imply that some regulation is proper. My point here is rather that except under special circumstances, there seems to be no particular claim to live in *this particular* community, paying *higher* rents and forcing out current tenants.

14. *See* ch. 1.

15. G.W.F. Hegel, Hegel's Philosophy of Right (Grundlinien der Philosophie des Rechts) §§ 41–71 (T. Knox trans. 1942).

16. I base this upon Hegel's treatment of the distinction between alienability and inalienability, in which he relies on a distinction between things external and things internal to the person; this seems to me a sharp divide between subject and object. *Id.*

17. How to characterize the species of objectivity needed, and how to make the required objective judgment about various categories of object-relations, are difficult problems. I think an ultimate context-dependency of the distinction between good and bad object-relations, and thus of the choice of moral categories of personal property, can be admitted without thereby rendering the matter subjective or merely conventional. The methodology of coherence or reflective equilibrium in ethics constantly requires attention to total context, but this does not render that which is justified subjective, nor does it entail conventionalism. I am influenced here, for example, by Hilary Putnam, Reason, Truth and History (1981).

18. The successful argument in recent tax limitation initiatives has been the appeal to save longtime homeowners from losing their homes because of property tax increases. The tax limitation schemes would in my view be more readily justifiable if the beneficiaries had in fact been limited to resident owners. The commercial beneficiaries are moral free riders.

19. There seems to be little empirical data on this point; *see* Richard F. Muth, *Redistribution of Income Through Regulation in Housing*, 32 Emory L.J. 691, 697–700 (1983).

20. Roberto M. Unger, Knowledge and Politics (1975) is perhaps representative ("theory of groups").

21. *See, e.g.,* Ronald R. Garet, *Communality and the Existence of Groups*, 56 S. Cal. L. Rev. 1001 (1983); Michael J. Sandel, Liberalism and the Limits of Justice (1982).

22. The evaluation here would be analogous to that involving the subclass of indifferent tenants (if any) discussed in note 12.

23. For a detailed discussion of various provisions of rent-control legislation, *see* Kenneth K. Baar, *Guidelines for Drafting Rent Control Laws: Lessons of a Decade*, 35 Rutgers L. Rev. 723 (1983).

24. An exception for "retaliatory eviction" is now part of the normal legal rule. In most jurisdictions, termination of a tenancy is disallowed if the landlord's motive is to retaliate against the tenant for complaining to housing authorities or exercising certain other rights.

25. But I do not believe such an exemption necessary to protect landlords, at least if they have bought the building for investment and never previously lived in it, for their interest is purely commercial. At best they are in a similar moral position to excluded would-be tenants.

26. In Fresh Pond Shopping Center Inc. v. Rent Control Board of Cambridge, 388 Mass. 1051, 446 N.E. 2d 1060 (1983), *appeal dismissed,* Fresh Pond Shopping

Center Inc. v. Callahan, 464 U.S. 875 (1983), local regulation preventing the land-lord from demolishing a rental building in order to build a parking lot was upheld. It was perhaps an important (though not recognized as such) circumstance in the case that the landlord was a corporation, and therefore not capable of claiming other than a fungible interest in the property. The Massachusetts Supreme Judicial Court has also upheld regulation prohibiting a landlord who acquires a rent-controlled condominium unit occupied by a tenant from later removing the unit from the rental market by taking up residency in it herself. Flynn v. City of Cambridge, 383 Mass. 152, 418 N.E. 2d 335 (1981). Under appropriate circumstances I think such a regulation could be defended on the ground stated in note 25. (Whether the appropriate circumstances are actually present in Cambridge, Massachusetts, is a question about which I do not have enough information to make a judgment.)

27. Birkenfeld v. Berkeley, 17 Cal. 3d 129 (1976).

28. *See* Margaret Jane Radin, *Risk-of-Error Rules and Non-Ideal Justification,* in NOMOS XXVII, JUSTIFICATION 33 (J. Pennock & J. Chapman eds. 1986).

29. *See, e.g.,* Robert M. Cover, *Foreword:* Nomos *and Narrative,* 97 HARV. L. REV. 4 (1983).

Chapter Three

1. R. EPSTEIN, TAKINGS: PRIVATE PROPERTY AND THE POWER OF EMINENT DOMAIN 95 (1985).

2. *Id.* ch. 14.

3. *Id.* ch. 8.

4. *Id.* at 202–09.

5. I have further commented on Epstein's views in chapter 4, "The Liberal Con-ception of Property: Crosscurrents in the Jurisprudence of Takings."

6. *Proceedings of the Conference on Takings of Property and the Constitution,* 41 U. MIAMI L. REV. 49, 176–78 (1986) [hereinafter *Proceedings*]. *See* D. HUME, A TREATISE OF HUMAN NATURE bk. III, pt. II, §§ I–IV (Lewis Selby-Bigge ed. 1978) (1740).

7. *Proceedings, supra* note 6, at 126–27.

8. EPSTEIN, *supra* note 1, at 304.

9. For example, the restraints imposed by the tenancy by the entireties, or, for that matter, by the fee tail. Epstein elsewhere takes an ambivalent attitude toward inalienabilities. It seems from his Columbia article, Epstein, *Why Restrain Alien-ation?,* 85 COLUM. L. REV. 970 (1985), that no deviations from free-market alien-ability are permitted unless they are required by efficiency; whereas it seems from a more recent pronouncement that any restraints are fine as long as imposed by indi-viduals and not the government. Epstein, *Past and Future: The Temporal Dimension in the Law of Property,* 64 WASH. U. L.Q. 667 (1986). *See infra* my discussion of the tension in his arguments in section II, "Time, Possession, and Alienation."

10. *See* C. DONAHUE, T. KAUPER & P. MARTIN, CASES AND MATERIALS ON PROPERTY: AN INTRODUCTION TO THE CONCEPT AND THE INSTITUTION 664–70 (2d ed. 1983).

11. EPSTEIN, *supra* note 1, at 65.

12. Civil Rights Act of 1964, 42 U.S.C. § 1971 et seq. (1982).

13. EPSTEIN, *supra* note 1, at 325–327.

14. *Proceedings, supra* note 6, at 187–197. [Recently Epstein has indeed argued

for repeal of civil rights laws insofar as they prohibit discrimination by private employers in a reasonably competitive market setting. R. EPSTEIN, FORBIDDEN GROUNDS (1992).]

15. J. BENTHAM, THEORY OF LEGISLATION 113 (R. Hildreth trans. 2d ed. 1871).

16. Timeless, changeless, and prepolitical practical consequences determine what property "is."

17. It seems entirely implausible that human nature and human society are so essentially fixed in the eighteenth-century market models that they have always and will forever practically arrive at private property and free contract, much less specific, detailed institutional manifestations of them.

18. EPSTEIN, *supra* note 1, at 138.

19. *Id.* at 174.

20. K. MARX, CAPITAL 41–81 (F. Engels ed. 1906).

21. Cohen, *Property and Sovereignty,* 13 CORNELL L.Q. 8 (1927). The distinction was earlier proposed by the British sociologist L.T. Hobhouse in *The Historical Evolution of Property, in Fact and in Idea,* in PROPERTY: ITS DUTIES AND RIGHTS 3 (2d ed. 1922).

22. Epstein, *Past and Future: The Temporal Dimension in the Law of Property,* 65 WASH. U. L.Q. 667, 667 (1986).

23. R. NOZICK, ANARCHY, STATE AND UTOPIA (1974).

24. This appears to be Epstein's view also; *see* Epstein, *supra* note 22, at 667–68.

25. *Id.* at 674–76.

26. In addition to the omission of this theoretical point of view, which is no doubt a matter of normative choice on Epstein's part, there are substantive omissions from his treatment of adverse possession that I believe should be included in any general discussion of the common law treatment of nonconsensual transfer of property rights over time. The most important omission is prescription, by which an adverse user creates a divided title where formerly there was one owner. It is difficult to use the standard rule-utilitarian treatment of adverse possession (i.e., that it clears titles and facilitates transactions) to justify prescription. The most one can say, perhaps, is that where a court has a choice between awarding an easement by prescription or awarding the entire fee interest by adverse possession, it ought to choose the latter. This could explain why those who build encroaching buildings are awarded a fee in the strip they have built upon, rather than an easement to maintain a building upon that portion of their neighbor's land. *See, e.g.,* Belotti v. Bickhardt, 228 N.Y. 296, 127 N.E. 239 (1920).

Another important omission is the problem of nonconsensual transfer between a private party and a governmental entity or the general public by means of adverse use. The problem goes both ways: how should we treat adverse possession against a government title; and how should we treat adverse possession or user by the general public? *See, e.g.,* Gion v. City of Santa Cruz, 2 Cal. 3d 29, 465 P.2d 50, 84 Cal. Rptr. 162 (1970); CAL. CIV. CODE § 1009 (Deering Supp. 1986).

27. Epstein, *supra* note 22, at 674. Epstein's argument is that the longer the lapse of time between relevant events and a legal decision, the greater the costs to the system. Specifically, the argument seems to run like this: (1) as time passes, it becomes more difficult to ascertain facts, and thus uncertainty increases; (2) the greater the uncertainty the greater the risk of error in any specific decision; (3) the

greater the risk of error the higher the costs associated with any specific decision; (4) therefore, the longer the time between relevant events and a legal decision, the higher the costs associated with that decision; and (5) therefore, the longer the time between relevant events and all legal decisions, the higher the costs associated with legal decisions in the aggregate. Perhaps perversely, I wonder whether the argument is as self-evident as Epstein seems to think. Might uncertainty sometimes decrease as time passes? (It might, if your normative theory of property tells you to look to productive use, settled expectations, or the bonds of personhood rather than first possession.) Might uncertainty ever decrease risk of error? (It might, if a right normative result does exist and we are steadfastly pursuing the wrong one.)

28. Indeed, "[t]he real questions are not whether a statute of limitations in the round works some Pareto superior move. Instead the harder question is one of fine tuning. What is the best way to structure the rules of adverse possession in order to maximize the general gain?" Epstein, *supra* note 22, at 680.

29. *See, e.g.,* J. BUCHANAN, THE LIMITS OF LIBERTY ch. 10 (1975) (arguing that constitutional "renegotiation" would be chosen as preferable to a revolution otherwise predictable in light of ongoing shifts in the underlying power balance among various groups).

30. Jeremy Bentham gives more recognition to this than does Epstein. *See* J. BENTHAM, THE THEORY OF LEGISLATION, PRINCIPLES OF THE CIVIL CODE pt. 1, ch. 10 (1789): "Everything which I possess, or to which I have a title, I consider in my own mind as destined always to belong to me. I make it the basis of my expectations, and of the hopes of those dependent upon me; and I form my plan of life accordingly. Every part of my property may have, in my estimation, besides its intrinsic value, a value of affection—as an inheritance from my ancestors, as the reward of my own labour, or as the future dependence of my children. Everything about it represents to my eye that part of myself which I have put into it—those cares, that industry, that economy which denied itself present pleasures to make provision for the future. Thus our property becomes a part of our being, and cannot be torn from us without rending us to the quick." Of course, this insight is also at the root of the personality theory of property. The personality theory can be conflated with a welfare theory that pays sufficient attention to "subjective" value, including attention to which subsets of property interests this kind of "subjective" value is likely to attach. In my treatment of personality theory I do not do this because I do not treat this kind of value as "subjective."

31. Although I think this is not so once a theory of rectification (corrective justice) is admitted as necessary.

32. Epstein seems to feel that the legal system is now doing without adverse possession, more or less, having developed better methods of dealing with the problem, but the 850 *appellate* opinions since 1966 examined by Helmholz seems to make this an overstatement; *see* Helmholz, *Adverse Possession and Subjective Intent,* 61 WASH. U. L.Q. 331 (1983). In any case, the better methods of dealing with the problem are modern conveyancing and recording practices, and these are (arguably) "better" only in a utilitarian, not a Lockean sense, because they make titleholders actively pursue the goal of remaining titleholders. Further, I imagine that these better practices deal less well with acquisition of less than a fee interest (i.e., prescription) than they do with acquisition of the fee by adverse possession. Hence, I would hypothesize that the volume of prescription cases has not diminished as much as the

volume of adverse possession cases, assuming their volume has in fact diminished. But this problem awaits investigation.

33. As Hegel puts this: "The form given to a possession and its mark are themselves externalities but for the subjective presence of the will which alone constitutes the meaning and value of externalities. This presence, however, which is use, employment, or some other mode in which the will expresses itself, is an event in time, and what is objective in time is the continuance of this expression of the will. Without this the thing becomes a *res nullius,* because it has been deprived of the actuality of the will and possession. Therefore I gain or lose possession of property through prescription." HEGEL'S PHILOSOPHY OF RIGHT § 64 (T. Knox trans. 1942).

In other words, for Hegel "actual" possession is needed to *keep* title as well as to gain it through adverse possession.

34. For example, much of Epstein's utilitarian reasoning assumes a knowing adverse possessor moving in on someone else's property. This assumption ignores the more common cases where people are simply mistaken.

35. *See, e.g.,* Lessee of Ewing v. Burnet, 36 U.S. (11 Pet.) 41 (1837).

36. *See, e.g.,* Ennis v. Stanley, 346 Mich. 296, 78 N.W. 2d 114 (1956). It is my tentative view, which it would take a Helmholzian endeavor to substantiate (*see* Helmholz, *supra* note 32), that permeation of reasoning appropriate to the "squatters" picture may have caused conflict and confusion in the law surrounding the kinds of cases that actually occur.

37. As Helmholz has shown, *supra* note 32, it appears that the practice of judges is to take into account state of mind more often than the doctrine in their jurisdictions would warrant.

38. This debate is usually put into the "hostile and under claim of right" part of the hornbook doctrine. If we are to understand "claim of right" in any ordinary language sense, then we tend toward position (2) (the "good-faith" standard), and must interpret "hostile" as meaning merely nonpermissive on the part of the "true owner." On the other hand, if we are to understand "hostile" in an ordinary language sense, then we tend toward position (3) (the "aggressive trespasser" standard), and must interpret "claim of right" to mean not claim of ownership, but merely nonsubservience to the claim of the titleholder. If we take position (1) (which I call the objective standard), then "hostile and under claim of right" must be taken just to negate permission.

39. Epstein argues that the subset of "bad-faith" adverse possessors, which would presumably include "squatters" and aggressive encroachers in boundary disputes, should be subject to a longer statute of limitations before acquiring title. The asserted utilitarian ground for this argument is that "parties who engage in deliberate wrongs constitute a greater threat than those who make innocent errors or are simply negligent: there is a greater danger that intentional wrongdoers will do it all again." EPSTEIN, *supra* note 1, at 686. But if the "wrongdoers" are productive and the titleholders are passive, are the "wrongdoers" so wrong in the utilitarian sense? And to carve out a subset of "bad-faith" cases makes evidence of "bad faith" relevant in every case. This is a cost to the system and will fail to clear some titles where an accusation of "bad faith" is wrongly made to stick. (I don't mean to suggest that making it harder to acquire property by adverse possession in "bad faith" is necessarily wrong, only that it is probably more readily supported by nonutilitarian than by utilitarian normative arguments.)

40. If we heavily weight the utilitarian concern with notice (ability to structure other transactions based upon foreseeable consequences), it is clear that the double message imparted when the lived boundaries differ from the record books is costly, but unclear which way the correction should go in order to eliminate the double message at least cost. If we heavily weight the utilitarian concern for choosing rules so as to steer behavior into paths creating fewer transaction costs, then perhaps we would think that the recorded boundaries should prevail: make people pay the price of failing to check official boundaries, because then they will more often check them before acting and conform their activities to them.

41. Epstein discusses this problem in detail, *supra* note 22, at 689–91, concluding on utilitarian grounds that there should be a longer statute of limitations for remaindermen than for holders of present possessory estates. Without going into detail here, I believe there is an equally persuasive utilitarian argument for cutting off remaindermen at the same time as the life estate holder (provided that future interest holders have a cause of action against trespassers, by analogy with the law of waste). Nevertheless, the two-tier result here is not as problematic from a utilitarian point of view as is the two-tier result on the issue of "bad faith," because whether or not there is a remainderman somewhere in the wings will not thereby become a submerged issue in every case.

42. For example, in Belotti v. Bickhardt, 228 N.Y. 296, 127 N.E. 239 (1920) it was sufficient to establish "open and notorious" adverse possession that the title-holder had seen the physical object (an encroaching building), even though no one knew that the building was over the boundary line because all parties relied on a mistaken map.

43. The common law tradition here is to grant extensions of the statute of limitations to those who are minors, insane, prisoners, or out of the jurisdiction, but only if this "disability" existed on the day the trespasser moved in. Epstein's reconstrual of these common law traditions in utilitarian terms leaves out prisoners' rights, and lacks an explanation of why the "disability" does not provide any extra time to sue if it occurs after the trespasser has moved in, but before the statute has run.

44. If an object is fungible it is perfectly replaceable with money or other objects of its kind. If it is personal, it has become bound up with the personhood of the holder and is no longer commensurate with money. The distinction—which of course really marks the endpoints of a continuum of kinds of relationships between persons and objects—may be symbolized as widgets versus wedding rings.

45. Might the long time required in common law England and in the colonies, and the shorter time required in the American West, be related to cultural differences in the time required to become attached to one's land?

46. In Epstein's view, "the only justification for restraints of private alienation is to prevent the infliction of external harms, either through aggression or the depletion of common-pool resources." Epstein, *supra* note 22, at 705; *see also* Epstein, *Why Restrain Alienation?* 85 COLUM. L. REV. 970 (1985).

47. It seems to me that one of the ways the common law reflected this conceptual tendency was in striking down restraints because they were "repugnant to a fee." In other words, free alienability was inherent in the concept of being a fee simple absolute, and a fee simple with strings attached was something of a contradiction in terms. (Of course, for a utilitarian this conceptualism seems to make a fee some kind

of metaphysical entity, when it is really only whatever turns out to be the most socially useful package of rights.)

48. Epstein's focus upon the Rule Against Perpetuities, which limits only certain kinds of future interests in persons other than the grantor (contingent remainders and executory interests), obscures both the scope of the problem of restraints upon alienation and the range of the common law's responses to it.

49. At least in the case of remainders, Epstein does argue that the restraint is inefficient; he professes puzzlement about why a grantor would want to create them. Epstein, *supra* note 22, at 706–07.

50. Note that Epstein holds at the same time that legally imposed restraints are forbidden, with the exception of necessary prevention of external harm. *See id.* at 705, quoted at *supra,* note 46. Thus his position is that government-imposed structuring of transactions between persons is forbidden, *unless* necessary to prevent externalities, while private (government-authorized) transactions between persons must be protected against government restructuring, *even if* they create restraints resulting in costly externalities. This position may ultimately be incoherent: for a utilitarian, an externality is an externality. At minimum, it places great weight on the problematic "public/private" distinction. From a libertarian point of view, there is no reason to suppose that publicly imposed restraints always represent rent-seeking by special interest groups; sometimes, especially in small local jurisdictions, they may really reflect uncoerced community consensus. There is likewise no reason to suppose that privately imposed restraints always represent uncoerced consensus; sometimes, especially if widely imposed and uniform, they may reflect rent-seeking by those with market power.

51. Johnson v. Whiton, 159 Mass. 424, 34 N.E. 542 (1893) (citing Co. Litt. 27).

52. Epstein, *supra* note 22, at 698–99 (footnotes omitted).

53. An insight about this difference between absolute property in widgets and in land seems to be the reason why nineteenth-century theorists like J.S. Mill and T.H. Green argued for limitations on property in land but not widgets.

54. Epstein, *supra* note 22, at 704–05.

55. Epstein, *Notice and Freedom of Contract in the Law of Servitudes,* 55 S. CAL. L. REV. 1353, 1360 (1982).

56. *See, e.g.,* Reichman, *Judicial Supervision of Servitudes,* 7 J. LEGAL STUD. 139 (1978); Sterk, *Freedom from Freedom of Contract: The Enduring Value of Servitude Restrictions,* 70 IOWA L. REV. 615 (1985). The term "residential private government" was coined by Reichman; *see* Reichman, *Residential Private Governments: An Introductory Survey,* 43 U. CHI. L. REV. 253 (1976).

57. In my view, this "optimal jurisdiction problem" is an interesting way to see the issue the court was wrestling with in Southern Burlington County NAACP v. Mt. Laurel, 67 N.J. 151, 336 A.2d 713 (1975), *cert. denied,* 423 U.S. 808 (1975) ("[T]he general welfare which developing municipalities like Mount Laurel must consider extends beyond their boundaries and cannot be parochially confined to the claimed good of the particular municipality.").

58. *Cf.* the treatment of "regret" as a moral reason to limit freedom of contract in Kronman, *Paternalism and the Law of Contracts,* 92 YALE L.J. 763 (1983).

59. *See, e.g.,* Reichman, *Judicial Supervision of Servitudes,* 7 J. LEGAL STUD. 139 (1978).

60. Perhaps the list of proscribed servitudes would include things that look like new feudalism, such as requirements that the resident always buy supplies at the grantor's store, serve in the grantor's employ, etc.; and things that look like discrimination by the relatively powerful against the relatively powerless, such as the formerly common servitudes specifying that the resident must be of the Caucasian race; and perhaps things that look like tying essentials of life (like housing) to important and disputed matters of conscience, like religion or political affiliation, etc. This list of moral limitations on servitudes correlates fairly well with Reichman's proposed rereading of the touch-and-concern requirements. *See* Reichman, *supra* note 59.

61. Perhaps this is why J.S. Mill in ON LIBERTY argued against freedom to sell oneself into slavery on the ground that "[t]he principle of freedom cannot require that [one] should be free not to be free. It is not freedom to be allowed to alienate [one's] freedom." J.S. MILL, ON LIBERTY ch. 5 (1849).

Chapter Four

1. *See* R. EPSTEIN, TAKINGS: PRIVATE PROPERTY AND THE POWER OF EMINENT DOMAIN (1985).

2. *Id.* at 304; *see also id.* at 58–59 (discussing the rights of ownership according to his conception).

3. *Id.* at 65.

4. *Id.* at 66–73.

5. "The right of disposition is a property right, in the same degree and manner as the right to exclusive possession. What a plaintiff demands is noninterference by the rest of the world in his dealings with any third party, X. . . . [A]t stake is the right to contract with X, which is good against the world." *Id.* at 74.

Epstein maintains that "[a]s a first approximation it appears that any restraint upon the power of an owner to alienate his own property should be regarded as impermissible." Epstein, *Why Restrain Alienation?*, 85 COLUM. L. REV. 970, 971 (1985); *see also* R. EPSTEIN, *supra* note 1, at 252–53 ("[T]he system of private property contains the right to dispose of acquired wealth," hence the rationale that workers' compensation statutes are justified on the basis of unequal bargaining power is "*constitutionally* defective" because the employers' property rights preclude such a forced wealth transfer.).

6. Epstein assumes that a bright line can be drawn between harm-causing nuisance-like activities and normal activities. *See* R. EPSTEIN, *supra* note 1, at 112–21. Epstein's critics have vigorously taken him to task for this and other philosophical camel-swallowing. *See, e.g.,* Grey, *The Malthusian Constitution*, 41 U. MIAMI L. REV. 21 (1986).

7. This is Epstein's version of the notion of reciprocity, in which those injured by regulations also receive offsetting benefits. R. EPSTEIN, *supra* note 1, at 195–215.

8. For example, Epstein indicates that although social security, Medicare, and other welfare programs are wrong in principle, they should not now be abruptly reversed. *Id.* at 324–29. "Where the reliance interest is powerful and pervasive, it must be respected, so caution, but not total inaction, is the order of the day. Where the reliance interest is weak, there is a strict constitutional duty to chip away more forcefully at the present structure." *Id.* at 326.

9. *Id.* at 22–25. *See* ch. 3, sec. I.

10. *Id.* at 26–29.

11. *Id.* at 25–26.

12. *Id.* at 24–25.

13. *Id.* at 24.

14. *Id.* at 20.

15. *Id.* at 23. Blackstone defined property as "that sole and despotic dominion which one man claims and exercises over the external things of the world, in total exclusion of the right of any other individual in the universe." *Id.* at 22 (quoting WILLIAM BLACKSTONE, COMMENTARIES *2). Blackstone also stated that property consists of "the free use, enjoyment, and disposal of all his acquisitions, without any control or diminution, save only by the laws of the land." *Id.* Epstein believes that these quotations "well capture[ ]" the "basic sense" of the word property. *Id.*

16. *Id.* at 230–31. For a trenchant critique of Epstein's approach, see Grey, *supra* note 6, at 29–31.

17. 444 U.S. 164 (1979).

18. *Id.* at 179.

19. *Id.* at 179–80.

20. 458 U.S. 419, 435–36 (1982).

21. *Id.* at 435 (quoting United States v. General Motors, 323 U.S. 373, 378 (1945)).

22. *Id.* at 435. In referring to an owner's bundle of property rights the Court was adopting the modern conceptualization of property as an aggregate of rights rather than a unitary thing. *See* Hohfeld, *Fundamental Legal Conceptions as Applied in Judicial Reasoning*, 26 YALE L.J. 710 (1917); B. ACKERMAN, PRIVATE PROPERTY AND THE CONSTITUTION (1977).

23. *Loretto,* 458 U.S. at 435.

24. I shall explain later why I believe this development to be deeply misguided, an artifact of the kind of conceptualism that tends to be associated with the neoconservative view of constitutional property. *See infra* notes 44–54 and accompanying text (explaining the problem of conceptual severance).

25. 438 U.S. 104 (1978).

26. Others are: the economic impact of the regulation and particularly whether it has interfered with "distinct investment-backed expectations," *id.* at 122; whether the regulation is an exercise of the taxing power, *id.*; whether it promotes public "health, safety, morals, or general welfare," *id.* at 123; whether it is reasonably necessary to the effectuation of a substantial public purpose, *id.* at 127; whether it may be characterized as for the purpose of permitting or facilitating "uniquely public functions." *Id.* at 128.

27. *Loretto,* 458 U.S. at 436. In its concern about the difficulty of line drawing, the Court was perhaps manifesting discomfort with the pragmatic approach in general. As discussed later, *infra* notes 62–75 and accompanying text, this discomfort is likely related to a conservative interpretation of the Rule of Law.

28. Penn Central Transp. Co. v. City of New York, 438 U.S. 104, 130–38 (1978).

29. Village of Euclid v. Ambler Realty Co., 272 U.S. 365 (1926). *Euclid* upheld the general constitutionality of local zoning regulations that resulted in a 75% diminution in the market value of Ambler Realty's 68 acres of vacant land. The case has come to stand for the notion that zoning regulation does not per se deny due process or "take" property.

30. *See, e.g.,* R. EPSTEIN, *supra* note 1, at 102 *passim.*

31. 444 U.S. 51, 64–68 (1979).

32. *See, e.g.,* R. EPSTEIN, *supra* note 1, at 76.

33. 481 U.S. 704 (1987).

34. *Id.* at 719 (Scalia, J., concurring).

35. *Id.* at 716.

36. Kaiser Aetna v. United States, 444 U.S. 164, 180 (1979). Previously an easement would more readily have been considered a restriction on use. Rehnquist's assimilation of easements to physical occupations bears fruit in Justice Scalia's opinion for the Court in Nollan v. California Coastal Commission, 483 U.S. 825, 831 (1987), *see infra* notes 46–53 and accompanying text.

37. Fresh Pond Shopping Center Inc. v. Callahan, 464 U.S. 875, 877 (1983) (Rehnquist, J., dissenting from dismissal of appeal).

38. 458 U.S. 419, 435 (1982).

39. 482 U.S. 304 (1987).

40. *Id.* at 312.

41. *Id.* at 318.

42. *See First English,* 482 U.S. at 328–334 (Stevens, J., dissenting).

43. *See* Loretto v. Teleprompter Manhattan CATV Corp., 458 U.S. 419, 426–38 (1982).

44. 482 U.S. at 319.

45. Penn Central Transp. Co. v. New York City, 438 U.S. 104, 142–44 (1978) (Rehnquist, J., dissenting); *see also* Keystone Bituminous Coal Ass'n v. DeBenedictis, 480 U.S. 470, 515–516 (1987) (Rehnquist, C.J., dissenting) (using conceptual severance to find that ground surface support regulation works a taking).

46. 438 U.S. at 130–31.

47. 483 U.S. 825 (1987).

48. CAL. PUB. RES. CODE §§ 30000–30900 (West 1986).

49. There was expert testimony that much of the access path was below the mean high tide line and thus within the public's right under California's public trust doctrine; there was also testimony that an access easement may have been acquired by the public in any case through its long use of the path. 483 U.S. at 862 nn.11–12.

50. 483 U.S. at 831.

51. Pennsylvania Coal Co. v. Mahon, 260 U.S. 393 (1922).

52. Goldblatt v. Town of Hempstead, 369 U.S. 590 (1962).

53. *See, e.g.,* B. ACKERMAN, PRIVATE PROPERTY AND THE CONSTITUTION, *supra* note 22, at 93–103; Michelman, *Property, Utility, and Fairness: Comments on the Ethical Foundations of "Just Compensation" Law,* 80 HARV. L. REV. 1165, 1229–34 (1967).

54. Conceptual severance is made possible by an anachronistic admixture of Lockean absolutism into the modern "bundle of sticks" image of property. Thomas Grey has pointed out that mixing these views of property intellectually mixes apples and oranges. Grey, *supra* note 6, at 30–31.

55. Reich, *The New Property,* 73 YALE L.J. 733, 774 (1964).

56. 438 U.S. 104, 138 (1978).

57. But the 1987 *First English* case might seem to be an exception to this proposition, because there the church was prevented from doing something on its own land (i.e., it was temporarily prevented from building on a flood plain). First English

Evangelical Lutheran Church v. County of Los Angeles, 482 U.S. 304 (1987). If, however, as Frank Michelman speculates, *Takings, 1987,* 88 COLUM. L. REV. 1600, 1619–21 (1988), the temporariness was illusory because the government announced no time limits on its restrictions, then the regulation in *First English* seems tantamount to government transfer of the land to itself for governmental use as a flood control area, rather than a mere negative servitude.

58. 2 WILLIAM BLACKSTONE, COMMENTARIES *2.

59. Thus, ultimately Charles Reich failed to convince the Court that entitlements of the welfare and regulatory state, because they serve the same function as traditional property, should be accorded similar constitutional treatment. *See* Simon, *The Invention and Reinvention of Welfare Rights,* 44 MD. L. REV. 1, 37 (1985) ("The New Property view of welfare rights is incoherent as jurisprudence and exhausted as politics."); Note, *Justice Rehnquist's Theory of Property,* 93 YALE L.J. 541, 541 (1984).

60. *Cf.* M. DAN-COHEN, RIGHTS, PERSONS, AND ORGANIZATIONS 5–6, 13–14, 199–200 (1986) (criticizing the tendency of legal theorists and practitioners to equate organizations with individuals for the purpose of ascribing legal rights).

61. Lochner v. New York, 198 U.S. 45 (1905). The *Lochner* Court found that state regulation of working hours for health and safety reasons was unconstitutional because it violated a substantive due process right to freedom of contract. *Lochner* and the constitutionalization of laissez-faire market principles were thoroughly repudiated during the New Deal era.

62. *But see supra* note 18 and accompanying text (Rehnquist's statement in *Kaiser Aetna* that certain "expectancies" are "embodied in the concept" of property).

63. Penn Central Transp. Co. v. New York City, 438 U.S. 104, 124 (1978).

64. *Id.*

65. *See, e.g.,* R. RORTY, THE CONSEQUENCES OF PRAGMATISM (1982); H. PUTNAM, REASON, TRUTH AND HISTORY (1981); H. PUTNAM, THE MANY FACES OF REALISM (1987).

66. *See, e.g.,* Stick, *Can Nihilism Be Pragmatic?,* 100 HARV. L. REV. 332, 383–85 (1986) (arguing that "nihilist" legal critics misunderstand pragmatism); Wells, *Tort Law as Corrective Justice: A Pragmatic Justification for Jury Adjudication,* 88 MICH. L. REV. 2348 (1990).

67. *See* Kennedy, *Form and Substance in Private Law Adjudication,* 89 HARV. L. REV. 1685, 1712 (1976); Schlag, *Rules and Standards,* 33 UCLA L. REV. 379, 383 (1985).

68. Michelman, *supra* note 57, at 1625–29.

69. *See* Radin, *Reconsidering the Rule of Law,* 69 B.U. L. REV. 781 (1989). In my view, pragmatism and the Rule of Law are not antithetical.

70. Michelman, *supra* note 57, at 1625.

71. I do not mean here to recapitulate the inconclusive debate about whether a preference for "rules" over "standards" signifies a conservative individualistic disposition. Duncan Kennedy asserted this psychological connection to be intuitively evident, Kennedy, *supra* note 67, but to others it does not appear so obvious. *See, e.g.,* Schlag, *supra* note 67, at 418–22 (claiming that arguments for rules can be generated by altruism as well as individualism).

72. The "model of rules" is Ronald Dworkin's term for the view that law consists of a body of rules. *See* R. DWORKIN, TAKING RIGHTS SERIOUSLY chs. 2–3 (1978).

73. The story I am telling in this paragraph about the judicial role in a Hobbesian conception of politics is basically the same as that told by Frank Michelman. *See* Michelman, *supra* note 57, at 1625–29; M. Tushnet, Red, White, and Blue: A Critical Analysis of Constitutional Law 8–10 (1988). The model of rules does not recommend itself so urgently to those who do not espouse such a Hobbesian outlook on self-government. The model of rules is (ideologically) a poor interpretation of the Rule of Law for those who find room in the democratic tradition for conceptions of legislatures that govern in the public interest and of judges who judge responsibly. Moreover, theoretical adherence to the model of rules causes inconsistencies for conservatives, because the complete rejection of judgment under "standards" cannot be maintained in practice even by conservatives, who under some circumstances argue strongly for case-by-case decisions as being the only way to vindicate individual just deserts. Perhaps most important for my purposes here, the model of rules is (logically) a poor interpretation of the Rule of Law if in fact government by means of formal rules is impossible. A body of philosophical thought roughly traceable to Wittgenstein suggests that even rules cannot have the formally decisive properties made necessary by the Hobbesian theory of politics. This line of philosophical argument is reviewed in Radin, *supra* note 69. All of this suggests that we should investigate whether pragmatism can be consistent with the Rule of Law. I do think that it can be, giving up some of the conservative assumptions about the nature of rules and the nature of politics, but I cannot yet display any grand theory about this. (In Radin, *supra* note 69, I venture some initial thoughts.)

74. T. Hobbes, Leviathan pt. 1, ch. XIV–XV & pt. II, ch. XXIV (1651); D. Hume, A Treatise of Human Nature bk. III, pt. II, §§ I–VI (1740); J. Bentham, The Theory of Legislation, Principles of the Civil Code pt. I, ch. II–XII (1840).

75. *See, e.g.,* R. Posner, Economic Analysis of Law 25 (3d ed. 1987) ("perhaps the most common" meaning of "justice" is "efficiency").

76. *See supra* note 25 and accompanying text.

77. *See* Michelman, *supra* note 53.

78. There is an interesting problem here lying in wait for those who think the body is property: can the government condemn kidneys at fair market value? *See* Andrews, *My Body, My Property,* Hastings Center Rep., Oct. 1986, at 28, 36.

79. In Hawaii Housing Auth. v. Midkiff, 467 U.S. 229, 240 (1984), the Court declared the scope of public use to be "coterminous" with the scope of the police power, which means that any government activity deemed to further a legitimate government purpose is ipso facto a public use.

80. Lochner v. New York, 198 U.S. 45 (1905). Fully constitutionalizing the liberal conception of property would be a return to *Lochner* to the extent that *Lochner* finds "in" the Constitution a right to unfettered freedom of contract regarding all of one's entitlements, whether referred to as property or not.

81. *See* R. Epstein, *supra* note 1, at 252–53.

82. Garet, *Comparative Normative Hermeneutics: Scripture, Literature, Constitution,* 58 S. Cal. L. Rev. 35, 44–46 (1985).

83. Gallie, *Essentially Contested Concepts,* 56 Proceedings of the Aristotelian Society 167 (1956). *But see* R. Epstein, *supra* note 1, at 22 (implicitly arguing that the meaning of property is uncontested).

84. Although the Supreme Court holds that just compensation "means in most

cases the fair market value of the property on the date it is appropriated," the Court occasionally acknowledges that this standard can fail under the circumstances to "make the owner whole." Kirby Forest Indus., Inc. v. United States, 467 U.S. 1, 10 & n.15 (1984). The market value quid pro quo standard is particularly ironic where the Court acknowledges that the government in taking land from people has "depriv[ed] them of their chosen way of life." United States v. Sioux Nation of Indians, 448 U.S. 371, 423 (1980).

85. In fact, this makes me sound rather Dworkinian, for Ronald Dworkin has stressed the distinction between concepts and various competing conceptions of them, and the role of contested concepts in constitutional thought. *See, e.g.* R. DWORKIN, *supra* note 72, at 134–36. I am certainly more Dworkinian than Epsteinian, although I have serious differences with Dworkin too that I need not catalogue here.

86. Thus, the Court could hold that extreme jet noise is a taking even if the planes do not invade the resident's airspace and still be able to distinguish this situation from Rehnquist's position in his *Penn Central* dissent. *See supra* note 45 and accompanying text.

87. In the case of the corporate owner, those injured by the noise might well be the corporation's employees—unless they must already wear ear protection—but their injury cannot easily be characterized as the taking of a property right.

88. *See* Singer, *The Reliance Interest in Property*, 40 STAN. L. REV. 611 (1988) (arguing that workers should have a property right which would allow them to purchase a plant slated for destruction).

89. In the useful terminology of Calabresi and Melamed, ownership is protected by a property rule if transfer must be voluntary, and is protected only by a liability rule if the entitlement can be taken from the owner against her wishes upon payment of compensation set by the government or some other authoritative entity. *See* Calabresi & Melamed, *Property Rules, Liability Rules and Inalienability: One View of the Cathedral*, 85 HARV. L. REV. 1089, 1092 (1972).

90. As long as efficiency or competition is thought to be served, the "public use" limitation on the eminent domain power does not prevent legislation from divesting A's title and making provision for it to be vested in B. *See* Hawaii Housing Auth. v. Midkiff, 467 U.S. 229 (1984). Nor is there necessarily anything wrong with this as long as A's interest is properly treated as fungible.

91. 410 Mich. 616, 304 N.W.2d 455 (1981).

92. 26 N.Y.2d 219, 257 N.E.2d 870, 309 N.Y.S.2d 312 (1970).

93. 431 U.S. 494 (1977).

94. *Id.* at 520 (Stevens, J., concurring).

95. *Loretto*, of course, is an exception, but I have explained why I believe *Loretto* is wrong. Conceptual severance and the per se rule for physical invasion allowed the Court to bypass both the balancing test and the "confiscatory" standard.

96. Who is "we"? *See* Minow, *The Supreme Court, 1986 Term—Foreword: Justice Engendered*, 101 HARV. L. REV. 10, 15 (1987). An important issue is whether "we" are indeed one ethical/political community. Is it appropriate to think of ourselves in any sense as only one community or does that do violence to heterodox groups that are less powerful hence less able to say who "we" are? *See* Sullivan, *Symposium: The Republican Civic Tradition: Rainbow Republicanism*, 97 YALE L.J. 1713 (1988) (politics should be conceived in terms of normative pluralism of private voluntary

groups). It seems to me that "we" are one community on the issue of whether two plus two equals four, but perhaps we are many incommensurate communities on other issues more readily regarded as ethical, religious, or political. Yet the normative hermeneutic significance of our having a constitution is to deny at least the furthest reaches of such pessimistic irreconcilable pluralism. We are one in at least some sense(s). There are some problems I pass over here that must be taken very seriously.

97. Frank Michelman's thought has evolved from a "liberal" to a "republican" understanding of the issue. In Michelman, *supra* note 53, at 1214–18, he argues that fear of systematic exploitation of the few by the many gives rise to unacceptable "demoralization costs," whereas he now characterizes the harm that justifies finding a taking to be corruption of public commitment to the values of self-government. *See* Michelman, *Tutelary Jurisprudence and Constitutional Property,* in Economic Rights and the Constitution: Yesterday, Today, and Tomorrow (1989); Michelman, *Possession v. Distribution in the Constitutional Idea of Property,* 72 Iowa L. Rev. 1319, 1329 (1987).

98. Michelman, *Possession v. Distribution, supra* note 98, at 1327–29.

99. More difficult is the question whether a landlord can permissibly be prevented from evicting tenants and moving in herself. If the landlord has never lived in the building, then her interest is not superior to a tenant's. But what if the building is the landlord's ancestral home and she is still attached to it, but now the tenant has become attached to it too? This is the kind of hypothetical that personhood theory cannot resolve very well. Yet it is perhaps one that we do not pragmatically face, because few people rent out their ancestral homes.

100. But note that this characterization does not raise any difficulty for considering *corporate* landlords' property to be fungible. Although I have not sought to elaborate it here, I believe there is a strong case for treating corporate property as fungible.

Chapter Five

1. Ludwig Wittgenstein, Philosophical Investigations § 255 (1958).

2. The "takings" clause of the Fifth Amendment reads: "Nor shall private property be taken for public use, without just compensation." Application of the "takings" clause often coalesces in important respects with the Fifth Amendment's due process clause, which provides that "[no person shall be] deprived of life, liberty, or property, without due process of law." The jurisprudence of these clauses restraining the federal government is applicable to state governments as well through the due process clause of the Fourteenth Amendment. State constitutions have their own "takings" clauses as well.

3. *See, e.g.,* Frank Michelman, *Property, Utility, and Fairness: Comments on the Ethical Foundations of Just Compensation Law,* 80 Harv. L. Rev. 1165 (1967); John Costonis, *Presumptive and Per Se Takings: A Decisional Model for the Taking Issue,* 58 N.Y.U. L. Rev. 465 (1983); and Leslie Bender, *The Takings Clause: Principles or Politics,* 34 Buff. L. Rev. 735 (1985).

4. In Pennsylvania Coal Co. v. Mahon, the Court stated that "while property may be regulated to a certain extent, if the regulation goes too far it will be recognized as a taking. . . . " 260 U.S. 393, 415 (1922).

5. *See, e.g.,* Michelman, *Property, Utility, and Fairness, supra* note 3. Richard

Epstein, Takings: Private Property and the Power of Eminent Domain (1985); and Bruce Ackerman, Private Property and the Constitution (1977).

6. *See, e.g.,* Cass R. Sunstein, *Lochner's Legacy,* 8 Colum. L. Rev. 873 (1987).

7. We also need to know how long Susan has been there, and whether the circumstances are such that we ought to treat Susan's claim as paramount to John's in view of the length of time she has been trespassing. If she has been trespassing long enough to have gained title by adverse possession, then she can be treated as the rightful owner. In cases that deviate from this kind of simple paradigm, however, it is much more difficult to say how we should weigh the length of time the wrongful claim has been exercised, as against its wrongfulness at its inception. I will have more to say about this problem in subsection A.3 below.

8. The problem is further complicated by the fact that it may matter whether the value is lowered only in the current holder's perception, or whether indeed the market value is lowered (that is, the value is lowered in the perception of what we would consider an "average" holder). It also may matter whether the injury appears normatively to be merely a lowering of monetary value, or whether the personhood of the holder appears to be infringed upon. (See subsection I.B below.) These concerns may pull in opposite directions, further complicating the issue. That is, we may intuitively feel that "mere" lowering of value in one's own perception is not entitled to as much weight as lowering of market value, yet we may feel that injury to personhood is entitled to more weight than "mere" lowering of market value.

9. *See* Restatement (Second) of Torts § 882 (1979). (For nontrespassory invasion to be the source of liability it must be (i) intentional and unreasonable, or (ii) unintentional and otherwise actionable under the rules controlling liability for negligent or reckless conduct, or for abnormally dangerous conditions or activities.)

10. The avenues of appropriateness explored in the rather extensive literature on nuisance are both utilitarian (focusing on economic efficiency) and nonutilitarian (focusing either on rights or on custom). *See, e.g.,* Robert G. Bone, *Normative Theory and Legal Doctrine in American Nuisance Law: 1850–1920,* 59 S. Cal. L. Rev. 1101 (1986).

11. *See* Michelman, *Property, Utility, and Fairness, supra* note 3.

12. 276 U.S. 272 (1928).

13. 239 U.S. 394 (1915).

14. 56 Wis.2d 7 (1972).

15. *See* Margaret Jane Radin, *Market-Inalienability,* 100 Harv. L. Rev. 1849, 1915–17 (1987).

16. *See* Louis Kaplow, *An Economic Analysis of Legal Transitions,* 99 Harv. L. Rev. 511 (1986).

17. The problem is further complicated by the question of the extent to which we might be morally inclined to honor holdings we come to recognize as wrongful, simply because of their entrenchment (this is the problem of "settled expectations" or "vested rights"). Even if we are not positivists, and admit that property rights are not properly accepted to be exactly what the government or society in general proclaims or allows, we still might think that (some of the time? always?) we should honor wrongfully granted or wrongfully condoned property claims. This could be either because we think repose is necessary (analogous to one strand of the rationale

for adverse possession), or because we think there is affirmative moral force to settled expectations that at some point can outweigh the wrong in holding (analogous to another strand in the rationale for adverse possession). This difficulty will be discussed in subsection A.3 below.

18. There is intuitive appeal in Austin's and Bentham's critique of the notion that a bad law is not a law. See H. L. A. Hart, *Positivism and the Separation of Law and Morals,* 71 HARV. L. REV. 593 (1958). We should face the fact that we do have some bad laws, and deal with it. Yet there is also intuitive appeal in the notion that people can have rights even if the government fails to recognize them, which means that property rights cannot be entirely positivist creatures. *See* ch. 6.

19. *See* J. S. MILL, PRINCIPLES OF POLITICAL ECONOMY (1848) bk. II, ch. II, § 2. For other strands of rationale about adverse possession, see chapter 3.

20. *See, e.g.,* Hadacheck v. Sebastian, 239 U.S. 394 (1915); Pendoley v. Ferreira, 345 Mass. 309 (1963).

21. Congress passed a special statute of limitations so that the Sioux Indians could sue today for the loss of the Black Hills in the time of Custer. We might want to say that even without the intervention of Congress we should not consider their claim to have lapsed. *See* United States v. Sioux Nation of Indians, 448 U.S. 371 (1980).

22. *See* Mugler v. Kansas, 123 U.S. 623 (1887) (upholding enforcement of a state prohibition on the sale of alcohol that destroyed plaintiff's brewery business).

23. G. W. F. HEGEL, PHILOSOPHY OF RIGHT, translated as HEGEL'S PHILOSOPHY OF RIGHT, § 41 (1942). *Cf.* § 39 ("[P]ersonality is that which struggles . . . to give itself reality, or in other words to claim that external world as its own [*jenes Dasein als das ihrige zu setzen*]."); ch. 1.

24. Charles Reich, *The New Property,* 73 YALE L.J. 733, 774 (1964); ROBERT NOZICK, ANARCHY, STATE AND UTOPIA (1974).

25. KARL MARX & FRIEDRICH ENGELS, *The Communist Manifesto,* in THE MARX-ENGELS READER 484–485 (R. Tucker ed., 2d ed. 1978).

26. For example, judicial decisions that enhance a tenant's entitlements and diminish the landlord's often find it significant that the tenant is a person with a home and the landlord is, or is assumed to be, a commercial business entity. *See, e.g.,* Javins v. First National Realty Corp., 428 F.2d 1071 (D.C. Circ. 1970), *cert. denied,* 400 U.S. 925 (1970). Landlords' claims that such diminutions of their entitlements vis-à-vis tenants are "takings" regularly fail. *See also* PruneYard Shopping Center v. Robins, 447 U.S. 74 (1980) (it is not a taking for California law to prevent commercial shopping centers from excluding people engaging in peaceful political speech).

27. A 75% diminution in market value was found not to be a taking in the classic case of Euclid v. Ambler Realty Co., 272 U.S. 365 (1926), which validated land-use regulation by zoning. Those theorists, often economists, who favor utilitarian or market-oriented tests for taking often find it absurd that the courts tolerate so high a percentage loss (often dismissing it as "mere diminution of market value"). I believe that one reason for this high threshold, which must be incomprehensible to those who conceive of all property as fungible, is that legal practice tacitly gives greater weight to personal interests.

28. Nor is justifiable personal connection expressed through a monetary estimation of consumer surplus. Where consumer surplus is traditionally conceived as a

dollar amount over market value that an individual would demand to relinquish an object or a right, justifiable personal connection is associated with and identified by the personal pain or anguish that occasions the loss of an object or right.

29. This would be analogous to the common law recognition of ameliorative waste, giving the right to future interest holders to receive the property in the same condition, even if the interim holder's changes increase its market value. The inquiry focuses on a substantial change in the character of property without reference to the resulting increase or diminution of market value.

30. Modern taking decisions have consistently found the right to exclude trumped by other rights. *See* PruneYard Shopping Center v. Robins, 447 U.S. 74 (1980) (political speech); State v. Shack, 58 N.J. 297 (1971) (access to counseling about federal rights).

31. 458 U.S. 419 (1982).

32. *See* ch. 4.

33. Kathleen M. Sullivan, *Unconstitutional Conditions,* 109 HARV. L. REV. 1413 (1989). Though not a core liberal ideological concern in the same way as personhood, we can see an analogy here in the connection between landholding and group religious or cultural identity. The Sioux Indians won only an ironic victory when, after one hundred years of effort, they persuaded the Supreme Court that the U.S. government had "taken" the Black Hills from them such that monetary compensation was due, for, as the Court itself recognized, they had been deprived of their chosen way of life. United States v. Sioux Nation of Indians, 448 U.S. 371, 423 (1980).

34. There is a difficult problem lying in wait here for those who argue that body parts are alienable property. *See,* for example, Lori Andrews, *My Body, My Property,* 16 HASTINGS CENTER REPORT, Oct. 1986, at 28, 36. (arguing thoughtfully for a "quasi-property" approach in which "human beings have the right to treat certain physical parts of their bodies as objects for possession, gifts, and trade"); Comment, *Retailing Human Organs under the Uniform Commercial Code,* 16 J. MARSHALL L. REV. 393, 405 (1983) (arguing that "society should not view the sale of human organs any differently than the sale of other necessary commodities such as food, shelter, and medication").

35. *See* PruneYard Shopping Center v. Robins 447 U.S. 74 (1986); note the tortured distinction of *PruneYard* in Nollan v. California Coastal Commission, 483 U.S. 825, 831 n.1 (1987).

36. In a case analytically similar to *PruneYard Shopping Center,* in that it involved state law diminishing a landowner's exclusion rights, the New Jersey Supreme Court declared, on normative grounds, that an agricultural landowner's property rights simply did not include the right to exclude Office of Economic Opportunity (OEO) workers who wished to counsel farmworkers about their federal rights. Hence the landowner could not claim trespass, or a deprivation of his supposed right to exclude others, when the federal workers entered his land without permission. State v. Shack, 58 N.J. 297 (1971).

37. In an article similar in spirit to this chapter, Carol Rose locates here (in the tension between liberal and republican theories of politics and property) the reason why the takings issue is still a "muddle." Carol Rose, *Mahon Reconstructed: Why the Takings Issue Is Still a Muddle,* 57 S. CAL. L. REV. 561 (1984).

38. *See* part II below on the Rule of Law.

39. The affinity between positivism and the interest-group theory of politics may simply lie in the compatibility of both with Hobbesian assumptions. *See, e.g.,* Frank Easterbrook, *Foreword: The Court and the Economic System,* 98 HARV. L. REV. 4 (1984).

40. *Cf.* Michelman, *Property, Utility, and Fairness, supra* note 3, at 1238 (sweepstakes discussion); Penn Central Transportation Co. v. New York City, 438 U.S. 104, 137 (1978) (Court's discussion of valuable rights afforded Penn Central through the City's transferable development rights program).

41. *See, e.g., Symposium: The Republican Civic Tradition,* 97 YALE L.J. 1493 (1988).

42. On occasion the courts are quite clear that that is how they understand their task. *See* Penn Central Transportation Co. v. New York City, 438 U.S. 104, 124 (1978) (taking decisions are "essentially ad hoc").

43. *See* Margaret Jane Radin, *Reconsidering the Rule of Law,* 69 B.U. L. REV. 781 (1988).

44. *See* JOHN RAWLS, A THEORY OF JUSTICE § 38, 235–43 (1971).

45. Mention of two ways of failing to render taking jurisprudence rule-like may be instructive. One way corresponds roughly to the liberal entitlement theory of property and one corresponds roughly to the liberal utilitarian view. Richard Epstein asserts that there is one canonical concept of property and any diminution of its scope is a taking. EPSTEIN, *supra* note 5, at 85; Richard Epstein, *An Outline of Takings,* 41 U. MIAMI L. REV. 1 (1986). This definitional coup might satisfy lay libertarians, but fails to convince any who understand property to be both a contested concept and one that evolves historically. *See* ch. 3; Thomas Grey, *The Malthusian Constitution,* 41 U. MIAMI L. REV. 21 (1986). It also fails to convince any who think the personal/fungible continuum both normatively significant and observable in our practice of property. *See* ch. 3. Epstein undermines his own attempt to make takings rule-like by admitting the issues of corrective justice (especially the nuisance aspect and the reliance aspect) and political reciprocity, for his attempts to render these issues rule-like in turn fail to convince.

Frank Michelman, in an early but still important article, found that a utilitarian solution to the taking problem would have a "quasi-mathematical structure." Michelman, *Property, Utility, and Fairness, supra* note 3, at 1214. But the algorithmic structure was achieved by excepting the class of cases in which corrective justice is relevant, without trying to demonstrate that the exception could be algorithmically delineated, and by ignoring (largely, though not completely) the problem of political contextuality, that is, the dynamic nature of the problem.

For reflections on the jurisprudential problems posed by the death penalty, *see* Margaret Jane Radin, *Risk-of-Error Rules and Non-Ideal Justification,* in NOMOS XXVIII, JUSTIFICATION 33, 41 (1985); Margaret Jane Radin, *Cruel Punishment and Respect for Persons: Super Due Process for Death,* 53 S. CAL. L. REV. 1143 (1980).

46. Nor am I addressing here the question whether it is possible to solve anything with rules. My own view is that a pragmatic reinterpretation of rules does indeed speak well to many legal situations; Radin, *Reconsidering the Rule of Law, supra* note 43. *See also* FREDERICK SCHAUER, PLAYING BY THE RULES (1991).

47. *See* Radin, *Reconsidering the Rule of Law, supra* note 43.

48. In other words, perhaps we possess an "overlapping consensus" about property. *See* John Rawls, *The Idea of an Overlapping Consensus,* 7 Oxford J. Legal Stud. 1 (1987).

49. Radin, *Reconsidering the Rule of Law, supra* note 43.

50. *See, e.g.,* Rolf Sartorius, Individual Conduct and Social Norms (1975).

51. *See, e.g.,* Richard Epstein, *Needed: Activist Judges for Economic Rights,* Wall Street Journal, Nov. 14, 1985, at 32; Robert Ellickson, *Suburban Growth Control,* 86 Yale L.J. 385 (1977).

52. *See* Frank Michelman, *Tutelary Jurisprudence and Constitutional Property,* in Liberty, Property, and the Future of Constitutional Development 127 (Howard Dickman & Ellen Paul eds. 1990).

53. Compare Susan Rose-Ackerman, *Against Ad-Hocery: A Comment on Michelman,* 88 Colum. L. Rev. 1697 (1988), with Frank Michelman, *Takings, 1987,* 88 Colum. L. Rev. 1600 (1989). Compare Penn Central Transportation Co. v. New York City, 438 U.S. 104, 124 (1978), (takings decisions are "essentially ad hoc") with Loretto v. Teleprompter Manhattan CATV Corp., 458 U.S. 419 (1982) and Nollan v. California Coastal Commission, 483 U.S. 825 (1987) (seeking a priori rules).

Chapter Six

1. 112 S.Ct. 2886 (1992).

2. 483 U.S. 825, 107 S.Ct. 3141 (1987).

3. 112 S.Ct. 1522 (1992).

4. 485 U.S. 1, 108 S.Ct. 849 (1988).

5. *See, e.g.,* Phillips Petroleum Co. v. Mississippi, 484 U.S. 469, 481–82 (1988) (mean high tide seaward is public trust); Kaiser Aetna v. United States, 444 U.S. 164 (1979) (navigational servitudes); Shively v. Bowlby, 152 U.S. 1 (1894).

6. *See, e.g.,* Summa Corp. v. California *ex rel.* State Lands Commission, 466 U.S. 198 (1984) (state interest may be terminated). *See also* Gilbert L. Finnell, Jr., *Public Access to Coastal Public Property: Judicial Theories and the Takings Issue,* 67 N.C. L. Rev. 627, 640 n.12 (1989).

7. State *ex rel.* Thornton v. Hay, 254 Or. 584, 462 P.2d 671 (1969). On the issue of whether such a judicial decision can itself count as an unconstitutional taking of property rights, *see* Barton H. Thompson, Jr., *Judicial Takings,* 76 VA. L. Rev. 1449 (1990).

8. Marks v. Whitney, 6 Cal.3d 251, 491 P.2d 374, 91 Cal. Rptr. 790 (1971). *Cf.* Matthews v. Bay Head Improvement Ass'n, 95 N.J. 306, 471 A.2d 355, 363–65 (1984) (public trust doctrine is "dynamic"; expanded to cover public shore recreation and use of privately owned dry sand areas as reasonably necessary).

In California the courts held public use rights to be broader than formerly thought in other ways as well. It was judicially found that public use rights over beach property under private title could be impliedly dedicated to the public if the owner's tolerance of incursion by the public permitted an inference that the owner intended to grant or recognize public rights. Gion v. City of Santa Cruz, 465 P.2d 50. It was found at the same time that public use rights could also be acquired by implied dedication in case the incursion was found to be without the owner's permission for the requisite time period at any time in the past. Dietz v. King, 2 Cal.3d 29, 465 P.2d 50, 84 Cal. Rptr. 162 (1970).

After *Gion-Dietz,* the California legislature responded by limiting the scope—or making clear the limited scope—of these judicial findings. Except for coastal property, implied dedication was limited to instances where government expenditures were visible and acquiesced in by the owner. Even for coastal property, periodic posting of signs, or compliance with other notice provisions, will prevent implied dedication. CAL. CIV. CODE § 1009 (West 1986). The legislature also made explicit that posting permission to pass will defeat prescription as well, CAL. CIV. CODE § 1008, although of course it cannot defeat prescriptive rights already gained in the past.

Since it was already understood under the common law of prescription that granting permission to pass would defeat a claim of right by adverse use, the effect of this legislation is to make it easier to prove that permission was granted. These legislative developments make it somewhat harder for the public to gain access rights without the owner's permission, but give owners strong incentives to grant permission. The legislation interacts with the courts' pronouncements both to express a cultural understanding that beach property is not exactly the same as other property, and that public access to beaches is to be encouraged.

9. California Coastal Zone Conservation Act of 1972, *superseded by* California Coastal Act of 1976, CAL. PUB. RES. CODE § 30000–30900 (West 1986).

10. State *ex rel.* Thornton v. Hay, 254 Or. 584, 595–97 (1969).

11. *Gion,* 2 Cal.3d at 43.

12. Marks v. Whitney, 6 Cal.3d 251, 259–60 (1971).

13. Lucas v. South Carolina Coastal Council, 112 S.Ct. 2886, 2890 (1992).

14. PruneYard Shopping Ctr. v. Robins, 447 U.S. 74, 100 S.Ct. 2035 (1980) (not a taking of private property rights under the Fifth Amendment to the U.S. Constitution for California to interpret its state constitution as granting access to shopping center premises for purposes of political expression, even though speakers do not have this right under the First Amendment).

15. Justice Kennedy, concurring in the judgment, was more willing than Scalia to recognize that such background principles may have already precluded activities that damaged the coastline: this property "may present such unique concerns for a fragile land system that the State can go further in regulating its development and use . . . . " *Lucas,* 112 S.Ct. at 2903.

16. In *Lucas* Justice Scalia is clear that in order to decide whether the government has acted to change property rights, first we must precisely identify the content of the prior regime. Government action that we perceive as confiscatory is, according to Scalia, justified only if it amounts to enforcement of the state's preexisting scheme: "Any limitation so severe cannot be newly legislated or decreed (without compensation), but must inhere in the title itself, in the restrictions that background principles of the State's law of property and nuisance already place upon land ownership." *Lucas,* 112 S.Ct. at 2900.

In many respects Scalia's position is consistent with mine, although we disagree about the current state of "our" culture. Serious disputes about these cultural background principles remain after *Lucas:* Are courts who declare (discover? create?) nuisance law to be the sole arbiters of "our" culture of property? (Why not the legislature? What about other sources of cultural understanding not embodied in nuisance law?) How are we to understand the evolving nature of "our" culture, and, particularly, how are we to understand the effect upon it of courts' own pronouncements? *See* Frank Michelman, *Construing Old Constitutional Texts: Regulation of Use as "Taking" of Property in United States Constitutional Jurisprudence* (forthcoming 1993). Isn't the assumption that "our" culture is nationally monolithic, with a sharp distinction between landownership and other ownership, merely a convenient ideological fiction?

17. For accounts of the revolution, *see, e.g.,* Mary Ann Glendon, *The Transformation of American Landlord-Tenant Law,* 23 B.C. L. REV. 503 (1982); Edward H. Rabin, *The Revolution in Residential Landlord-Tenant Law: Causes and Consequences,* 69 CORNELL L. REV. 517 (1984).

18. This development is nicely illustrated in Haar and Liebman's casebook, C. HAAR & L. LIEBMAN, PROPERTY AND LAW ch. 8, 287–386 (2d ed. 1985).

19. This process can be seen, for example, in Robinson v. Diamond Housing Corp., 463 F.2d 853 (D.C. Cir. 1972), in which Judge J. Skelly Wright elaborated the retaliatory termination defense, relying in part on local regulations which had in turn been promulgated by the District of Columbia commissioners in response to one of his earlier decisions.

20. *See* Lucie E. White, *Representing "The Real Deal,"* 45 U. MIAMI L. REV. 271 (1990–91).

21. Lindsey v. Normet, 405 U.S. 56, 73–4 (1972).

22. 256 U.S. 135, 41 S.Ct. 458 (1921).

23. 485 U.S. 1, 108 S.Ct. 849 (1988).

24. Landlords lost yet again in Yee v. City of Escondido, 112 S.Ct. 1522 (1992). *Yee* was decided on the issue of whether local rental control on trailer park spaces, in the context of state law that prevented the landlord from negotiating a new rent when the mobile home was sold to a new tenant, was a "physical invasion" of the landlord's property. If the answer was yes, then the landlord could take advantage of a per se rule that all physical invasions are takings, but the answer was no. In this decision the Court did not reach the issue of whether a regulatory taking could be found in these circumstances, so there is still a glimmer of hope for conservatives. *See infra* note 51.

25. *See, e.g.,* RICHARD EPSTEIN, TAKINGS: PRIVATE PROPERTY AND THE POWER OF EMINENT DOMAIN (1985).

26. In Lochner v. New York, 198 U.S. 45 (1905) the Court declared that substantive due process protected absolute freedom of contract so that New York could not limit the work week of bakers for health and safety reasons. *Lochner* and its brand of substantive due process fell into extreme disfavor with the change in the Court under Roosevelt.

27. *See, e.g.,* Michael S. Moore, *The Semantics of Judging,* 54 S. CAL. L. REV. 151, 265–70 (1983).

28. Interstate Commerce Commission v. Kroblin, 348 U.S. 836, 75 S.Ct. 49 (1954), which asks the question, "Is an eviscerated chicken a manufactured product?" is reprinted in the innovative casebook, W. BISHIN & C. STONE, LAW, LANGUAGE & ETHICS (1972), and plays a prominent role in courses in Law, Language and Ethics at the University of Southern California.

29. Unless we are public choice extremists. *See infra* sec. III.

30. The useful distinction between "public interest" and "public choice" views of government is due to Frank Michelman, *Political Markets and Community Self-Determination: Competing Judicial Models of Local Government Legitimacy,* 53 IND. L.J. 145, 148–54 (1977–78); *see also* Gregory S. Alexander, *Takings, Narratives, and Power,* 88 COLUM. L. REV. 1752, 1770–71 (1988) (contrasting republican and public-choice views of government in the context of judicial evaluation of land-use regulation).

31. As indeed Hobbesian economic theorists tend to advocate; *see, e.g.,* Robert C. Ellickson, *Suburban Growth Control: An Economic and Legal Analysis,* 86 YALE L.J. 385 (1977).

32. As is evident from his opinions in *Lucas* and *Nollan,* Justice Scalia is extremely suspicious of at least some kinds of government activity when individuals claim that the activity invades property rights. But he seems largely to lack these suspicions when the individual claim against the government involves a nonproperty right, such as freedom of religion, freedom of speech, or liberty. Explaining why Scalia mistrusts government in the property field to a greater degree than in other fields is a puzzle beyond the scope of this essay. At least it is clear that the turn to public choice theory is not the whole answer, because nothing intrinsic in public choice theory would dictate such a distinction between property and nonproperty rights.

Perhaps a mythology of property salient at the framing of the Constitution is, as Jennifer Nedelsky suggests, still ordering the political views of Justice Scalia and his many sympathizers. *See* JENNIFER NEDELSKY, PRIVATE PROPERTY AND THE LIMITS OF AMERICAN CONSTITUTIONALISM (1990). But how can this traditional ideological hierarchy, if indeed it is still at work in our legal culture, be squared with the tendency of law-and-economics adherents (including public choice theorists) to think of *all* rights as "property"?

There are many other questions having to do with the judicial turn toward public choice theory which should be investigated, including the following: Are executive or administrative decisions more or less suspect than legislative decisions? Are legislative decisions at the local level more or less suspect than legislative decisions at the state or federal level?

33. First Evangelical Lutheran Church v. County of Los Angeles, 482 U.S. 304, 107 S.Ct. 2378 (1987).

34. Agins v. City of Tiburon, 447 U.S. 255, 100 S.Ct. 2183 (1980).

35. Nollan v. California Coastal Comm'n, 483 U.S. 825, 837 (1987).

36. *Id.* at 837 n.5.

37. The minor premise of the syllogism reflects Scalia's perception that in this case there was indeed an instrumental failure. That Scalia perceived matters this way does seem to reflect his predisposition to view the Commission's activities with extreme suspicion, because a more benign perception of the means/end connection was clearly possible.

38. For interesting thoughts on the ways in which traditional legal discourse has used the idea of "germaneness" of conditions imposed by governmental entities, see Kathleen M. Sullivan, *Unconstitutional Conditions,* 102 HARV. L. REV. 1413 (1989).

39. *Nollan,* 483 U.S. at 838.

40. *Id.* at 836, 840.

41. Lucas v. South Carolina Coastal Council, 112 S.Ct. 2886, 2895 (1992).

42. *Id.*

43. *See* note 16, *supra*.

44. I know that we *might*, if we had a Hobbesian view of the person, think until we saw a way the action was instrumentally suited to breaching the person's duty and lining her own pockets. I think that in ordinary life we do not consistently see persons as Hobbesian, nor could we and maintain ordinary life. But I cannot argue for this here.

45. 483 U.S. at 841 *passim*.

46. My impression is that this is the dominant implicit theory among practitioners of law and economics. *See, e.g.*, RICHARD A. POSNER, ECONOMIC ANALYSIS OF LAW (3d ed. 1986).

47. Hall v. City of Santa Barbara, 833 F.2d 1270, 1281 n.26 (9th Cir. 1986). *cert. denied*, 485 U.S. 940 (1988). In *Hall*, Judge Kozinski's holding was that local mobile home rent control constituted a physical invasion of the landlord's reversionary interest (and therefore a per se unconstitutional "taking") in the context of a state law that prohibited landlords from refusing to lease at the controlled rent to creditworthy successor tenants. (Because of the controlled rent, the tenant in possession when rent control was enacted was able to charge a higher price for selling the mobile home to the new tenant, and thus pocket a gain that otherwise would have been reaped by the landlord in higher rent.) The California state courts refused to follow the Ninth Circuit in construing this situation as a physical invasion, so, even though certiorari had been denied in *Hall*, the U.S. Supreme Court stepped in to resolve the matter. It did so in a common sense way: when a landlord loses money because of rent control, nothing has been physically taken. Yee v. City of Escondido, 112 S.Ct. 1522 (1992).

48. Pennell v. City of San Jose, 485 U.S. 1, 20 (1988).

49. *Id.* at 20.

50. *Id.* at 22.

51. In *Yee v. City of Escondido* there was a possible *Nollan*esque view of matters. Since the local rent control measure had been enacted by initiative, one might infer that the measure was mere rent-seeking on the part of tenants in possession at the time of the election. In light of the background state law allowing them to sell their mobile homes to new tenants whose site rent would remain controlled, and in light of the lack of price control on the mobile home itself, the tenants in possession were, it could be inferred, merely voting themselves a monetary gain at the expense of the landlord rather than enacting anything of general benefit to tenants as a whole.

Justice O'Connor's opinion for the Court in *Yee* skirted this issue by finding that regulatory taking was not properly before the Court; the Justices were deciding on physical invasion only. Her opinion hinted that when regulatory taking is the issue such a *Nollan*esque analysis will be relevant: "[A] typical rent control statute will transfer wealth from the landlord to the incumbent tenant and all future tenants. By contrast, petitioners contend that the Escondido ordinance transfers wealth only to the incumbent mobile home owner. This effect might have some bearing on whether the ordinance causes a regulatory taking, as it may shed some light on whether there is a sufficient nexus between the effect of the ordinance and the objectives it is supposed to advance." 112 S.Ct. at 1530 (citing *Nollan*).

Still, it may be significant that Justice Scalia chose not to (or did not have the votes to) reach out for this issue. Perhaps he is less willing to engage in activist review of measures enacted by direct democracy. Perhaps "physical invasion" really mattered in *Nollan* (as Professor Michelman said at the time)—the lateral easement involved people actually physically walking on land the Nollans claimed to own. *See* Frank Michelman, *Takings, 1987,* 88 COLUM. L. REV. 1600, 1608–14 (1988). At any rate, it becomes clear from this passage in *Yee* that *Nollan* is to be taken as a case about how to infer illegitimate motive in general and not as a case about unconstitutional conditions.

    52. 485 U.S. at 22.

Chapter Seven

    1. Peter Berger and Stanley Pullberg sound a warning against conflating the Marxist meaning of alienation with merely subjective feelings of estrangement, which is the dominant ordinary language sense of the word. "To say that man is alienated is not the same as saying that he is 'anomic' or that he feels psychologically estranged. On the contrary, some of the most important examples of alienated consciousness can be taken from the magnificent *nomoi* of human history, such as the religious interpretations of the human world as merely a reflection of a divine world . . . . Nor is it necessary or even likely that an alienated consciousness is subjectively experienced as psychological conflict, anxiety, or lostness . . . . If [psychological 'health'] is defined in alienated terms, then only those who share this definition will be psychologically 'healthy.'" Berger and Pullberg, *Reification and the Sociological Critique of Consciousness,* in 4 HISTORY AND THEORY 196, 200 (1965). Since I am not in this essay tackling the problem of pervasive false consciousness, I am content to let my analysis address only those relationships or social arrangements where there is at least some dissonance caused by an admixture of "better" and "worse" views of the self vis-à-vis the world about us, and hence some subjective feeling of unease.

    2. In German there are two different words, *Entäusserung* and *Entfremdung.* Hegel referred to the alienation accomplished by withdrawing one's will from an object (part of the process of contract) as *Entäusserung, see* GRUNDLINIEN DER PHILOSOPHIE DES RECHTS § 65 *passim* (1821), translated by T. Knox as HEGEL'S PHILOSOPHY OF RIGHT (1942), while Marx referred to *Entfremdung, Entfremdete Arbeit* and *Selbstentfremdung.* The latter two terms are translatable either as "alienated labor" or "estranged labor," and "self-alienation" or "self-estrangement." Marx also used the term *Entäusserung,* but he apparently meant the process of working-up the material world through human interaction with it, and not the idea of trading of objects. The term *Entäusserung* in Marx is sometimes translated as "alienation" or "objectification," but the latter is open to confusion with *Vergegenständlichung. See* R. Tucker, *Note on Texts and Terminology,* in THE MARX-ENGELS READER xxxix, xli (R. Tucker ed., 2d 1978).

    3. K. MARX, CAPITAL ch. I, § 4 (1889).

    4. J. LOCKE, SECOND TREATISE OF GOVERNMENT ch. IX, § 123 (P. Laslett ed. 1960) (1690). The better-known passage from chapter V, § 27, that everyone "has a Property in his own person," might be better understood in conjunction with this definition of "the general Name, *Property.*" On the very broad meaning of the term property in Locke, *see* J. TULLY, A DISCOURSE ON PROPERTY 111–116 (1980).

    5. There are longstanding philosophical debates about whether it is permissible to sell oneself into slavery or commit suicide. The debates seem to be interminable (in the sense suggested by Alisdair MacIntyre in AFTER VIRTUE (2d ed. 1984)).

This seems to me largely because the disputants are unclear on the issue of whether (and which) properties of persons can also be thought of as objects separate from the person. In other words, they are unclear on the boundary between attribute-properties ("inside" the self) and object-properties ("outside" the self). The disagreement between John Rawls, A THEORY OF JUSTICE (1971), and Michael Sandel, LIBERALISM AND THE LIMITS OF JUSTICE (1982), can likewise be seen as a disagreement about where to place the boundary between attribute-properties and object-property when considering the necessary content of personhood. For Sandel, Rawls's characterization of personhood is too thin; in the terms I am suggesting here, Rawls places too much in the object-property realm.

6. On the subject/object dichotomy, that is to say the worldview that postulates a sharp divide between the world of physical objects ("out there") and the world of mental subjects ("in here"), engendering the idea of the *Ding-an-Sich* (thing-in-itself), the "reflection" theory of knowledge, and the "mind-body" problem, *see, e.g.,* R. RORTY, PHILOSOPHY AND THE MIRROR OF NATURE (1979).

7. G. HEGEL, PHILOSOPHY OF RIGHT §§ 44, 45 (T. Knox. trans. 1942) [hereinafter PR].

8. PR § 65.

9. PR § 66.

10. PR § 66R.

11. *Id.*

12. PR § 45.

13. PR § 73.

14. The term "disaggregation" is used in C. Edwin Baker, *Property and Its Relation to Constitutionally Protected Liberty,* 134 U. PA. L. REV. 741 (1986).

15. *See* chapter 1, and writers discussed there in section IV; *see also* Baker, *supra* note 14.

16. The matters in this paragraph are further explored in Margaret Jane Radin, *Market-Inalienability,* 100 HARV. L. REV. 1849 (1987).

17. It is my understanding that this give-and-take between cause and symptom is part of what it means to give a functional or dialectical explanation. This idea seems incoherent or circular to traditional empiricists, even including some who view themselves as followers of Marx; *see, e.g.,* J. ELSTER, MAKING SENSE OF MARX ch. 1 (1984).

18. For more of my thoughts on the issues in this paragraph, see Radin, *supra* note 16; Margaret Jane Radin, *Justice and the Market Domain,* in NOMOS XXXI, MARKETS AND JUSTICE 165 (J. Chapman ed. 1986); and Margaret Jane Radin, *Rent Control and Incomplete Commodification,* 19 PHIL. & PUB. AFF. 80 (1988).

19. Calabresi & Melamed, *Property Rules, Liability Rules and Inalienability: One View of the Cathedral,* 85 HARV. L. REV. 1089, 1125 (1972). *See also* Richard Posner, *An Economic Theory of Criminal Law,* 85 COLUM. L. REV. 1193 (1985) (the purpose of laws against rape is to protect property rights in women's persons). I should note here that if one were to name the most thoroughgoing proponents of treating sexuality (and family life, and everything else) in terms of market rhetoric, the name of Gary Becker would be much higher on the list than that of Dean Calabresi. *See* GARY BECKER, A TREATISE ON THE FAMILY (enlarged ed. 1991). In later work Calabresi has not adopted an explicit universal commodification approach. *E.g.* GUIDO CALABRESI & PHILIP BOBBITT, TRAGIC CHOICES (1978).

Index